Politics, Identity, and Mexico's Indigenous Rights Movements

Drawing on years of field research and an original survey of more than 5,000 respondents, this book argues that, contrary to claims by the 1994 Zapatista insurgency, indigenous and non-indigenous respondents in southern Mexico have been united by their socio-economic conditions and land tenure institutions as much as, or more than, by their ethnic identities. The prevalence of communitarian attitudes in rural Chiapas – as compared with neighboring Oaxaca – is the result of centuries of peasant repression, the form land tenure institutions take, and indigenous identity. Contrary to many analyses of Chiapas' 1994 indigenous rebellion, Todd A. Eisenstadt argues, using a comparison with Oaxaca, that structural factors like social and economic history can trump ethnic identity in the formation of individuals' attitudes regarding individual and collective rights. The book finds that in Oaxaca, where indigenous communities have been less repressed and where land tenure institutions emphasize individual property rights, indigenous and non-indigenous survey respondents adopt individual rights-favoring positions, rather than those favoring collective rights. Further evidence for this argument is found by comparing the non-indigenous 2006 anti-government social movement in Oaxaca to Chiapas' 1994 Zapatista insurgency, which acquired a strong indigenous rights platform, but only after an initial discourse of class-based revolution.

Todd A. Eisenstadt is Associate Professor of Government at American University, where he also serves as chair of the department. He is the author of *Courting Democracy in Mexico* (Cambridge, 2004) and has published dozens of articles and book chapters and co-authored or edited several books on democratization, identity and social movements, public opinion, political parties, elections, and campaign finance, mainly in Latin America. Professor Eisenstadt has been a visiting scholar at Harvard University's David Rockefeller Center for Latin American Studies, the Centro de Investigación y Docencia Económicas (CIDE) and El Colegio de México in Mexico City, the Latin American Social Science Faculty (FLACSO) in Quito, Ecuador, and the Center for U.S.-Mexican Studies of the University of California–San Diego. Formerly an award-winning "police beat" newspaper reporter, he has also consulted for international development agencies and worked as a legislative aide on Capitol Hill.

Cambridge Studies in Contentious Politics

Editors

Mark Beissinger, *Princeton University*
Jack A. Goldstone, *George Mason University*
Michael Hanagan, *Vassar College*
Doug McAdam, *Stanford University and Center for Advanced Study
in the Behavioral Sciences*
Suzanne Staggenborg, *University of Pittsburgh*
Sidney Tarrow, *Cornell University*
Charles Tilly (d. 2008)
Elisabeth J. Wood, *Yale University*
Deborah Yashar, *Princeton University*

Title in the Series

Ronald Aminzade et al., *Silence and Voice in the Study of Contentious Politics*
Javier Auyero, *Routine Politics and Violence in Argentina: The Gray Zone of
State Power*
Clifford Bob, *The Marketing of Rebellion: Insurgents, Media, and
International Activism*
Charles Brockett, *Political Movements and Violence in Central America*
Christian Davenport, *Media Bias, Perspective, and State Repression: The
Black Panther Party*
Gerald F. Davis, Doug McAdam, W. Richard Scott, and Mayer N. Zald,
Social Movements and Organization Theory
Jack A. Goldstone, editor, *States, Parties, and Social Movements*
Tamara Kay, *NAFTA and the Politics of Labor Transnationalism*
Joseph E. Luders, *The Civil Rights Movement and the Logic of Social Change*
Doug McAdam, Sidney Tarrow, and Charles Tilly, *Dynamics of Contention*
Sharon Nepstad, *War Resistance and the Plowshares Movement*
Kevin J. O'Brien and Lianjiang Li, *Rightful Resistance in Rural China*
Silvia Pedraza, *Political Disaffection in Cuba's Revolution and Exodus*
Eduardo Silva, *Challenging Neoliberalism in Latin America*
Sarah A. Soule, *Contention and Corporate Social Responsibility*
Yang Su, *Collective Killings in Rural China during the Cultural Revolution*
Sidney Tarrow, *The New Transnational Activism*

(continued after the index)

Politics, Identity, and Mexico's Indigenous Rights Movements

TODD A. EISENSTADT

American University

CAMBRIDGE
UNIVERSITY PRESS

CAMBRIDGE UNIVERSITY PRESS
Cambridge, New York, Melbourne, Madrid, Cape Town,
Singapore, São Paulo, Delhi, Tokyo, Mexico City

Cambridge University Press
32 Avenue of the Americas, New York, NY 10013-2473, USA

www.cambridge.org
Information on this title: www.cambridge.org/9781107001206

First published 2011

Printed in the United States of America

A catalog record for this publication is available from the British Library.

Library of Congress Cataloging in Publication data
Eisenstadt, Todd A.
    Politics, identity, and Mexico's indigenous rights movements / Todd A. Eisenstadt.
        p.   cm. – (Cambridge studies in contentious politics)
    Includes bibliographical references and index.
    ISBN 978-1-107-00120-6 (hardback)
    1. Indians of Mexico – Politics and government.   2. Indians of Mexico – Ethnic
identity.   3. Indians of Mexico – Civil rights.   4. Civil rights movements – Mexico.
5. Indians of Mexico – Statistics.   6. Social surveys – Mexico.   7. Land
tenure – Social aspects – Mexico.   8. Mexico – Ethnic relations.   9. Chiapas
(Mexico) – Ethnic relations.   10. Oaxaca (Mexico : State) – Ethnic
relations.   I. Title.   II. Series.
    F1219.3.P7E36   2011
    305.800972–dc22   2010031516

ISBN 978-1-107-00120-6 Hardback

*To Planting Trees with Guapasan, and the Many
Other Adventures that Await*

Contents

List of Tables and Figures   *page* x

Preface and Acknowledgments   xi

1 SURVEYING THE SILENCE: TRADITIONAL
    SOCIETIES, INDIGENOUS RIGHTS, AND THE
    STATE IN SOUTHERN MEXICO   1

2 A TALE OF TWO MOVEMENTS: COMPARING
    MOBILIZATIONS IN CHIAPAS 1994 AND
    OAXACA 2006   18

3 INDIVIDUAL AND COMMUNITARIAN IDENTITIES
    IN INDIGENOUS SOUTHERN MEXICO: A
    THEORETICAL AND STATISTICAL FRAMEWORK   45

4 AGRARIAN CONFLICT, ARMED REBELLION,
    AND THE STRUGGLE FOR RIGHTS IN CHIAPAS'
    LACANDON JUNGLE   77

5 CUSTOMARY PRACTICES, WOMEN'S RIGHTS,
    AND MULTICULTURAL ELECTIONS IN OAXACA   104

6 FROM BALACLAVAS TO BASEBALL CAPS: THE
    MANY HATS OF "REAL WORLD" INDIGENOUS
    IDENTITIES   129

7 RECONCILING INDIVIDUAL RIGHTS, COMMUNAL
    RIGHTS, AND AUTONOMY INSTITUTIONS:
    LESSONS FROM CHIAPAS AND OAXACA   157

Bibliography   181

Index   203

Tables and Figures

Tables

2.1. Comparison of *Ejido* and *Tierras Comunales* Land
  Tenure Regimes   *page* 31
3.1. Survey Questions Used to Construct Communitarian
  and Pluralist Clusters   58
3.2. Summary of Hypothesized Causes of Pluralist Attitudes   60
3.3. Reporting Split Sample Probit Models   64
4.1. Land Redistributions by Presidential Decree, 1918–1992
  (and beyond)   85
4.2. Distribution of Land Indemnities under Different
  Compensation Schemes   99
5.1. Scope of Issues Discussed at UC Electoral Assemblies   109
5.2. Oaxaca's and Mexico's Post-electoral Conflicts,
  1989–2007, by Local Election Cycle   111
5.3. Participation in Customary Governance Institutions   114
6.1. Monetization of *Usos y Costumbres* Institutions   145

Figures

3.1. Oaxaca Municipalities Surveyed   66
3.2. Chiapas Municipalities Surveyed   67
4.1. Map of Chiapas Showing Lacandon Communal
  Land Zone Claims   79
4.2. Map of Lacandon Area Showing Land Claims (2005)   80
4.3. Autonomous Municipalities and Their Corresponding
  "Official" Municipalities, circa 1997   92
4.4. Map of Lacandon Area Showing Ethnic Group
  Divisions (2005)   95

Preface and Acknowledgments

Every student of Mexico has an opinion about the 1994 Zapatista uprising in Chiapas and its role in Mexico's recent political history. For that reason, this has not been an easy topic to research or an easy book to write. But for that same reason, it was an extremely rewarding book to write, and I hope I was up to the challenge. While a whole generation of cool-headed analysts is coming of age, some of the early scholarship treated these social movement underdogs as a cause to fight for rather than as a phenomenon to study. Activism definitely has its place, but I have tried here to focus mostly on scholarship. I must confess great personal sympathy for the movement when I started taking research trips to southern Mexico as part of my dissertation research in the mid-1990s.

By the late 1990s, I was hooked on the story unfolding in Chiapas and found several excuses to return even before I was formally working on this book. The Zapatistas have faded, although they can claim many accomplishments. But the scholarly community, led by several brave researchers in San Cristóbal de las Casas and a few in Mexico City, has started reckoning more objectively with the strengths and weaknesses of that movement, its broader lessons, and what it has portended for southern Mexico's development model and for the indigenous autonomy model the Zapatistas so articulately advocated.

If I am able to contribute to this discussion, it will have been by arriving in Chiapas by way of Oaxaca. As a complement to the superlatives of Chiapas, I was lucky to find in Oaxaca a less politicized environment (at least before 2006), clever but unpretentious colleagues with whom to discuss important issues, and an empirical counterpoint to the polemical academic battlefields of Chiapas (and all international events relating to Chiapas). Although I only started framing the comparison between the polarized and centralized movement in Chiapas with the workaday, bottom-up movements in Oaxaca after the 2006 Oaxaca urban revolt (which was devoid of indigenous identity issues), I was making implicit connections well before then. Not to mention that the less-studied (and hence less intellectually pigeonholed) context of Oaxaca offered an emotionally and intellectually vibrant balance against the hyper-intensity of Chiapas.

Both field research environments were fascinating respites from my more mundane university office back in the United States, and they beckon me still. Colleagues from around the hemisphere have read and commented on portions of this manuscript, and I thank all of them, with the usual caveat that any mistakes in this text are mine and mine alone. First, I thank friend and colleague Shannan Mattiace who allowed me to use a grant proposal we co-authored as the basis for several pages in Chapter 7, gave me access to her archive of Zapatista movement founding documents, and offered friendly advice and support throughout the process, as well as a good critical read. Next, I thank my outstanding doctoral student, Michael S. Danielson, whose own dissertation in some regards grew out of paths stemming from research we jointly conducted (with our Oaxacan colleagues) for this book and papers we have written. Danielson generously contributed his growing expertise to this project, as did my former undergraduate research assistant, Viridiana Ríos, whose own doctoral career in political science has also prospered since we worked together in Mexico City on postelectoral conflicts in Oaxaca. Jennifer Yelle has stepped in very ably to index, proofread, and otherwise serve as research assistant for the completion of this volume. She is also emerging as an outstanding researcher in her own right, and the last (but far from least) student I have had the privilege of working with on research related to this book.

Departed friend Donna Lee Van Cott offered her usual intense editing assistance to try to bring the manuscript up to snuff. I miss her, as do many in our discipline, but am pleased, in retrospect, that this work was still able to benefit from her extensive talents and high standards. Other colleagues who have been extremely generous in reading, commenting, and otherwise encouraging this work include: Raúl Avila, Diego Ayo, Moisés Jaime Bailón Corres, Allyson Benton, Catherine Boone, Charles Brockett, Araceli Burguete, Roderic Camp, Miguel Centellas, Matthew Cleary, Erik Cooke, Federico Estévez, Marco Estrada Saavedra, Manuel Garza, Edward Gibson, Agustina Giraudy, Jorge Hernández-Diaz, Maria Inclán, Rene Kuppe, Jason Lakin, Laura Langbein, Carl Le Van, Soledad Loaeza, José Antonio Lucero, Raúl Madrid, Eric Magar, Victor Leonel Juan Martínez, Carmen

Martínez Novo, Lourdes Morales, David Recondo, Alain de Remes, Luis Miguel Rionda, Jan Rus, Brian Schaffner, Andreas Schedler, David Shirk, Willibald Sonnleitner, Carlos Sorroza, Guillermo Trejo, Miguel Angel Vásquez de la Rosa, Peter Ward, Jeffrey Weldon, Gloria Zafra, and several anonymous reviewers.

Burguete is a field research guru, spirited writer, and prolific social scientist who helped me establish contacts and contexts, and was a consistent source of good advice for navigating the contentious politics of studying Chiapas. Dedicated former Secretary of Agrarian Reform, Chiapas Representative Martha Cecilia Díaz Gordillo, and her resourceful and clever policy analyst, Fermín Ledezma, tirelessly explained the nuances of the post-1994 land reforms, and took me with them to the Lacandon jungle to watch them conduct negotiations. Their tasks were herculean, but with persuasion and diligence, they resolved a lot of stalemates. I also thank them for letting me use some of their graphics in the book.

In Oaxaca, my work would not have been possible without the encyclopedic knowledge and constant patience of several colleagues at the Benito Juárez Autonomous University (UABJO): Moisés Jaime Bailón Corres, Manuel Garza, Victor Leonel Juan Martínez, and Carlos Sorroza, as well as help from public servant Cipriano Flores Cruz, former electoral institute director and presently the director of Oaxaca's successful adult literacy program. With Bailón Corres, Sorroza, Juan Martínez, and Danielson, I ran a successful USAID-HED project in Oaxaca, which, in addition to the provision of fellowships, training, and research, allowed me to learn a lot in a limited period of time. My colleagues at UABJO were exemplary partners from the moment we commenced the project, even when co-director Bailón Corres' UABJO office was inaccessible because of the 2006 teachers' protest. I also wish to thank Services for an Alternative Education (EDUCA), a dedicated non-profit group in Oaxaca that has boldly challenged Oaxaca's authoritarian government by meticulously documenting human rights abuses and by proposing and lobbying for policy alternatives. EDUCA let me use the cover photo of this book, which came from their comprehensive multimedia documentation of Oaxaca's customary law elections over the last decade.

Our project was profiled by Higher Education in Development (HED) as a "success story" because of my colleagues' resourcefulness and determination to succeed, even in the unstable political environment we initially faced. I will never forget working with Flores Cruz, but I will never remember exactly how much of the *mezcal* from his village I actually did drink before getting sick at a dinner celebrating the collaboration between

UABJO and American University. Katya Salazar and Laura Park of the Due Process of Law Foundation, our other institutional partner on the HED project, were also very productive and helpful.

Exemplary program directors Jene Thomas and Elisabeth Bauch of the United States Agency for International Development (USAID) and Manny Sanchez and Jennifer Sisane of HED graciously allowed me to complement policy-related work with academic research, yielding the survey featured in Chapter 3, which undergirds the rest of the analysis and, as part of a project with the UABJO, allowed us to help train hundreds of lawyers and social scientists in Oaxaca between 2006 and 2009.

The Center for US-Mexican Studies at the University of California, San Diego, under the able leadership of Christopher Woodruff, Graciela Platero, and Erik Lee (and more recently under the excellent new direction of Alberto Díaz-Cayeros and Platero), welcomed me back to UCSD in 2005–2006, as did my UCSD dissertation chair Wayne Cornelius (emeritus director of that Center and another), Stephan Haggard, and Matthew Shugart. In the summer of 2010, several researchers at the Latin American Faculty for the Social Sciences (FLACSO) received me in Quito, which helped me broaden my comparative horizons at just the right moment. Thanks in particular to Eduardo Kingman, Santiago Basabe, Fernando García, Luis Verdesoto, Carmen Martínez Novo, and Werner Vásquez.

Back at American University, Dean William LeoGrande and associate deans Meg Weekes and Gamze Zeytinci supported this project with faculty improvement grants for more summers than I would care to enumerate. Director Eric Hershberg of the Center for Latin American and Latino Studies offered encouragement and contacts hemisphere-wide, which helped me enhance my comparative perspective. Government chairs Saul Newman and Candice Nelson also helped me compete for internal grants, including one from the Dean of Academic Affairs. Government Department Professor James Thurber helped me get in touch with his bright and friendly son Mark Thurber in Ecuador and offered sound advice at many stages on a wide range of issues. Rachel Pentlarge and Niloo Spencer helped me manage the external USAID/HED grant that let me complete this book, and here too, Danielson and Yelle made a big difference.

Most recently, as chair myself, I counted in 2009–2010 on the extremely able assistance of Jenna Bramble. Knowing that Bramble was on the beat allowed me to excuse myself from the university a day or two a week while writing this manuscript in favor of my cozy home office, where the distractions were fewer and the coffee stronger. Sara Ghebremichael took over that job with a lot of enthusiasm and promise as this book was going to press. I also wish to thank my friendly, knowledgeable, and straight-shooting project editor at Cambridge University Press, Eric Crahan; his assistant Jason Przybylski; project director Bindu Vinod; and super text editor Elizabeth Goldberg for bringing this project together with care and precision.

Portions of Chapter 3 were drawn from Todd A. Eisenstadt, "Agrarian Tenure Institution, Conflict Frames, and Communitarian Identities: The Case of Indigenous Southern Mexico," 2009. *Comparative Political Studies*, Vol. 42 (1) January: 82–113. I thank that journal for its liberal reprint rights policy, elaborated at http://www.sagepub.com/journalsPermissions .nav (link to "authors re-using their own work"). The book benefited from various presentations at the American Political Science Association, Latin American Studies Association, and Midwest Political Science Association annual meetings; the 2010 meeting of the Latin American Network of Legal Anthropology (RELAJU); and invited talks and conference presentations at American University, the Autonomous Technological Institute of Mexico (ITAM – Mexico City), the Benito Juárez Autonomous University (Oaxaca), the Center for Economic Research and Teaching (CIDE – Mexico City), Harvard University's David Rockefeller Center for Latin American Studies, the Latin American Faculty for Social Sciences (FLACSO – Quito), the Japan Institute for International Affairs, the Mexican Congress, the University of California–San Diego's Center for US-Mexican Studies, and the University of Texas at Austin's Teresa Lozano Long Institute of Latin American Studies.

On a more personal note, my parents Mel and Pauline Eisenstadt have given me many things, including a passion for writing and for trying to make a difference. Most importantly, they have given their love and support for whatever I do. My "Renaissance Man" brother Keith "Keegan" Eisenstadt, his wonderful wife Kristy Pilgrim, and their beautiful kids – son Spencer and daughter Holly – are also a constant source of encouragement. My own marvelous and increasingly autonomous daughters, Natalia and Paola, give me unending inspiration and perspective, and offer the single best antidote to any rough day at the office. Most of all, I'd like to thank my lovely wife and *confidente* Mireya Solís, who holds our family together with discipline, virtue, and intellect; excels at many things (showing our daughters that "you can do it all"); and graces my life with love, elegance, and joy. I dedicate this book to her.

1

Surveying the Silence

TRADITIONAL SOCIETIES, INDIGENOUS RIGHTS, AND THE STATE IN SOUTHERN MEXICO

For nearly two decades, leaders of the Zapatista social movement in Chiapas, Mexico, have claimed to speak on behalf of the region's disenfranchised rural dwellers. The Zapatistas, led by the ubiquitous and awe-inspiring Subcommander Marcos, have claimed to give voice to the voiceless. On January 1, 1994, the Zapatista Army of National Liberation declared war on the Mexican state, demanding radical class warfare (immediately) and pan-indigenous self-government and autonomy (eventually). This uprising was immediately met with violent suppression by Mexican authorities, but the Zapatistas have continued to be a force for political, economic, and social change in Chiapas.

Much has been written about the organization's violent beginning. Comparatively little has been written about the indigenous jungle dwellers in whose name the Zapatistas took up arms. This book gives these rural Chiapas residents voice, finally, through a comprehensive survey and case study. Among the questions addressed are: How many followers do the Zapatista leaders actually represent? How many of Chiapas' poor, dispossessed peasants actively participated in the Zapatista cause in the late 1990s? How many shared the movement's objectives but did not participate? How many opposed the armed rebellion in 1994? How many have lost faith in the succeeding years?

This book also uses the Zapatista movement as a model for refining a theoretical understanding of collective action. The failure of social movements and other expressions of collective action to reach their goal of social change is often blamed on the "free-rider" problem. Free-riders are people who agree with the movement's ends, but do not share leaders' zeal and believe they can remain on the sidelines and still reap the public benefits of a movement's eventual success. This theory was famously described in the 1960s by the late Mancur Olson. In the case of the Zapatistas in southern Mexico, indigenous peasants who were presumed to sympathize with the movement for greater political autonomy and took no action have been characterized as free-riders. But even in the decade since the 1994 Chiapas uprising, little has been heard from these indigenous citizens who comprise the majority of Chiapas' rural residents. Indeed, their silence raises the question: does a pro-Zapatista silent majority, implied in much of the sympathetic academic literature, even exist?

Building on Olson's work, this book suggests that passive bystanders may sometimes actually be misrepresented by the movement leaders who claim to speak for them. José Antonio Lucero, writing about Andean indigenous rights movements in 2008 (19 – quoting Jenkins), asked "whether social movements constitute a direct [form] of representation resembling classic conceptions of participatory democracy, a device for representing the underrepresented and countering entrenched oligarchies, or an elite group of self-appointed advocates." In Chiapas, for example, Zapatista leaders overstated the collectivist identity of indigenous residents, compromising, ironically, the very autonomy the Zapatistas said they were fighting to enhance. In this vein, our study of social movements may need to question leaders' presumed commitment to communitarian rights more closely. Exploring the ways that individuals' beliefs are subsumed by leaders' public discourse might reveal how silent majorities are manipulated by group leaders the world over and how social movements can undermine individual expression.

This book and the survey of indigenous public opinion on which it is based are intended, essentially, to audit three interrelated claims frequently made by the Zapatista leadership. First, Zapatista leaders assert they are supported by and speak for all of the indigenous people of Chiapas. Second, Zapatista leaders contend (for both political and ideological reasons) that indigenous Chiapanecans have a "communitarian" identity, meaning their primary definitions of self and self-interest are defined by their communal attachments and community's needs. Third, Zapatista leaders argue that they are the natural interpreters and representatives of this communitarian cultural frame.

In order to assess these claims, we conducted a survey of more than 2,000 indigenous and 3,000 non-indigenous Mexicans and performed in-depth case studies in two Mexican states. The survey was designed to measure respondents' level of support for communitarianism. For the sake of comparison and context, I surveyed residents in the states of

Chiapas, Oaxaca, and Zacatecas. Chiapas and Oaxaca are both heavily indigenous and Mexico's most historically unequal states in terms of wealth distribution. Chiapas has a history of widespread repression of peasants, particularly indigenous peasants, by an oligarchy of governing *ladino* [non-Indian] elites. Oaxaca, by contrast, has a history of de facto indigenous autonomy going back centuries, and conflicts are more often between indigenous communities than between indigenous communities and the state. Zacatecas is a poor but non-indigenous state in northern Mexico and serves as a control case.

My central findings are provocative and tend to disprove the Zapatista leadership's claims about the indigenous people of Chiapas. (Detailed survey results are presented in Chapter 3.) With regard to the strength of their support, only some 15 percent of Chiapanecan respondents say they "trust" the Zapatistas, and the movement is trusted less than either the police or dominant political parties. Responses were similar in both Oaxaca and Zacatecas. With regard to the degree of communitarianism, interestingly, indigenous respondents articulate social values based on individual rights (rather than communitarian rights) perspectives to the same degree as non-indigenous respondents. By surveying the rural dwellers in Chiapas and Oaxaca, I am able to discern that whereas indigenous identity may have some effect on whether respondents are more communal-rights or individual-rights oriented, factors such as local land tenure institutions and political history have even more causal impact on respondents' world-views. Based on the survey data and case studies, I argue that indigenous Chiapanecans are neither lock-step communitarians as represented by Zapatista leaders nor liberals in the strictly Western tradition. As this book will show, they can adopt either of these positions, depending on the need. Moreover, I examine how misrepresentations by movement leaders of the indigenous population's views impacted Chiapanecans and how similar dynamics between leaders and their so-called followers are playing out in social movements throughout Latin America.

My findings regarding indigenous Chiapanecans' political and cultural identity speak to one of the central debates in contemporary social science scholarship: whether rights are afforded on a communitarian or individual basis. Pioneers of indigenous rights studies, including Van Cott (2000), Mattiace (2003), and Yashar (2005), argue that indigenous rights movements have been a refuge for communitarians in the post–Cold War era as "the idea of social rights was everywhere challenged by conservative politicians and neoliberal economists who successfully reframed it as an expensive and unsustainable entitlement rather than a fundamental right of the citizenry" (Yashar 2005, 47). By this argument, the international appeal of indigenous rights movements like the Zapatistas has been that they have reformulated the case for communitarian rights after the communist version was discredited by the implosion of the Soviet Union (Brysk 2000; Mattiace 2003; Plutarch 2004). The Soviet pursuit of group equality has been replaced by the Zapatista pursuit of group autonomy. This refashioning has made indigenous rights movements likewise acceptable to neoliberals, as long as the indigenous groups do not challenge the primacy of individual rights.

One of the first scholars to try to interpret the Zapatista movement was anthropologist Gary Gossen. His 1994 work took a steadfastly primordial view of ethnic identity, arguing identity is the result of ascriptive characteristics such as race and language. Gossen romanticized the Zapatista struggle as being the awakening of a new Mayan identity replete with a "distinctively Mesoamerican vision of self, society, and ethnic identity" (Gossen 1994, 568). In contrast, more subjectivist scholars (those who emphasize the malleability of identity) such as Higgins (2004), Stahler-Sholk (2007), and Jung (2008) view indigeneity as situational and post-modern, and argue that the Zapatistas' emphasis on identity politics and autonomy compliments traditional Marxist class-based identity. They write that this is 21st century movement in that it redefines rights, adopts new international electronic communications strategies, and situates oppressed groups in the world of flux wrought by globalization rather than in old materialist Marxist categories based on economic and social class. Indeed, this generation of constructivists (who view indigeneity as malleable, but within a finite domain) allowed for the possibility that citizens could identify as members of a particular group, like the Tzeltales or the Tzotziles, but without possessing the type of pan-indigenous identity the Zapatistas envisioned. The Zapatistas generally supported this broad pan-ethnic indigeneity even as regional and local leaders disaggregated this position into one of supporting only their linguistic or ethnic group.

Primordialist/essentialist views have dominated Chiapanecan studies for several generations. Starting with the fabled Harvard Project in the 1950s, hundreds of anthropology graduate students from the United States have been sent to document the "closed corporate communities" in Zinacantán in south central Chiapas on the premise that these communities foster strong, inward-looking collective cultures that protect them from cultural degradation by the outside world (Rus 2002). Corporate communities are, according to Wolf (2001, 156–158), peasant organizations which limit privileges to insiders and discourage member involvement in the outside community. This stylized ethnographic narrative, repeated in many dissertations in the 1970s and 1980s, presaged the Zapatistas' post-1996 emphasis on recognition of a communal ethnic identity rights. Zapatista leaders relied on this construct well after research had come out in the 1990s debunking the inward-looking-communities thesis in favor of one that recognized labor exploitation (even enslavement) and human rights abuses were the principal determinants of rural Chiapanecan identities (Rus 2002). Of course, as pointed out by Estrada Saavedra's ground-breaking research, the vast majority of scholarship on the Zapatistas has been polemical rather than objective (Estrada Saavedra 2007, 568). In the following section, we further explore the theoretical starting points of some of this literature.

In the Name of Zapata or Jacinto Pérez?[1]

The Rural Class Cleavage and Zapatista Leaders, Followers, and Bystanders

The Zapatistas' "First Declaration," issued on January 1, 1994, was a call for revolutionary class warfare. Close observers have noted that ethnic identity was not originally part of the Zapatista discourse (Estrada Saavedra 2007; 386–388; Ruiz interview 2004; Mestries Benquet 2001, 139). Indeed, the geographical and membership restrictions posed by the movements' subsequent focus on indigenous rights have recently forced the group to return to its origins on the anti-capitalist left (Estrada Saavedra 2007, 599–601). Not only did the Zapatista insurgency originally ignore the plight of indigenous groups (in contrast to their initial attention to oppressed peasants), the Zapatistas and indigenous groups sometimes directly clashed over resources and the provision of social services. This was especially true where the Zapatistas conscripted livestock, resources, and people into their cause.

Evaluated as a class-based revolution, the Zapatistas failed. They did not break Chiapas' entrenched oligarchical elites. Similarly, as an

---

[1] Jacinto Pérez "Pajarito," a political leader in Chamula, Chiapas, led an important indigenous uprising against Chiapas' non-indigenous *ladino* elites in 1911. The followers of moderate General Venustiano Carranza, Mexico's eventual president after the constitutional convention, killed Pérez during the Mexican Revolution out of fear that he might incite further social upheaval. Other famous national leaders of indigenous movements whose names advocates might have chosen include colonial-era heroes Kanek and Moctezuma.

ethnic movement, they did not obtain many real concessions to advance indigenous autonomy, rhetorical amendments to the Mexican Constitution notwithstanding. However, as an agrarian movement, they were wildly successful – much more successful than the Mexican Revolution or President Lázaro Cárdenas' game-changing land reforms way back in the 1930s. The post-1994 land redistributions by state and federal authorities reallocated more than 6 percent of the state's surface area from land-holding elites to squatters, Zapatistas, and other previously landless peasants, increasing the number of *ejidos* (public farm collectives) by more than 40 percent statewide (Chiapas State Government, Secretary for Rural Areas 2006). Chapter 4 details the story of that remarkable transformation from the perspective of the peasants who were involved.

A prominent Chiapas social movement leader whose main struggle was for land not ethnic recognition openly acknowledged "taking advantage of the Zapatistas' cover" after the 1994 insurgency and using the state government's fear of further instability to their own ends (Gómez Hernández 2004 interview). A 1992 amendment to Article 27 of the federal constitution had decreed that there would be no new land reform, only resolution of the thousands of pending land actions in Chiapas, which had the greatest backlog.[2] Another pressure valve was clearly needed. As the Zapatistas and the Mexican Army ceased hostilities in the spring of 1994, belligerent copycat groups sprung up around the state. Long-time petitioners for social change capitalized on the state government's sudden fear of instability and its willingness to bargain. These groups occupied private land and then persuaded the government to buy it from the private owners and donate it to the social movement squatters. The number of land invasions in Chiapas doubled from some 1,000 in 1994 to 2,000 in 1995 (Mattiace 2003). While indigenous rights and autonomy finally became headline issues during the San Andrés Dialogues (which resulted in a 1996 peace accord signed between the Zapatistas and President Ernesto Zedillo), demands made by a dozen outside groups helped ensure the creation of mechanisms for redistributing land.

Prior to 1994, the Chiapas State Legislature had tacitly encouraged social movements to mobilize and demand land reforms and measures to decrease political instability. Seasoned leaders on the political left lived by

[2] Although it contained only 3 percent of the national population, in the early 1990s Chiapas accounted for fully 25 percent of the federal government's caseload of unexecuted agrarian distribution claims (Monroy 1994, 18).

6

this formula: "mobilization + storming of town halls = creation of an interim municipal council" (Eisenstadt 2004, 216). Essentially, well-focused political pressure yielded concessions. Squatters or others on the political left could march on town squares and either change who governed or receive concessions in exchange for ceasing their pressure tactics. Indeed, Araceli Burguete has shown that such overthrows of mayors and elected town councils happened in Chiapas scores of times. (Burguete 2006, 135–186, cites thirty-one cases of "decreed" mayoral changes within Chiapas' 118 municipalities between 1996 and 2001 alone.)[3]

Before the Zapatista insurgency, government controlled the behavior of both agrarian elites and peasants. The peasants received direct subsistence aid from the government in exchange for their passivity and acceptance of authoritarian regimes and hierarchies defined in terms of land ownership. Consistent with the documented importance of "side payments" (Olson 1971), peasants were not usually offered group benefits; rather, the state coerced participation by granting individual rewards through group membership. Citizens who joined the state peasant union and its affiliated political party (the long-ruling Party of the Institutional Revolution, or PRI) received preferential access to fertilizers, farm machinery, other agrarian subsidies and inputs, and (in Chiapas) access to the all-important union-sponsored mechanisms to petition for land. In regards to this system, the Zapatistas did help end state corporatism in Chiapas. Of course, the 2000 gubernatorial victory by the first non-PRI candidate since before World War II, the economic crisis of the 1980s, and the agrarian crisis in the 1990s also had enormous impacts.

Corporatism in this context refers to the mechanisms of state control by manipulating support from interest groups. Inclusionary corporatism creates structures within the state that allow communitarian group interests to be represented. Exclusionary corporatism is also predicated on communitarianism, but seeks to consolidate political authority by co-opting and/or repressing opposing views rather than allowing them expression. In the case of Mexico, political control was exercised through exclusionary corporatism and coerced membership in government-sanctioned unions (Reyna and Wienert 1977, 161). To defuse class conflicts, the ruling class would accede to moderated versions of peasants' and workers' redistributive

---

[3] In 1999, seven new municipalities were added in Chiapas, bringing the total to 118. Analysts Leyva and Burguete (2007) argue that the creation of new municipalities was part of the state's counterinsurgency strategy to divide and conquer Zapatista-occupied areas.

demands. In the countryside, this meant rural residents were compelled to participate in local branches of the official peasants' union, and squatters were regularly co-opted by state governments through quiet backdoor land deals. Peasants who joined the union received carrots in the form of agricultural subsidies, social programs, and preferential treatment in applying for (although not necessarily receiving) land. Those who did not join the PRI-backed organizations got the stick of repression. Resisters were jailed without formal charges (often for months or even longer), and a few were even killed.

In this way, Mexico's federal and state governments fomented class identity at the expense of ethnic identity. No such rewards existed for identifying oneself as Indian. To the extent that indigenous groups were acknowledged at all, they were encouraged to assimilate into the *raza cosmica* [cosmic race] and subscribe to the myth of national unity that put Mexican nationalism above indigenous ethnic identities. In some ways, the PRI-dominated state succeeded in molding rural dwellers into corporate peasants. After all, these identities have withstood numerous efforts by indigenous rights activists to make ethnic identity more important than land tenure structures in determining how citizens see their relationship to the state and, more specifically, whether their rights are essentially individual or collective.

The survey data show that there is variation in levels of communitarianism among Mexican respondents: Chiapanecans express more strongly communitarian views than Oaxacans. But the differences do not correspond to a division between indigenous and non-indigenous citizens. Rather, the differences are best explained by variables relating to respondents' economic well-being, whether they live in rural areas, and, if they do, whether the dominant land tenure institutions are the state-penetrated *ejidos* of Chiapas or the more autonomous federally-recognized communal lands of Oaxaca. Stark differences between liberal pluralists and traditional communalists are apparent when latent attitude clusters are constructed (as described in Chapter 3). But, again, the distinctions are more the result of class rather than ethnicity.

According to this and other research, it seems that individuals consciously choose to prioritize their indigenous identity in some circumstances and class-based identity in others. Thus far, however, the process and mechanisms of how individuals make that decision have not been systematically drawn out. Most of the literature does not even differentiate among the various strategic considerations that inform individuals' decisions to adopt indigenous or peasant identities. Most existing literature, especially social movements literature, focuses on the consciousness-raising work activists undertake after they have established an indigenous collective identity rather than on the processes that leads people to prioritize one identity over another. This book offers a corrective. I will systematically examine individuals' attitudes and then discuss how these views aggregated into a social movement, instead of making inferences about individuals' attitudes by disaggregating group outcomes.

Differentiating Individual and Communitarian Citizenship Rights

In the context of southern Mexico in the late 20th century, the demand for indigenous rights was basically synonymous with a demand for communitarian rights. As per Adelfo Regino Montes, an Oaxacan Mixe intellectual, "It is important to recall that before the arrival of the Spanish the collectivities present in these lands were peoples, with their own culture and social, political, economic, and judicial institutions.... They believed, as some continue to affirm today, that these categories and concepts should impose themselves on the essence of things" (Regino Montes 1996). His argument to the National Indigenous Forum, based on this strong concept of collective rights, was that "the recognition of our collective rights is necessary so that we can truly enjoy our individual rights" (Regino Montes "Taller 2 – Libre Determinación de los Pueblos Indígenas" n.d.). Regino Montes attended that summit to defend Oaxaca's de facto autonomy and argue for its enhancement, and his approach was characteristically Oaxacan. While they participated actively in the Zapatista-facilitated debate over autonomy, the Oaxacan delegation advocated gradualism where the Zapatistas of Chiapas pushed for more radical and urgent action.

The essence of Zapatista communitarianism can be understood from reading the group's statement on autonomy presented at the National Indigenous Forum:

We are peoples, not ethnics or populations; by recognizing us thusly, with the collective rights which correspond to us for our difference, conditions are created for us to enjoy all the rights and liberties which correspond to us as people.... We do not ask anyone to grant us this autonomy. We have possessed it and continue to do so.... But we have not been able to fully exercise this liberty, not in colonial times nor in independent Mexico. We have always had to do it [exercise these rights] against everything and against everyone, in a long struggle of resistance. (National Indigenous Forum 1996, 1)

Although a more communitarian flag would be difficult to raise, even in this statement the Zapatistas recognized the need for recognition of individual rights. But to the Zapatista polemicists at the National Indigenous Forum, individual and collective rights were not coequal. Collective rights precede individual rights; individual rights extend from collective rights. This concept of the relationship between an individual and the collective is fundamentally different from the Western concept of citizenship rights as born out of the Enlightenment and French Revolution.

Both the role of the state and the role of the citizen are vastly different in communitarian versus liberal societies. Deborah Yashar developed four heuristic definitions of citizenship[4] in her 2005 exploration of ethnic identities and political contestation. She concluded that the form and content of participation must be considered alongside the rules that determine who actually qualifies for citizenship. According to Yashar, political participation is itself a product of interest intermediation. She argues, therefore, that access to political associational space and pre-existing political networks determine whether citizenship in a given nation assumes an ethnic dimension. For Yashar, the issue becomes one of identifying whether individuals (as in pluralist models) or groups (as in corporatist and consociational models) are privileged:

Liberalism … is an individual affair. Rights and responsibilities inhere in the individual. And it is the individual who relates to and is regulated by the state. Ethnicity and multiculturalism are irrelevant to a discussion of citizenship and the formal mechanisms of interest intermediation…. But citizenship has obviously not been confined theoretically or empirically to a set of individual rights and responsibilities. Groups have also assumed a formal role in defining some state-society relations…. Indeed, communitarians argue that identities, interests, preferences, meanings, and capacities are socially constructed and are rooted in communities. (Yashar 2005, 43)

The implications of these divergent worldviews are dramatic. For liberals, the individual is primary, and the state exists to protect its citizens from encroachment on their individual liberties. Such liberal republicanism is best exemplified by the French Revolution's Declaration of

---

[4] These four principles are: the "Aristotelian ideal," or according such rights to all who can reason and interpret the community's general will; *jus sanguinis*, which grants citizenship based strictly on "bloodlines" and kinship; *jus soli*, the standard territorially-based means of granting citizenship to all who reside in a geographic area; and a universal or open borders approach that accords citizenship to everyone, as per the United Nations (Yashar 2005, 36–39).

the Rights of Man, the social contract treatises of the Enlightenment (including works by Rousseau, Hobbes, Locke, and Montesquieu), and the defense of individuals' rights to "life, liberty, and the pursuit of happiness" in the U.S. Declaration of Independence. For communitarians, groups are the best and most legitimate intermediaries between citizens and the state. Economic, political, religious, and ethnic groups (among others) are recognized as possessing rights that supersede and encompass those of individuals. Social rights, including the "right to a modicum of economic welfare and security to the right to share to the full in the social heritage and to live the life of a civilized being according to the standards prevailing in a society" (Marshall 1973, 70, 106, as cited in Yashar), are communitarian in nature.

Inclusionary corporatism (as described by Europeanists like Molina and Rhodes 2002) is a communitarian phenomenon; exclusionary corporatism, such as that used by the Mexican government to divide and conquer PRI-state opponents, is not. By disaggregating incentives and forcing members of a collective to make individual cost-benefit calculations about side payments, the Mexican government ensured that rural peasants in Mexico behaved just as Vietnamese peasants had in Sam Popkin's landmark study, *The Rational Peasant*: "Whether a self-interested peasant will or will not contribute to a collective action depends on individual – not group – benefits" (Popkin 1979, 251). The subversion of class interests to side payments actually undermined the Mexican countryside's traditional communitarianism and forced peasants to be pluralists.

The dichotomy between individual and communitarian rights is, on some level, artificial in that most democratic societies possess considerable elements of both. European democracies, for example, combine strong communitarian rights (pensions, labor rights, and free access to public education and universal health care) with the same pluralistic individual rights (freedom of speech and assembly, writ of habeas corpus and other judicial due process guarantees, property rights protections) afforded in more strictly liberal democracies like the United States. For the purposes of this research, however, the dichotomy is useful precisely because indigenous rights movements and their promoters cast themselves as exclusively communitarian. For the first five chapters, I will maintain this dichotomy in order to highlight and characterize individualistic behaviors undertaken in supposedly communitarian settings. In the last two chapters, I will adopt a more integrated approach and attempt to represent the complex mix of communal and individualist attitudes evidenced on the ground.

Outline of the Book

In Chapter 2, I contrast the histories of Chiapas and Oaxaca and discuss why their recent respective movements for indigenous rights have been so different in design and character. In Chiapas, the movement for indigenous rights was the result of long and severe repression by the state government, extending back centuries. In Oaxaca, the Spanish conquest was followed by centuries of benign neglect by state officials that actually allowed the indigenous populations to largely govern themselves. This history goes a long way toward explaining why the 1994 Chiapas insurgency was so much more intense and communitarian than the subsequent Oaxacan movement in 2006. The chapter details the process by which the Zapatistas came to make their indigenous rights claims and compares it to the fact that in Oaxaca the leadership never framed grievances in a particularly communitarian way. I introduce the idea that the relative autonomy afforded the Oaxacans under Mexican rule actually fostered the development of more individualistic attitudes and left Oaxaca's indigenous communities without a communal conception of rights or grievances. Understanding the differences between Chiapas and Oaxaca is critical for interpreting the survey data presented in Chapter 3.

Chapter 3 presents the book's core statistical analysis. I categorize the responses of more than 5,000 survey participants through a technique called latent variable clustering. The results demonstrate that non-indigenous and indigenous respondents cluster in individualistic and communitarian types at similar rates. This data allows me to statistically disconfirm the existence of a strong correlation between ethnic identity and communitarian values. Using a probit model based on survey-derived variables, I conclude that ethnicity is less important in shaping political attitudes than class, rural land tenure systems, and agrarian state corporatism. Supporting this conclusion is the fact that corporatist peasant identities have withstood efforts by indigenous rights activists over the last two decades to reconstitute a communitarian ethnic identity.

Chapters 4 and 5 present qualitative case studies about the indigenous rights movements in Chiapas and Oaxaca. In both chapters, I attempt to disaggregate the so-called communitarian outcomes in order to understand the specific motivations, attitudes, and incentives of the individuals involved. Chapter 4 includes a close study of the Lacandon communal lands case, which was a flash point for Zapatista mobilization. The Lacandon was a patchwork quilt of polarized groups by 1994, with ethnic identity being one important social cleavage, but far from the only one. I describe the tumultuous origins of the Lacandon conflict and how it fostered an us-against-them type of solidarity among the diverse local groups who confronted the state. I argue that this solidarity transcended ethnic identity, which, in that region, had gone from being ethnically monolingual (Lacandon) to ethnically trilingual (also Chol and Tzeltal) over the preceding 30 years. After elaborating on the Lacandon case, I generalize some of its characteristics to the rest of Chiapas in the pre-Zapatista and Zapatista eras.

Chapter 5 contrasts Chiapas's indigenous movement with the one in Oaxaca, where closed corporate communities (recall Wolf's term)[5] fought over common borders in battles that pitted one cohesive ethno-geographic community against another. Chapter 5 closely considers the Mexican government's decision in 1995 to recognize Oaxaca's *usos y costumbres* [elections via customary norms rather than through political parties] as an acceptable means of selecting municipal civic leaders (mayors and city councils). *Usos y costumbres* was intended to be a moderate multicultural policy, allowing the Oaxacans to be more locally communitarian than Mexico as a whole. Recognition of this traditional means of selecting leaders has been widely credited with giving government institutions greater credibility and fostering ethnic pride. But this process has also accommodated individual and pluralist interests as well as communitarian imperatives. Using cases of postelectoral conflicts, I highlight how *usos y costumbres* elections disenfranchise women and residents outside the municipal seat, often for the benefit of individual political bosses, but in the name of group solidarity. I will explore this and other ways in which individual rights have become increasingly explicit factors in how Oaxacans conduct their political lives.

While most of the book maintains a dichotomous view of communitarianism and individualism, in Chapters 6 and 7 I take a more holistic view and show how these two political approaches co-exist on a continuum. Southern Mexico's Indians have been able to pragmatically integrate communitarian and individualistic orientations, for example, in *usos y costumbres*

---

[5] Wolf argues that peasant organizations in Mesoamerica and Java were similar in that "in both areas they are corporate organizations, maintaining a perpetuity of rights and membership; and they are closed corporations, because they limit these privileges to insiders and discourage close participation of members in the social relations of the larger society" (Wolf 2001, 148). It is important to note that even as this famous article described the closed and communitarian nature of peasant communities, Wolf argued that the communities' inward focus was a defensive reaction against exploitation by European colonists. To Wolf, social threats forced the peasants to evolve these communitarian organizations (Wolf 2001, 156–158).

observance, by recognizing individual property rights under communitarian land tenure, and by providing public education in Zapatista-held areas. The fact that indigenous residents operate easily in both communitarian and liberal rights systems further supports the survey results: 1) indigenous respondents possess the same individualistic inclinations as non-indigenous respondents, and 2) ethnicity is a less salient predictor of where one falls on the communitarian-individualism continuum than economic condition. Chapter 7 continues to probe the ways that communal- and individual-rights orientations can be integrated by broadly evaluating indigenous rights movements, but in Bolivia and Peru. I conclude by assessing the value of autonomy and considering the implications of indigenous rights movements' theoretical success.

Throughout this book, it will become clear that the views of indigenous people in Mexico are at once more diverse and more nuanced than the Zapatistas and other indigenous leaders claim. Whereas some rural dwellers no doubt remain loyal to the landmark movement and its arguably just cause, others have sought to reconcile ideological demands for autonomy with pragmatic imperatives for state services. Some Chiapanecans have migrated due to political opposition or economic need. (Indeed, some have been forced to flee by Zapatista conscriptions or anti-Zapatista "white guard" vigilantes.) The vast majority, however, simply persist, trying to provide for their families and improve their own futures. They are neither leaders nor followers of the collective actions taken in their names. Rather than speak on their behalf, this book tries to let the indigenous residents of southern Mexico start to speak for themselves.

Conclusion

This book attempts to measure and catalogue the opinions of a certain population of political followers at a certain point in time and compare that to representations made by the leaders of a political movement about that population. It tries to understand the attitudes of indigenous citizens in Chiapas and Oaxaca and the confluence of objective circumstances that led to these views. This work does not seek to undermine the grievances of the Zapatistas or question the justness of their cause. The insurgency was born from decades of repression and economic deprivation that came after a century of outright enslavement by ruthless land-hoarding elites (see, for example, Wasserstrom 1983; Benjamin 1996; Collier and Quaratiello 1999). I scrutinize the Zapatistas in order to understand the attitudes of

their supporters and rural residents in Zapatista-dominant areas, the mea-
surable conditions that led to the 1994 uprising and how the insurgency
was perceived by the rural populations it affected.

My approach is similar to that of the anthropologist David Stoll, who
took issue with many factual inconsistencies in Nobel Laureate Rigoberta
Menchú's epic autobiography, *I, Rigoberta Menchú*. Stoll was roundly
attacked by critics sympathetic to Menchú's political goal of stopping the
Guatemalan military's massacres.[6] In a response to these critics, Stoll (in
Arias 2001, 402) sought to separate the political from the scholarly:

> The laureate received the Nobel Peace Prize for her work as an indigenous human
> rights activist, not as an author. She and her editor Elisabeth Burgos-Debray were
> trying to persuade readers to stop massacres, not to create world literature. That
> they managed to do both is a huge accomplishment, but not one that can protect
> Rigoberta from obvious questions.... If everyone has the right to a preferred truth,
> how do we refute the Guatemalan army's version of events? If scholars like our-
> selves do not have the authority to evaluate contradictory versions of events, how
> can outsiders intervene in human rights cases?

Public opinion is subjective, of course, but strong patterns of response must be
assumed to be attributable to objective circumstances, to discernible truths. In
the politicized world of Zapatista study, Stoll's defense of the quest for objectivity has sometimes not been heeded. Along those lines, this work seeks to
extend beyond the preferred truth of the Zapatista leaders and the generation
of sympathetic scholars who accompanied their rise. Instead, I seek to com-
prehend the views of the region's actors (and free-riders) themselves.

Survey research, volatile and chaotic though it may be, serves a critical
role in characterizing baseline views of a broad universe of respondents,
including movement leaders, followers, free-riders, and silent bystanders.
Indeed, the rigorously analyzed survey is a valuable source of independently
generated information of the kind that was not available to Stoll, for example, as he waded through contrary testimonials to understand the truth
about gut-wrenching events. My objective is not to discern an objective

---

[6] The Guatemalan massacres perpetrated by the military authoritarian regime on innocent
civilians (87 percent of whom were Mayan) may have been the most bloody event in the
Western Hemisphere since World War II. The Commission for Historical Clarification
(CEH) identified 42,275 victims (23,671 were executed arbitrarily and 6,159 were
"disappeared") and estimated total casualties at 200,000. The severity of the violence lent
great urgency to Menchú's task and won her latitude, according to many, for writing a
polemical composite testimonial rather than a biography that could withstand rigorous
fact checking. See the CEH's summary report at http://shr.aaas.org/guatemala/ceh/report/
english/conc1.html

truth; I want to understand the attitudes of indigenous and non-indigenous Mexicans and determine whether conventional primordialist assumptions about their communitarianism hold. Some may criticize on political grounds the scholarly decision to question the strength of Zapatista claims about communitarianism and ethnic unity among followers. I hope these critics will also recognize the virtue of recognizing agency among individual indigenous actors and of disregarding the usual assumption, tacit or explicit, that indigenous people are simply passive followers ready to be led by paternalistic leaders. Contrary to that stereotype, survey respondents often said they felt empowered by finally being asked for their views.

This book fits a growing trend that sees the Zapatista leadership's framing of an indigenous identity as more instrumental and strategic (see Bob 2005; Inclán 2009; Trejo 2004; Plutarch 2004; Sonnleitner 2001; Viqueira 2002) and less primordialist than movement leaders, media, and public policy depictions have suggested. This is not an exercise in second-guessing Zapatista leadership, which brilliantly guided the movement and shined national and international light on the dire needs of its constituents. From a tactical point of view, the Zapatistas were smart to reframe their struggle as one of ethnic identity, once their initial class conflict and Mexican nationalism frames failed to generate the desired effects. (As a result, during the 2000 gubernatorial election, the Zapatistas helped replace one of Mexico's most repressive state governments with one of the country's most progressive.) Rather, this work seeks to demonstrate that the communitarian frame was not, in fact, reflective of the views of most of the indigenous survey respondents in Chiapas.

Of course, this conclusion is itself a generalization, drawn from stylized versions of pluralist versus communitarian respondent types described in Chapter 3. In reality, southern Mexico's Indians are less dichotomously pluralist-individualist or communitarian than this or any survey model can reflect. As is true for all attitude surveys, most respondents fall between extremes on a continuum. Whether an individual projects a more individualistic or communitarian bent depends largely on the social situation in which they are currently operating. Survey research can provoke respondents to reply as if engaged in certain interactions, but only social experiments beyond the scope of this study (such as those suggested by Corstange 2005) can actually simulate such responses. This book relies on case studies to flesh out the survey data. By describing the complex mix of communitarian and pluralist attitudes in populations in Chiapas and Oaxaca, it becomes clear that identity among southern Mexico's rural dwellers is neither singular nor static. Rather than an expression of pessimism about the disunity of the Zapatistas, this is a beacon of hope. People in the rain-forests of Chiapas and the remote valleys of Oaxaca weigh information and make decisions, when given the chance, rather than passively following anyone. This is an appeal for understanding them on their own terms, and, in the conclusion, a bid for moderation, for a constructivist understanding allowing outsiders also to advocate for them, or, better yet, advocate with them, in a plural manner that includes anyone willing to speak. Their story, the story which follows, is one of dynamism, creativity, and agency against the structural odds.

2

A Tale of Two Movements

COMPARING MOBILIZATIONS IN
CHIAPAS 1994 AND OAXACA 2006

At a series of protests over several months in 2006, hundreds of thousands of protesters in Oaxaca, Mexico, dared authorities to arrest them by taunting the authoritarian state government and calling for the governor's resignation. Military police and tanks stormed the city, taking prisoners and threatening bystanders, and violent melees broke out on several occasions. It sounded like the onset of another protracted conflict in poor, indigenous southern Mexico, the region that globalization forgot. Indeed, the Oaxaca 2006 protests bore a strong resemblance to the Chiapas 1994 uprising in intensity and high degree of initial public support. But unlike the Zapatista insurgency, which over a few short years transformed itself from a class-based struggle to one focused on indigenous rights and autonomy, the Oaxaca movement, in one of Mexico's most indigenous states, did not assume any multiculturalist frame whatsoever. Why not? What was different about the Oaxaca 2006 movement, and did its lack of a unifying indigenous rights message have any bearing on its broader failure?

The indigenous rights movement by the Zapatistas in neighboring Chiapas galvanized imaginations continents away; It is now referred to as the world's first "Internet War" (Ronfeldt et al. 1998). Furthermore, it catapulted Chiapas into an extremely prominent position on Mexico's domestic policy agenda, garnering for Chiapas, after prolonged negotiations, a doubling of federal social spending and a redistribution of over 6 percent of the state's land area. The uprising in Chiapas is also credited with instigating indigenous rights reforms in Mexico's constitution in 2001 and with legal reforms in twenty-two of the country's thirty-two states.[1]

---

[1] Many argue that the constitutional reforms have not been fully implemented, rendering the legislative accomplishment nothing more than a formality. Nonetheless, the reforms did pass the national Congress on the heels of a dramatic Zapatista march to Mexico City.

18

The short-lived Oaxaca uprising led to no such benefits. In fact, for all its intensity, the Oaxaca conflict did not even have a central, articulated set of objectives beyond demands for the governor's resignation.

More than three years after the Oaxaca conflict, human rights groups were still seeking investigations into several slayings, seven disappearances, scores of injuries, more than a dozen allegations of torture, and a dozen cases of aggression toward journalists (Castro Rodríguez et al. 2009, 39–49, 117–118). By a vote of seven to four in October 2009 the Mexican Supreme Court voted to hold Oaxaca's governor responsible for the state police's human rights violations during the 2006–2007 conflict. However, the Court did not include either then-President Vicente Fox or any of his cabinet members among those "named," and neither current-President Felípe Calderón nor the Mexican Congress has taken further action, despite widespread denunciations of Oaxaca's authoritarianism during the summer and fall of 2006 as Calderón was preparing to take office.

This chapter explores the context of these two movements, arguing that structural and historical conditions help explain the communitarian solidarity in Chiapas and its absence in Oaxaca. Furthermore, I explore why the Chiapas insurrection assumed an indigenous character, while no such identity was part of the movement in the more heavily indigenous Oaxaca. I evaluate the historical institutions and contingent, contemporary conditions that set the parameters for social movement frames in both the largely rural Zapatista insurgency and the more urban social movement in Oaxaca City, the state's capital. This chapter establishes the constructivist nature of southern Mexico's recent collective rights movements (between static primordialists, on the one hand, and subjectivists, on the other). The trajectories of these movements also set the stage for understanding the political realities in 2002–2003, when I conducted the survey research discussed in the next chapter.

I argue that the Zapatistas had a clearly articulated manifesto and that their grievances turned sharply toward the ethno-cultural within two years of the uprising. Despite references by Oaxaca activists in 2006 to the Paris Commune of 1871 the French case was more a matter of spontaneous revolt than social movement. Testimony from participants in Mexico's movements, quoted in the pages that follow, show that the Oaxaca "commune" had little or no guiding doctrine and was in fact so fragmented that a consensus never even formed around who was leading it. This chapter offers a preliminary empirical affirmation that, particularly in multilingual Oaxaca, ethnicity alone was insignificant as a rallying point for the state's most important social movement ever.

In Chiapas, well-articulated communitarian peasant identities took shape even in the remote Lacandon region and ultimately formed the basis of Zapatista ethnic identity and autonomy claims. In Oaxaca, the 2006 movement was primarily led by teachers and urban activists who were resentful of the lack of turnover in Oaxaca's monopoly PRI electoral system and of government failures to respond. In addition, Chiapas had a much more extensive system of communitarian land tenure institutions in the form of *ejido* farms. Oaxaca has a history of less hostile relations between the state and indigenous communities. Land there was divided largely by "communal holdings," or *tierras comunales*, which were parcelled out to families to manage autonomously. This goodwill was reinforced by the legal recognition by the state in 1995 of the Oaxaca customary law of *usos y costumbres*. Ironically, allowing indigenous communities to run their own elections may actually have undermined the rule of law regarding fair elections and weakened groups who opposed the dominant PRI.[2]

My overall finding is that, whereas indigenous populations in Chiapas were victimized by widespread environmental degradation; class and ethnic conflict instigated by oppressive elites; and human rights abuses by authorities, most of the violence visited upon Oaxaca's indigenous people has historically been at the hands of indigenous people themselves. The Zapatistas' ingenious reconfiguration of a "long lost" indigenous identity in Chiapas through a figurative and symbolic effort was intended to give people a broader "repertoire of contention," using Tarrow's term (1998, 20),[3] and to offer a claim that would garner national and international attention. In Oaxaca, the 2006 movement was not framed in terms of indigenous identity; in fact, the communitarian indigenous rights movements in Oaxaca have been less publicized and more passive. As detailed in Chapter 5, legislation was passed in 1995 and amended in 1998 in Oaxaca (perhaps as a consequence of the uprising in neighboring Chiapas) to legalize the existing practice of selecting leaders via customary law in Oaxaca's indigenous communities. Since then, the Oaxacan state has largely ignored indigenous populations.

In Chiapas, indigenous communities have long been decimated by forced relocation, debt peonage, and outright slavery by powerful owners

---

[2] See Eisenstadt (2007b), Danielson and Eisenstadt (2009), Anaya Muñoz (2002), and Recondo (2007).

[3] Tarrow (1998) (, 20) argues that "social movements are repositories of knowledge of particular routines in a society's history, which help them to overcome the deficits in resources and communication typically found among the poor...."

of huge land tracts. Large landowners and the state also attempted to co-opt communities of indigenous citizens and peasant laborers in the mid-20th century by imposing aggressive assimilation policies (Rus 1994, Pineda and Pineda 2002). These attempts at assimilation were resisted in the 1970s and 1980s by peasant land petitioners who were often violently repressed (see, e.g., Burguete Cal y Mayor and Montero Solano n.d., Guillén 1998, Gómez Cruz and Kovic 1994). As mentioned in the last chapter, land distribution in Chiapas was unequal, with rich absentee landowners holding the state's best land and instigating conflict between peasant groups and the state. In Oaxaca, assimilation efforts began earlier, but were less coercive. Oaxaca's land distribution inequality was also much lower. Indigenous people often possessed colonial-era land titles that gave them control over communal lands. Conflict with the state virtually never escalated to epic proportions, although lethal land struggles often occurred between indigenous communities. These differences explain why a strong communitarian ethnic identity developed in Chiapas but not in Oaxaca.

Oaxaca 2006: An Uprising Without an Ideology

The Oaxaca uprising of 2006 followed, for the most part, a corporatist logic common in the 20th-century Mexican countryside at that time.[4] In 2006, Ulises Ruíz, one of Latin America's most famously authoritarian governors (Benton 2006; Gibson 2005; Giraudy 2009), failed to assuage striking teachers and actually violated a long-standing truce between the state and social activists by not budgeting funds for social movement operatives to travel from Oaxaca's agrarian regions to protest in the capital. For more than six months, an ad hoc group called Asamblea Popular de los Pueblos de Oaxaca (APPO), a loose-knit confederation of social movement leaders and operatives from around the state, occupied the streets of Oaxaca City. Outgoing-President Fox, a lame duck after the July 2, 2006 elections, hesitated to intervene, but finally sent federal riot police backed by helicopters to Oaxaca City on October 28, 2006 after three people, including a freelance American journalist, were killed during violent protests with authorities.

After these slayings, the federal police forced APPO to retreat, but the conflict continued for another month. The final showdown occurred on

---

[4] As discussed in Chapter 1, corporatism in the Mexican countryside meant compulsory participation in local branches of the official peasants' union and co-optation of rural squatters by state governments through offers of land negotiated through the union.

the campus of the Benito Juárez Autonomous University in late November. APPO claimed that approximately twenty of its members were killed by authorities during the conflict, and three times as many were disappeared (Martínez Vásquez 2007, 262–264). By the end of November, federal authorities had detained more than 140 activists. The Mexican Supreme Court later refused to open inquiries about violations of the rights of these APPO detainees.

APPO's movement overlapped with, and may have benefited from, the teachers' strike. But the two were not as closely related as some contend. This should have been evident as early as July 2006, when a portion of Teachers' Local 22, the union chapter with the longest history of anti-state activism, ended the strike that had been in effect since May (Martínez Vásquez 2007, 160). The state police successfully repressed the strikers in a violent action on June 14 that injured more than ninety people. The government's heavy-handedness focused sentiment against Governor Ruíz, whose orders were viewed overwhelmingly as groundless and inhumane (Martínez Vásquez 2007, 205). Despite their common cause in advocating for the removal of Governor Ruíz, the teachers' union, under changed leadership, voted in late October to officially end its walkout and abandon APPO, which continued to try to mobilize. On December 3, the teachers' union leadership confirmed the break with APPO, stating that "they [the APPO] decided not to be there [in negotiations with the federal government], escalate to another level, and insist that Fox sit down with them, and now they have to face their decisions and consequences" (Martínez Vásquez 2007, 163). Having never consolidated any leadership or ideological platform, APPO members "shouted down" their leader in Oaxaca City's central square on November 25. Flavio Sosa stepped down and said, "The situation is uncontrollable, the rebellion is uncontrollable, the leadership of APPO has been superseded" (Osorno 2007b, 56).

The teachers' strike was an annual spring rite in Mexico. For years, Latin America's largest union, Mexico's National Union of Education Workers (SNTE), had walked out as part of a nationwide protest to force the state to raise salaries. (Salaries vary by zone, but Oaxaca's have long been the lowest in Mexico.) In 2006, Local 22 was also particularly agitated about Oaxaca's poor working conditions. The collapse of the PRI–federal government nexus in 2000 and subsequent polarization in Oaxaca (one of the PRI's last bastions) during the 2006 elections exacerbated tensions. The left-leaning Party of the Democratic Revolution (PRD) candidate Andrés Manuel López Obrador's challenge of his narrow defeat in the July presidential election also contributed to APPO's grievances.[5] But the national teachers' union head, Elba Ester Gordillo, who had broken from the PRI in 2004 to support the 2006 President-elect Felípe Calderón from the center-right National Action Party (PAN), co-opted Oaxaca union leadership by recruiting political moderates to form a new Local 59 and granting the remaining Local 22 teachers' demands in order to remove them from the conflict.

Governor Ruíz, by many accounts insensitive to social conditions and to the rule of law, was dismantling Mexico's old corporatist system by refusing to play ball with operatives in regional interest groups who had under previous governors received payoffs in exchange for persuading protesters to desist. Ruíz's predecessors, notably his immediate predecessor, José Murat, had been known for appeasing social movement leaders, some of whom led up to three protests per week (Osorno 2007a, 49), including APPO activists and leaders like Flavio Sosa (Osorno 2007a, 157). Local 22 member and APPO activist Sylvia Hernández Fernández said, "Murat was corrupt, but when the water threatened to overflow the dike, he tried to lower its level. Ulises [Ruíz], no. He saw the flood was going to carry us all away and he didn't care" (interview 2009).

In the 1990s, a small but tangible percentage of Mexico's budget was designated for "social peace," addressing social demands by delivering cement or fertilizer to protesters as a way of quelling potential disturbances (Hernández Fernández and Arnaud Viñas interviews 2009). But Ruíz refused to pay up and threatened activists that "this government is prepared for the worst scenario" (Hernández Fernández interview 2009), thereby conveying that there would be no concessions. Governor Ruíz tried to break down old corporatist structures without creating new ones; he sought to reduce the power of social interest groups to consolidate his own dominion.

The movement in Oaxaca was made up of two groups whose activities happened to coincide in time and place: the teachers and the APPO. Neither advocated for indigenous rights or even included indigenous activists as members. APPO leader and long-time Oaxaca indigenous rights advocate Marcos Leyva acknowledged that few "spaces" existed in APPO for indigenous voices (interview 2008). "The indigenous intellectuals arrived

---

[5] Several interviewees cited rumors that President Calderón had traded the removal of Ruíz and another besieged governor in the neighboring state of Puebla for the PRD's help in certifying Calderón's victory in the federal Congress. That deal was apparently never consummated. For more on the postelectoral conflict staged by PRD candidate Andres Manuel López Obrador, see Eisenstadt (2007a).

late," said Leyva. The APPO directorate member confirmed that his allied nongovernmental organization, Servicios para una Educación Alternativa (known as EDUCA), had an extensive agenda of reforms to improve governability, democracy, and representation in Oaxaca, but that APPO was "stuck" on simply forcing the resignation of Governor Ruíz and could not agree on more profound platforms (Leyva interview 2008). Similarly, APPO street barricade leader Tania Fernández said:

The indigenous movement was one more position. It was not favored in practice, but only in rhetoric. *Indigenismo* sells. It was a selling point [of the movement]. APPO sought to show that it was replicating an indigenous means of taking decisions in a communal assembly. But in the majority of instances, the assemblies took on their own logic, sometimes as fronts [in which each group achieved votes commensurate with the number of people it brought to the assembly]. (Interview, 2009)

APPO's constituency was urban and based in Oaxaca City. It ranged from middle-class political moderates to Leninist intellectuals to anarchists, making agreement on a common agenda extremely unlikely. Oaxaca's indigenous groups and other rural Oaxacans were excluded from the movement and, in many cases, did not even know about APPO (Cohen 2009, 12). They did know about the coinciding teachers' strike and lamented the fact that their children's schools were closed for months (Arellanes interview 2009). This strike led many pragmatic rural citizen parents to oppose the entire movement.

But was there a latent indigenous rights agenda in Oaxaca? One long-time analyst, Oaxaca state education advisor, Samael Hernández, said that Local 22 did have a grand reform agenda, which the Oaxaca teachers presented at meetings in the spring of 2006. It included proposals for mitigating poverty in Oaxaca's indigenous communities, among other things. But after the police actions on June 14, 2006, when state police cracked down on teachers during their annual march on Oaxaca City's central square, the broader agenda was forgotten in the immediate efforts to try to sanction the governor and state security apparatus. To Hernández, "Ulises [Ruíz] broke protocol in his relations with the teachers' union. The government tried to penetrate the structure of the union directly. He should have respected the 'ritual of mobilization' and put up with it" (Hernández interview 2009). Instead of promoting a radical but concrete list of reforms, the teachers were left just trying to free their prisoners, "as is usually the case after movements are repressed" (Hernández interview 2009). The Oaxaca movement has been widely seen as failing to promote an agenda for change, despite the fact that political activists and teachers did receive a much more favorable wages and work conditions settlement than usual. The Zapatista movement in Chiapas did not suffer the same fate.

Chiapas 1994: The Model Indigenous Rights Movement

In Chiapas, the roots of the movement lie much deeper. Precursor movements began in the 1960s and 1970s as peasant mobilizations for land. Organized peasant groups grew dramatically during the 1970s and 1980s, seeking resolution to land conflicts and, increasingly, an end to government repression that had reached extreme proportions.[6] Zapatista leaders borrowed ideas from these movements, as well as from the left-leaning Catholic Church and antiregime activists elsewhere in Mexico. On January 1, 1994, the Zapatistas launched their first attack against a half dozen towns, briefly taking three of them through violent acts that killed dozens of people during the first several days (although wildly conflicting accounts differ on the number of towns attacked and casualties suffered in the surprise attacks). The Zapatistas declared that they would overthrow the upper-class overlords in Mexico on behalf of the poor and oppressed.

A reprisal against the National Zapatista Liberation Army (EZLN – the group's military wing) by the Mexican State followed, and human rights groups and other arbiters, having missed the first salvo, sought to bear witness. Some 300 were killed in President Salinas' counter-attack in the spring of 1994, including 13 Mexican army soldiers, 38 state police, 70 of an estimated several thousand Zapatista fighters, and between 19 and 275 civilians (Womack 1999, 43–44). After internal jostling and a series of retreats prompted by an overwhelming army retaliation, the EZLN settled into a diminished military presence but with a galvanizing ideological and propaganda presence, as Subcommander Marcos' inspired, scathing, and humorous newspaper columns and communiqués with the Mexican public were carried worldwide over the Internet.

---

[6] Under the government of one of Chiapas' most ruthless governors, General Absalón Castellanos Domínguez, Burguete Cal y Mayor and Montero Solano (n.d., 56) documented 102 political assassinations, 327 disappearances, 590 arbitrary detentions, 427 kidnappings and/or tortures, and 40 families expulsions from land in Chiapas between 1982 and 1987. Expulsions and relocations increased under Governor Patrocinio González Garrido, as some 300 families were expelled from lands via squatter relocations between 1989 and 1993. There were 472 arbitrary detentions as well, although the number of politically motivated homicides dropped to 29 (Gómez Cruz, and Kovic 1994, 61, 91).

By way of this clever outreach through the new media (which was still really new in 1994), Subcommander Marcos and the Zapatistas articulated a coherent Marxist class conflict frame. Several years into the campaign, however, they shifted to an indigenous rights focus.[7] Marcos himself acknowledged as much in his statement, which also conveys his own frustration with indigenous movement leaders: "A movement that grows in darkness, isolated from everything, prepares to come into the world, and ... surprise! The world isn't the one you prepared for. We confronted the indigenous problematic and experienced a disconnect because the first that emerged from the indigenous movement was not the communities themselves, but the 'professional Indians ...'" (Mestries Benquet 2001, 138). But transitioning from a classist ideology to an indigenous rights perspective was not so simple. It required overcoming profound differences over religion, as the indigenous communities were strong Catholic adherents and the Marxist-oriented rebels were not. Ultimately, the Zapatistas had to be more flexible to overcome this difficulty.

The San Andrés Accords, negotiated between the Mexican government and Zapatista rebels and signed in 1996, laid out constitutional changes that awarded collective rights to indigenous groups within prescribed territorial boundaries, as per international standards established by the International Labour Organization Treaty 169 (or ILO 169) in 1989 and ratified by Mexico in 1990. The government acceded, in most regards, to the Zapatistas' position, although not completely. The unfulfilled Zapatista agenda for indigenous rights recognition largely concerned land tenure reform.

The Accords were severely tested when President Ernesto Zedillo's government did not submit the negotiated legislation for congressional ratification. Some 70,000 soldiers started amassing in what came to be known as the zone of conflict in the central and eastern parts of Chiapas, as the Mexican military dispatched roughly one-third of its troops to quiet the insurgents and also the vigilante groups – usually working for land barons with ties to the PRI – known as "paramilitaries." In late 1997, these agrarian conflicts, mixed with religious tensions and the struggle between the Zapatistas and pro-government vigilantes boiled over in the Tzotzil village of Acteal, Chiapas, where forty-five people were massacred.

Soldiers stationed at a nearby military base failed to intervene during the attack; some activists argue that the military, the PRI, and its state and

[7] Interview with Margarito Ruíz (2004).

federal executives were accomplices to these murders, which resulted in dismissals of a governor and federal Interior Secretary (widely regarded as the most powerful position in the Mexican government aside from the president). Perhaps even more frustrating to human rights activists than the Supreme Court's decision to not pursue allegations related to Oaxaca 2006 was the Supreme Court's August 2009 decision to release twenty of the eighty vigilantes convicted for perpetrating the Acteal massacre.[8] The release was based on procedural violations in evidence collection during the investigation and trial. The lack of accountability regarding Acteal mirrored the lack of formal progress the federal government made in implementing the Chiapas peace accords and resulting indigenous rights constitutional reforms.

The truncated San Andrés peace process coincided with efforts by policymakers in Oaxaca, led by then-PRI Governor Diódoro Carrasco, to legalize *usos y costumbres*. Whether the political objective of the legislation, passed in 1995 and revised in 1997, was to promote indigenous culture, protect PRI strongholds, or prevent an imagined Zapatista-style indigenous uprising,[9] indigenous leaders praised the new law for legally recognizing cultural practices and allowing them collective authority over resources and land they had stewarded for centuries. The federal government seemed to be conceding some enhanced rights for native peoples, recognizing that earlier government efforts had failed to protect indigenous minorities' rights or ensure access to state resources.

Individual Versus Communitarian Rights in Chiapas and Oaxaca

To many authors in the communitarian tradition (Escárzaga and Gutiérrez 2005; Jackson and Warren 2005), indigenous rights are communitarian

---

[8] The eighty individuals were from neighboring communities near Acteal and were directly involved in the attack. According to Amnesty International, fourteen junior public officials were convicted and served sentences of between three and eight years, but no senior government, military, or PRI party official has been held to account. See http://www. amnesty.org/en/for-media/press-releases/mexico-new-investigation-acteal-massacre-essential-20090813

[9] Several indigenous movements emerged in the years immediately prior to the Zapatista rebellion, and Oaxacan indigenous leaders participated prominently in the San Andrés Accord negotiations. Perhaps more importantly to the federal and state governments in Oaxaca, the Popular Revolutionary Army (EPR), an internal insurgency claiming indigenous identity (among other things), emerged in 1996. This armed movement's ideological justification was never clearly articulated nor published in Oaxaca.

rights by definition. For these theorists, politics is not just the aggregation of individual preferences (as it is for liberal individualists), but derives from preferences articulated by groups who represent the beliefs and attitudes of their constituents more effectively and coherently than each member could do individually. In the following sections, I use a loose paired-comparison approach to demonstrate that the diverging histories of Chiapas and Oaxaca are at least partially responsible for the survey respondents' views regarding communitarianism and individual rights. Survey results (as detailed in Chapter 3) show that Chiapanecan respondents are more communitarian than those in Oaxaca, which I argue has a number of historical causes.

First, whereas Oaxaca's indigenous communities suffered dislocation and discrimination during the colonial period, they were mostly ignored by the central government in the 19th and 20th centuries. Chiapas' indigenous communities, on the other hand, were enslaved and destroyed as recently as the 19th and 20th centuries. They were heavily repressed by a series of authoritarian governors and collaborationist economic elites throughout the decades leading up to the Zapatista rebellion (and, to a lesser degree, since that rebellion). Peasant groups mobilized in Chiapas to contest land disputes by staging hundreds of squatter protests, which fostered a communitarian identity and sense of ethnic solidarity. In Oaxaca, indigenous communities were allowed to reconstitute themselves as a result of the state's benign neglect. Communal properties were easily divided into individual and family parcels.

Oaxaca is known for a development pattern respectful of indigenous autonomy (Díaz Montes 1992, 101–103), as well as for fierce intervillage conflict in indigenous areas (Dennis 1987; Greenberg 1989). State authorities reinforced their harmonious relationship with indigenous people when it codified *usos y costumbres* in 1995.[10] On a state level, Oaxaca's less polarized relations between indigenous and non-indigenous citizens contrasts

---

[10] The Oaxaca state government recognized the long-standing practice in traditional communities of selecting leaders through routes other than through partisan local elections. For example, supporters of candidates were asked to line up behind their candidate, local mayors were selected via municipal plebiscites where at least some citizens were empowered to vote, or decisions were made behind closed doors by a tribal council of elders. As of 1995, these practices assumed a legal status for local mayoral selection in majority indigenous municipalities (418 out of Oaxaca's 570 municipalities as of 1998), and political parties have been banned from participation. Eisenstadt (2007b) argues, based on systematic evidence from 1995, 1998, and 2001, that the new system has actually increased electoral conflict.

sharply with the conditions in Chiapas. In Oaxaca, violent conflict has more often been among indigenous groups than between indigenous people and the state.[11] The significance of this from a political history perspective cannot be overstated. According to historian John Chance (1986, 180), "The Spaniards were most concerned with replacing Indian structures above the community level, and, in Oaxaca, where these were either tenuous or non-existent, a substantial portion of the indigenous sociopolitical organization survived the conquest years."

Consequently, perhaps, Oaxaca has more communal land than any other state in Mexico. Communal land claims have been granted when community leaders could credibly claim "primordial title," either by displaying a colonial-era deed or by obtaining a presidential decree stating that the community had held the lands since deeds were recorded. As further elaborated in Chapter 4, nearly five million hectares (or 50,000 km²) of Mexico were nationalized and collectivized between the Mexican Revolution and the constitutionally-mandated end of agrarian reform in the early 1990s; 94 percent of these lands were designated as *ejido* collective farms, whereas only 6 percent (constituting more than half of Oaxaca's distribution) were given the legal status of "communal" land.

Overall, more than 30 percent of Mexico (lands expropriated after the Revolution plus those which were already publicly held) was classified as "social" property in 2004. (Correspondence with the Attorney General for Agrarian Affairs, Office of Studies and Publications, September 30, 2004). In total, 77 percent of Oaxaca's territory is now designated public land, and the vast majority of these acres are in collective farms. Fifty-three percent of nonprivate properties are held as communal lands, whereas 47 percent have been constituted as *ejidos*. By 2004, only 49 percent of Chiapas' 7.6 million hectares was nonprivate (Attorney General for Agrarian Affairs, Office of Studies and Publications), with nearly a quarter of Chiapas' state-owned lands held in the protected Montes Azules Biosphere and other Lacandon area reserves, which are considered in Chapter 4. Regarding the

---

[11] Anthropologists like Dennis (1987) and Greenberg (1989) classify this intra- and inter-village violence as intergenerational "blood feuds." Human rights authorities argue that the state's authoritarian governments have allowed and on occasion even committed violence against social movement activists since the 1970s and 1980s. According to Minnesota Advocates for Human Rights (1996, 3): "Oaxacan state officials also violate basic human rights through their significant omissions. The chronic failure of Oaxaca's law enforcement apparatus to perform its duty to carry out the law is perhaps the principal method by which human rights guarantees are offended in the state."

remainder, eighty-eight percent of Chiapas' nonprivate farmlands were divided into *ejidos*, and only 12 percent carried the "communal land" designation. See Table 2.1 for distinctions between *ejidos* and communal lands and the prevalence of each in Chiapas and Oaxaca.

Much of the conflict over land in Chiapas can be traced back to the Mexican government's failure to consolidate control of Chiapas during the Mexican Revolution. In the late 20th century, it penetrated Chiapas' large landholder economy much more aggressively than it did Oaxaca's, which was organized into more egalitarian and self-governing, but less productive communal lands (*tierras comunales*) relatively soon after the Spanish conquest. The initial lack of penetration by the revolutionaries, achieved in much of Mexico by the 1950s, but in Chiapas' remote regions only in the 1970s and 1980s, has been associated with the failure of the federal government to successfully resist former-President Lázaro Cárdenas' redistribution of a third of Mexico's cultivated land in the 1930s (Hansen 1971, 34).

In Chiapas' central highlands, the PRI-state consolidated power in the 1940s, when the government decreed that only religious officials were allowed to sell alcohol in indigenous communities, thereby granting religious elders a profitable monopoly as compensation for empowering young interlocutors of the state. Bilingual teachers became the new political bosses and performed constituency services, lent money, and enforced loyalty to the PRI (Rus 1994; Pineda Pineda 2002). In the more remote Lacandon rainforest, where the Zapatistas hid for years before their 1994 emergence, corporatist arrangements were less apparent and the state's permeation less thorough. Here, even in the early 1980s, the Catholic Church was still the main political institution. Urban guerrillas who had failed to gain traction in Mexico City were drawn to the Chiapas' rainforest by promises that their existing social networks could be retooled in this environment and lead to successful rebellion (Trejo 2004).

This pattern in Chiapas of challenging state control over rural lands contrasts markedly with the forms of protest undertaken in Oaxaca. Land tenure structures in Oaxaca were mediated during much of the post-revolution 20th century by Mexico's National Peasant Confederation (CNC), the most important corporatist arm of the PRI. Struggles for land by indigenous communities were not prevalent, although mobilizations to challenge the CNC and the PRI did start to occur in the 1970s when independent peasant unions emerged as part of the broader political mobilization occurring nationwide after the 1968 student movement and the massacre of hundreds of students at Tlatelolco in Mexico City

Table 2.1. *Comparison of Ejido and Tierras Comunales Land Tenure Regimes*

Criterion	Ejidos	Communal Lands
How Government Recognition is Granted	Presidential decree creating new public lands based on a petitioning process which often involves mobilization	Presidential decree recognizing pre-colonial titles – usually just a matter of municipalities showing the proper paperwork
Restrictions on Private Use	May be used only on usufruct basis by stake-holders, based on membership list held by local government agent	May be used only on usufruct basis by stake-holders, but is usually parceled to families and individuals
Inheritance of Lands	Descendents may inherit *ejidatario* claims, but usually depends on collective vote	Descendents do not usually inherit *tierras comunales*, but this depends entirely on internal decisions
Governing Body	An *asamblea ejidal* convenes, each stake-holder votes. An *ejido* commissioner manages on behalf of this body.	An *asamblea communal* convenes, each stake-holder votes. A municipal commissioner of *bienes comunales* manages on behalf of the body.
Relationship to Municipality	None, as *ejidos* may overlap several municipalities or be contained entirely in one.	Strong, as only one commissioner of *bienes comunales* may be named per municipality, and they often manage most community resources, as the correspondence is often one communal holding per municipality.
Percentage of Mexico's Public Lands Under this Regime (Note: 31.21 percent of all lands are public)	93.54%	6.46%
Percentage of Chiapas' Public Lands Under this Regime (Note: 49 percent of all lands are public, but this also includes parks and reserves)	88.19%	11.81%
Percentage of Oaxaca's Public Lands Under this Regime (Note: 77 percent of all lands are public, but this also includes parks and reserves)	52.71%	47.29%

Sources: National Institute of Statistics, Geography, and Information Processing (INEGI) 2000 (2001a in bibliography); Attorney General for Agrarian Affairs, at http://www.pa.gob.mx/estadisticas_agrarias_2004/ini.htm; Attorney General for Agrarian Affairs, Office of Studies and Publications author correspondence, "Controversias por municipio en los Estados de Chiapas, Oaxaca y Zacatecas para el periodo 1992–30 de septiembre de 2004, Procuraduría Agraria (pedido expreso de Todd Eisenstadt a la Dirección de Estudios y publicaciones de la Procuraduría Agraria)."

(Moreno Derbez 2009, 55–56). Even some of the traditional political bosses, or *caciques*[12], had grown more independent by the 1980s and 1990s, as political opposition rose. But squatter mobilizations in rural Oaxaca (unlike the anarchic APPO in urban Oaxaca City) were always hierarchical and limited by clientelist ties between the leaders and followers. In Chiapas, particularly in the Lacandon wilderness and other remote areas, small groups of people banded together without preestablished hierarchies to oppose the authoritarian regime. Snyder (2001) captured the distinction by characterizing Oaxaca's system of interest articulation during this period as "corporatism from below," based on peasants' ties to the state, and Chiapas' system as "peasants against oligarchs."

Ejidos *Versus Communal Lands: The Difference Property Rights Make*

Mexico's 20th-century land reform movement at least partly passed Chiapas and almost completely passed the Lacandon rainforest area, where the Zapatistas began. As detailed in Chapter 4, President Lázaro Cárdenas (1934–1940) quintupled the amount of public land during his administration, although only about half was distributed during his term. Presidents since Cárdenas have re-granted the same land, leading to multiple claims on a single property and a notorious backlog in the actual titling of land that has been so generously bestowed ... and bestowed. Increased demand for land in the 1960s and 1970s corresponded with more presidential pledges of land. These pledges came in the form of populist decrees by presidents Gustavo Díaz Ordaz (1964–1970) and Luis Echeverría (1970–1976) who were trying to diffuse challenges to Mexico's authoritarian government by massive student movements and leftist urban insurgencies.

After decades of haphazard land granting processes, President Carlos Salinas (1988–1994) tried to keep some of those promises. But, in 1992, an

---

[12] Knight offers an extensive discussion of the definition of *cacique*, especially as distinguished from *caudillo*. While *caudillos* were more grandiose and violent and worthy of the 'warlord' or 'man on horseback' term, the *cacique* is thought of as more of an intermediary. To Knight (2005, 10): "In colonial Mexico, *caciques* were indigenous rulers, vital cogs in the machinery of colonial administration. During the nineteenth century, however, *'cacique'* came to mean a political boss, who – according to some – stood at the interface between 'traditional' communities and the new ostensibly 'modern' institutions of the (usually republican) nation state. Thus, *'cacique'* was detached from its indigenous roots and came to denote a form of political boss, mediator, or broker." In contemporary rural Mexico, I would add, *caciques* are ubiquitous and synonymous with 'PRI agent/representative.'

amendment to Article 27 of the Mexican Constitution officially ended the distribution of new lands, although existing claims would continue to wind through the system. By the end of President Zedillo's term (1994–2000), 14 percent of all the hectares pledged as *ejidos* and *tierras comunales* via presidential decree had still not been delivered; Chiapas alone accounted for 25 percent of that national backlog (Monroy 1994). President Calderón (elected in 2006), in order to close down the land distribution channels once and for all, actually did abolish the Agrarian Reform Ministry in 2009. Some rural citizens have resisted efforts to gain title to their lands because they feared the state would take their lands or at least put them up for sale, contributing to the uncertainty over property rights in rural areas.

The historically unequal distribution of land holdings in Chiapas was not notably improved by the Mexican Revolution in 1917, leading some to conclude that the revolution never came to Chiapas.[13] As late as 1960, 52.5 percent of the land was owned by 2.4 percent of landholders (Gómez Cruz and Kovic 1994, 43). After decades of agrarian reform barely reaching Chiapas (Benjamin 1996, 179), some of the Soconusco coffee plantations in southwest Chiapas were expropriated by the state in the mid-20th century, although the resulting redistribution was not widely significant, and it occurred far from where the Zapatistas would burst forth. Hundreds of new *ejidos* were created in Chiapas. But the rural *ejido* dwellers remained desperately poor, because they were not able to benefit from the boom in international demand for agricultural products in the way that large-scale producers of cattle, coffee, sugarcane, cacao, and cotton could.[14]

The state's elite land owners who emerged in the mid-20th century also benefited greatly from the federal government's decision in 1948 to start channelling the provision of all rural services through the National

---

[13] The Mexican Revolution did not really affect the interests of Chiapas' large landlords, consisting of approximately 300–500 people in the 1920s, 72 of whom owned 20 percent of all the state's private property. In 1930, the 500 farms and ranches of more than 500 hectares possessed 79 percent of the state's land, while the 67 *ejidos* in the census possessed 3 percent (Benjamin 1996, 150–151, 179).

[14] To Benjamin (1996, 226): "All indices point to the underdevelopment of the *ejidal* sector. In 1960, for example, while some 900 *ejidos* supported 92,000 families, as compared to about 30,000 landowning families, the *ejidal* sector earned one third as much, owned one tenth as many tractors, and possessed land valued at one third of the amount of the private sector. Although the *ejidal* sector increased its landholdings substantially, most *ejidos* were overpopulated by the 1960s. Many if not most *ejidal* parcels were too small to support a family, which forced members to work on neighboring estates or as migrant laborers."

Indigenous Institute (INI). Complimenting the work of the CNC (the PRI-state's corporatist peasant union), the INI sought "respectful, noncoercive integration" (Mattiace 2003, 60) of indigenous services across a range of administrative agencies. This was ultimately another very powerful means by which the federal government could permeate and subordinate indigenous populations to the PRI-state. The INI, however, failed to penetrate some of Chiapas' more remote areas, including the Lacandon communal land zone. It has been argued that this failure, coupled with generalized anger over the federal land title backlog and the economic strains posed by new waves of Chol and Tzeltal migrants, pushed the Lacandon colonists into the arms of jungle-based social service providers, including politicized Protestant and Catholic churches,[15] agrarian activists, and, ultimately, the Zapatistas.

A panoply of agrarian civil society groups emerged in Chiapas in the 1970s and 1980s. Most of these groups were co-opted by the CNC, which was authorized by law to review and validate all land claims prior to the creation of agrarian tribunals in 1992 (Hardy 1984, quoted in Trejo 2004, 133). But some independent organizations thrived and, by the early 1980s, were organizing hundreds of land mobilizations a year.

In response to sincere, albeit limited, federal efforts by President Salinas in the late 1980s to make good on presidential land grants, Chiapas' authoritarian local government (pressured also by the powerful landed elite) pushed back. They devised three institutional loopholes that helped maintain their already extreme land advantage. First, the government found a way, through the Agrarian Rehabilitation Program (PRA), to compensate landowners handsomely for launching fake invasions on their less fertile or otherwise undesirable lands, thereby ridding them of economic burdens. Second, Governor Absalón Castellanos Domínguez, perhaps the most corrupt of a bad lot, issued more certificates of non-affectability (2,932) in the 1970s and 1980s, removing land from the reach of redistribution, than any of his post-1934 predecessors (4,112 combined) (Reyes Ramos 1992, 119). Third, the Chiapas penal code was selectively used to punish land-seeking peasants. By the early 1990s, some 90 percent of Chiapas' prisoners were indigenous peasants, even though this group comprised only 30 percent of the population. Private landholders prosecuted *comunero* and *ejiditario*

---

[15] Trejo (2004, 140–145) argues that incursions by Protestant ministries, which had consciously selected Latin America as a potential area for expansion, prompted a Catholic reprisal and forced the Catholic Church to provide more social services.

peasants for chopping wood (illegal under the penal code), and peasants languished indefinitely in jail while interested parties took over cultivation of land the prisoners had previously occupied (Thibault 1998, 41). These efforts by Chiapas' regional elites to preserve the status quo coupled with new international declarations about the rights of indigenous peoples worldwide gave Chiapas' peasants a new means of framing their grievances and a new source of hope. And the federal government's failure to reign in the corrupt state governments along with the growing strength of independent activists mostly hidden in plain sight, laid the groundwork for the Zapatistas' public emergence in the early 1990s.

Before 1994, squatter groups had often succeeded in gaining access to land that previously has been off limits. But, with the 1992 reform to Article 27, declaring that there would be no new land redistribution, that line of protest was cut off. This was a huge blow to the social activist groups and a real source of frustration to the rural communities who were left empty handed. (Emiliano Zapata's battle cry during Mexico's first social revolution in the early 20th century was "land and liberty!") In 1994, the Mexican government turned to the corporatist CNC for help in trying to contain and diffuse the anger Article 27 had generated. It granted the official peasant union some three-quarters of the area the government redistributed immediately after 1994 (Villafuerte Solís et al. 1999, 156, fn 3).

At the same time, a land trust was created through a federal-state partnership that would buy land from private owners in Zapatista-occupied areas (where the owners could not access their land anyway), grant them cash indemnities, and help the former landowners relocate. The state would then conduct quiet ad hoc negotiations with individual squatter groups to informally redistribute the land. This practice peaked between 1994 and 1996, but lasted through 2005. Consistent with the PRI-state's strategy of co-optation, a majority of the 240,000 hectares bought by the state (Luna Lujan interview 2002) was given to pro-regime peasant or *campesino* groups[16] (Villafuerte Solís et. al. 1999, 195, 196; Ruíz 2004, interview). Roughly 20 percent of the land was given to independent Chiapas squatters. The state government also tried to address the Zapatistas' land-related claims by loaning an additional 65,000 hectares (or about 250 square miles) to Zapatista squatters (Luna Lujan interview 2002). And recall that Zapatista sympathizers at this time probably numbered in the hundreds of

[16] Violent "white guard" squatters' groups have also occupied large properties of absentee owners, and, in some cases, were organized by the owners themselves to "counter-invade" lands under the control of squatters.

thousands, as did refugees from the zones of conflict. But the Zapatistas themselves (at least the original Zapatistas who launched the movement), usually the beneficiaries of these land distributions, never numbered more than a few thousand.

These post-Zapatista rebellion informal land reforms have been credited with diminishing anger over land tenure in Chiapas. Overall, the Zapatistas provoked the government to redistribute more than 300,000 hectares (or 1,100 square miles), including the lands bought by the state trust and resold. This is more than 290,000 hectares that were redistributed in Chiapas as a result of President Lázaro Cárdenas' much-lauded 1930s agrarian reforms (Reyes Ramos 1992, 133). Moreover, federal social spending also increased dramatically in Chiapas after the uprising. According to Villafuerte Solís et al. (1999, 373), social spending increased greatly from 26 percent of state gross domestic product (GDP) in 1989 to 42 percent of GDP in 1994. Similarly, Chiapas' share of Mexico's federal rural development spending grew from 1.4 percent in 1991 to 2.3 percent, on average, from 1993 to 1996 (Villafuerte Solís et al. 1999, 374).

The Colonial Roots of Indigenous Communal Lands Autonomy in Oaxaca

Unlike in Chiapas, where the Spanish conquest was met with fierce resistance, Oaxaca's indigenous communities surrendered quickly (after a few short-lived rebellions) and were then mostly ignored by the Spanish. According to Bailón Corres, "The Zapotecs, Mixtecs and other Oaxacan indigenous groups had developed forms of political, cultural, and ethnic organization which gave them consistent but passive resistance against colonial dominance; this permitted them to conserve their lands and even initiate old agrarian disputes with neighboring communities and peoples" (2008, 21). The indigenous communities were exploited indirectly via the extraction of tribute payments, rather than through the direct servitude imposed in Chiapas. This allowed Oaxacans to retain the integrity of their lands and communities. In Chiapas, land was privatized and overtaken by national and international agrarian elites (Recondo 2007, 79). The land reform following the Mexican Revolution had some impact on Oaxaca, where many of the large land holdings were confiscated by the state and redistributed as *ejidos*. In Chiapas, *ejidos* were formed in much smaller numbers and land was further concentrated into a few hands. In Oaxaca, the vast majority of lands not privately owned stayed in the possession of communal stewards, called *comuneros*, based on pre-colonial claims.

This image of corporate integrity, reminiscent of Eric Wolf's prototype of "closed corporate communities," dissolves, however, under close examination. Common land holders in Oaxaca's closed communities subdivided the land in whatever manner best suited them. In some cases, such as Ixtlán de Juárez, one of the most prosperous Zapotec towns of Oaxaca's northern mountains, the public land commission is more powerful than the municipal government, and commons holders receive dividends every year from their jointly held ventures that comprise the vast majority of the local economy (Zenteno interview 2005).[17] Observers throughout Oaxaca remarked on how families had divided communal lands among themselves and argued, sometimes successfully, for the right to pass property to the next generation or to sell land to outsiders who would agree to go through the commission's internal titling process without any state involvement. One Ixtlán business shareholder, manager of an award-winning trout fishery and restaurant, acknowledged that provisions are in place for his children to inherit his share, and that the incentives provided by the commons-holder commission are a mix of individual and communal. He insisted, though, that in Ixtlán, purely private property does not exist (Jiménez Gaeta interview 2005).

Oaxaca's land rights movement, at least in indigenous areas, was largely driven by indigenous communities seeking recognition of their pre-colonial claims. As noted by Bailón Corres (2008, 23), "[B]etween the *ejido* and communal land owner exist structural differences. One receives land from the state, and the other receives recognition of what has always been in possession." This crucial difference goes far in explaining distinctions between Chiapas (majority *ejido* and hence subject to the state corporatist policies in place during much of the 20th century) and Oaxaca (majority communal lands for which ancestral claims were enough to get titles by presidential decree).

In Oaxaca, communal land governance was an internal matter for the public land commissioners and the commons holders; in Chiapas, it always involved the state, which perpetrated patron-client relations by keeping the list of *ejido* members in each community and, thus, the power to

---

[17] The community's economic interests include an ecotourism venture, gas station, general store, transportation company, trout fishery, and restaurant.

mobilize communal farmers who want to ensure their family's continued position on the government-controlled membership roster. Oaxaca had a more formal corporatist structure, but this was largely due to the pervasive influence of the one-party state. Oaxacans had a clear understanding of who owned land de jure and who owned it de facto, and could resolve internal contradictions to their own satisfaction among themselves. In Chiapas, the confounding regifting of the same lands over and over created cartographic chaos and led to the filing of thousands of agrarian court claims that dragged on over decades.

Demographic changes also speak to the comparative cruelty of the Spanish occupation in Chiapas relative to Oaxaca. In 1792, Oaxaca's indigenous population alone was estimated at slightly more than 400,000 people. This number increased to 600,000 by 1810 and to nearly 950,000 by 1901 (Bailón Corres 2008, 21). In Chiapas,[18] the total population in 1521 was estimated to be 1.7 million. By 1550, that number had dropped 70 percent to just 400,000 (Bailón Corres 2008, 26). Oaxaca grew steadily whereas Chiapas' population was decimated by colonial (and post-colonial) mistreatment.

Oaxaca's indigenous communities also benefited from the liberal reforms of the 19th century. Under those reforms, the Mexican government expropriated many of the Catholic Church's extensive land holdings and altered its federal pact with the states. In Oaxaca, indigenous leaders managed to ensure that their new state-level constitution protected the ability of local governments to administer communal lands in both indigenous and non-indigenous towns (Bailón Corres in Hernández-Díaz ed. 2007, 106–107). As stated by Recondo, "[T]hroughout the 19th Century, during the liberal reforms, the communities of Oaxaca did not just manage to stop the privatization of their lands, but also utilize the law to fortify their collective properties … The [indigenous] communities maintained control of their territory more or less disguised as collective property, utilizing, above all else, the figure of the municipality" (2007, 79). Indeed, a rough correspondence exists between municipal and communal boundaries in many Oaxacan communities. To this day, indigenous communities have been able to maintain their local autonomy over their communal lands by basing their legal claim on pre-colonial land titles and agreeing to be subsumed by the Mexican State for all extra-community purposes.

---

[18] There was no census of just Chiapas (which was divided into two political units at that time, current day Chiapas and Soconusco). The pre-independence data is for Chiapas, Soconusco, and Yucatán.

By the 20th century, the firewall protecting Oaxacans from the Mexican government's intrusion into matters of land distribution was sufficiently strong that the Mexican government found that it had to offer a clientelist bargain by which peasants voted for the PRI, and in exchange, the PRI-state left Oaxaca's rural towns alone between elections. Given the autonomy of what would ultimately become *usos y costumbres* communities, assimilationist economic development policies carried out by the National Indigenous Institute (INI) and the PRI's National Peasant Confederation (CNC) did not seem to penetrate Oaxaca's indigenous communities as well as in other rural areas with little autonomy, like Chiapas and Yucatán.[19] Mexico's agrarian reform, which had created new *ejidos* throughout much of the nation in the 1930s and 1940s, had a diminished impact in most of Oaxaca's indigenous regions. The indigenous communities actually used the opportunity to consolidate their communal autonomy, demonstrated by the fact that 80 percent of the state's community land claims at the time were sought as communal lands rather than *ejidos* (Recondo 2007, 79).

An informal bargain seems to have been struck in Oaxaca between the PRI and Oaxaca's indigenous communities. The local communities would continue to be left to govern themselves and only be forced to involve the state in dealings with neighboring communities, regional issues, or those with statewide or national implications. In exchange, the federal government would receive "tribute" from the winner of indigenous elections in the form of party membership. Those candidates would run unchallenged as the candidate of the ruling party and govern under that party's banner (even if the state party had no further contact with them until the next election). Several scholars (Aziz Nassif et al., 1990; Snyder 2001; Giraudy 2009) have identified Oaxaca's relationship with Mexico's ruling party from 1929 to 2000 as the definition of a one-party state. The PRI still dominates in Oaxaca; every governor since World War II has been a PRI member. Recondo (2007, 80–81) recently characterized the relationship with regard to Oaxaca's indigenous communities as a "perfect interdependence" in which "the corporatist unanimity of the communities is a guarantee of PRI hegemony, which in turn preserves their [physical] integrity."

To the outside world, however, the indigenous communities appear to be upholding their end of the corporatist bargain. Nearly 72 percent of Oaxaca's 496 municipalities possess only one or two "social lands" (*ejidos* or designated communal land) per municipality, and 49 percent possess

---

[19] On Yucatán, see Mattiace (2009).

only one. So, the *comuneros*, those on the all-important list of communal inheritors, are a powerful group. They give votes to the state in return for the state's continued absence, allowing these *comuneros* to manage Oaxaca's internal affairs, sometimes arbitrarily and without accountability. In many cases, the group of *comuneros* consists only of men, one heir per family. In some cases, only the families with the oldest land claims are allowed to participate in land administration. In Oaxaca, 350,000 people statewide are estimated to hold formal titles (Moreno 2009, 51), which is 10 percent of the state's population. Even if all of those holders are assumed to be from indigenous communities, it would still mean that only one-third of the indigenous population held title to land. So, while they are much better off than Chiapas' utterly disempowered and disinherited indigenous peasants, Oaxaca's indigenous people still suffer under a system of inequitably distributed land.

Individual and Collective Rights in the Recent History of Chiapas' Struggle

If Oaxaca's indigenous public land commissions are the self-appointed stewards of the cultural, economic, and political life in their communities, the Zapatistas have tried to claim this role for themselves in Chiapas. They have only been marginally successful. Having recruited members from repressed religious and ethnic minorities in the demographic patchwork quilt of the Lacandon rainforest, the Zapatistas have failed to retain those alliances. After 1994, it was said that "the loyalty of the new Zapatistas would be to the *guerrilla* and not to the Church or the *ejido* unions" (Estrada Saavedra 2007, 458). Some conflicts occurred when citizens withdrew from the Zapatistas but kept land gained as a result of the uprising. Others defections occurred when citizens sought to bypass Zapatista bans on sending their children to public schools or accepting government subsidies.

With the passage of time came increased need for basic services from the government, but the Zapatistas would not allow government intervention. This meant membership was now measured by "'strategic loyalty' rather than an 'ethic based on conviction'," and local chapters of grassroots groups, like Unión Tierra y Libertad, and the CIOAC were forced to abandon group-based allegiances so that they did not conflict with the support role forced upon them in Zapatista-dominant areas (Estrada Saavedra 2007, 461–462). To doctor and grassroots activist Gerardo González, the issue was simple: "[T]he Zapatistas could not resolve peoples' problems. By the turn of the millennium, a lost generation of young people had bet their futures on *Zapatismo* and realized the movement was going nowhere" (interview 2007). Furthermore, according to Burguete Cal y Mayor, the younger sons of Chiapanecan indigenous families who often did not inherit land, were particularly disadvantaged by Article 27. Land acquisition for them became a zero-sum game (interview 2008). Before then, land acquisition, even during population booms, had always been a positive sum game using the tools of squatter's protest and legal advocacy.

The collective aspirations of *Zapatismo* also suffered setbacks because supporters started to feel that the insurgency was taking too much of their livelihoods. The new distribution of production caused additional defections:

The collective way is to distribute work together on a piece of land to harvest corn and beans. The harvest is not distributed but stored in a house. This way the most destitute, the old, the orphans and widows can take their corn. This is how we were doing it for a time, but here in Tabasco [Chiapas] we were not accustomed [to collective work] because we saw that not everything goes fairly, that some work well and others do not, because everyone has a small piece [to work]. But not everyone produces the same, because some know how to work and some produce less. So we never accepted the idea of being a collective (Estrada Saavedra 2007, 463).

Most of Estrada Saavedra's ex-Zapatista interviewees were ambivalent about the movement. They appreciated its overall success at getting the government "to take its hand out of its ear," but regretted that the Zapatistas often appropriated cattle from their supporters as well as from landed ranchers and that the Zapatistas were unwilling to formalize post-1994 land titles won by peasants, such as in Buena Vista Pachán, even though community residents suffered for the insurgents' refusal to sign legal documents and end decades of uncertainty over land titles.

Even though the federal government had signed the San Andrés Accords in 1996, recognizing the Zapatistas and reinforcing indigenous and agrarian rights, the federal Congress never ratified it. Shortly after the 2000 election of Vicente Fox, Mexico's first non-PRI president since 1929, the political wing of the Zapatista movement, the EZLN, announced conditions for renewed dialogue and said that a delegation would be marching to Mexico City. Negotiations did not resume, but Congress did ratify the previous agreements, and the law went into effect in 2002. Despite having been fundamental to its creation, the Zapatistas did not find the new law to be sufficient.

In response to the new law, the Zapatistas set up loosely connected institutionalized autonomous governments, called the Juntas of Good Government, which opened their doors in 2003. Although largely ineffective as a substitute for the state government, the Juntas of Good Government offered the organizational structure that had been missing in the dwindling number of Zapatista-controlled areas and provided a much-needed public access point to the Zapatista leadership. Estrada Saavedra's many respondents conveyed to him that the Juntas of Good Government, which sought to consolidate remaining Zapatista authority in the eastern Lacandon jungles and the central Chiapas highlands, served two main purposes: 1) tightening discipline in the movement and establishing an organizational hierarchy through which policy decisions could be made; and 2) redefining relations between the Zapatista, social organizations, the government, and the people (Estrada Saavedra 2007, 541).

Junta jurisdictions were designated by highway signs, and ordinances were passed authorizing taxation, establishing conflict-resolution procedures, and outlawing the transit of area wood products, guns, drugs, or alcohol in junta-controlled areas (also known as *caracoles*, or "snailshells"). Zapatista sympathizers, while trying to retain their movement allegiance, increasingly turned to the state for services. The state, for its part, actively campaigned to bring the needy back into its sphere of influence through the provision of aid. Although supporters praised the Zapatistas for their efforts to listen to the people and institutionalize the leadership structure, a year later even junta leaders (who were appointed by commanders) openly acknowledged that "there isn't an economic plan to benefit us" (Estrada Saavedra 2007, 553).

The Zapatistas' decline by the late 1990s as a real political force was further hastened in 2000 by the election of the first non-PRI governor of Chiapas since before World War II (following the election of PAN-candidate President Vicente Fox to the presidency). Winning on a left-right, PRD-PAN alliance, Governor Pablo Salazar (2000–2006), a PRI dissident himself, engaged in informal dialog with the Zapatistas even as the federal San Andrés peace talks stalled. Salazar encouraged the government land trust that had been established by state and federal agencies to execute additional informal land reforms, parcel by parcel, after the end of land reform in 1992.[20] Salazar also sought to "disarm" Chiapas' hinterlands

---

[20] In 2009, the Agrarian Reform Secretariat was dissolved by Calderón (elected in 2006).

by forbidding area police from carrying guns (Luna Lujan interview 2002), and he maintained contact with the Zapatistas and other regime opponents through the Chiapas Secretariat for Indigenous Peoples and the office of Juan Esponda, commissioner of peace and reconciliation. Salazar's successor, Juan Sabines (2006–2012), also a PRI opponent, is widely viewed as a less competent or experienced administrator, but has continued the course of his predecessor with regard to relations with the Zapatistas.

Conclusions: The Decisiveness of Historical Trajectories and Land Tenure Institutions

The historical institutions of land tenure differ enormously between Chiapas and Oaxaca, as do the two states' historical relationships with the federal government. These differences have not only had a material impact on the economic health of each state's indigenous population, but also on the character of their respective indigenous rights movements. Land tenure and land distribution go a long way toward explaining why the Zapatista insurgency adopted a more communitarian frame than the corresponding movement in Oaxaca. The origins of this communal framing of Zapatista solidarity are rooted in the centuries-old repression of peasants waged by *hacienda* owners and their government allies. In Oaxaca, on the other hand, indigenous peasants were largely ignored by the Spanish colonizers and Mexican nation builders. In response to the brutal repression in Chiapas, peasants had to build networks and communal solidarity to survive. The relative autonomy enjoyed by Oaxacan indigenous peasants did not require the same degree of interconnectedness or cooperation.

One matter for further research in Mexico, the Latin American Andes (Urioste and Pacheco as quoted in Zoomers and van der Har 2000), and Sub-Saharan Africa (Boone 2007 and Onoma 2006) is the effect of land tenure systems on individual and group political attitudes. More specifically, is the strong correlation between communitarian attitudes and land tenure institutions in Chiapas and Oaxaca the result of membership in similar agrarian institutions (here, the *ejidos*) or similar political dynamics? Either way, it is important, moving forward, to look beyond movement leaders' articulated objectives in order to understand why bystanders become followers. Too much emphasis has been placed on the importance of movement leaders like the Subcommander Marcos and the duplicitous APPO leader Flavio Sosa. The state's extensive influence over land distribution, especially in the resource-poor countryside, must be reckoned with and given consideration. The ethnographic evidence presented here suggests that indigenous citizens will use traditional local institutions and modern state institutions interchangeably, depending on who can solve the problem at hand. They do this pragmatically and without the long-assumed ideological predisposition to "turn inward."

3

Individual and Communitarian Identities in Indigenous Southern Mexico

A THEORETICAL AND STATISTICAL FRAMEWORK

A debate currently rages in academia about identity formation and, more specifically, how much agency one has over the existence and nature of one's own ethnic identity. The contemporary generation of ethnic-conflict scholars who come from a rational-choice tradition (Hardin 1995; Lichbach 1994; Fearon and Laitin 2003; Chandra 2004) are to some degree, at least, proponents of an instrumentalist theory under which individuals are constantly making choices (consciously or subconsciously) about when to emphasize, for example, an Indian versus a peasant identity. This understanding is very much at odds with anthropologists' and collective studies scholars' primordialists claims (Geertz 1973; Escárzaga and Gutiérrez 2005; Gossen 1994) that ethnic identity is inherent and central. Primordialists argue ethnicity is at the core of individuals' decision-making behavior, particularly in indigenous cultures like those of southern Mexico. In the middle position are the constructivists, who believe in the malleability of ethnic identities, but within a constrained domain of possibilities.

Up until now, there has been little individual-level primary data gathered about identity formation that could inform the debate. This book is among the first to marshal empirical, quantifiable evidence for the claim that external factors (such as state built corporatist institutions) are more influential in individuals' political and economic decisions than either endogenous ethno-cultural identities or a movement's organization and structure. My key finding, that historical trajectories and the form of land tenure institutions correlates more closely with communitarian attitudes than ethnicity, suggests that the comparative study of institutions could be an important source of additional data.

Social movement studies of late 20th-century Chiapas – and beyond - have tended to provide little context and to overstate the role of leaders and their ideas. "The core elements of movement beliefs might be played out against the sincere situation and conditions in which the movement leader developed, but a kind of determinism or epistemic realism guided the analysis" (Zald 1996, 262–263). I have attempted here to reconceptualize social movement theory as an interaction between internal dynamics and external contexts (Whittier 2002, 293), building on the earlier work of Snow and Benford (1988) and Tarrow (1998). Upon demonstrating that land tenure patterns as well as indigenous identities shaped individual attitudes toward communal and individual rights, I will argue that when the Mexican state became responsible for setting land tenure systems in the 20th century, it became a primary force in conditioning individuals' worldviews.

Before delving into the survey results, however, it is important to position the survey questions themselves in the proper academic framework. Therefore, I review three bodies of literature that dichotomize aspects of the debate between individualism and communitarianism as they relate to indigenous rights movements. On a normative level, the questions sought to differentiate between multiculturalism (communitarian rights) and pluralism (individual rights); on an empirical level, between primordialism (or essentialism) and instrumentalism; and, on a policy level, pros and cons of ethnic rights recognition. Describing how these basic theoretical constructs relate to indigenous Mexicans will provide a basis for better understanding individuals' processes of identity formation.

Pluralism Versus Multiculturalism: The Normative Debate

Even though pluralism has achieved hegemony in U.S. political science (Yashar 2005, 43), the proper responses to group claims for recognition are still hotly contested in more culturally diverse and divided societies. Should existing cultural differences be legally recognized, empowering group identities and supporting the survival of heterogeneity in the face of globalization? Or, rather, should the malleability of culture be emphasized in order to better incorporate individual rights, diminish differences between groups, and prioritize individual potential? Charles Taylor aptly summarized both positions in his 1994 treatise on multiculturalism:

For [the politics of universal potential], the principle of equal respect requires that we treat people in a difference-blind fashion. The fundamental intuition that humans command this respect focuses on what is the same in all. For [the politics of multiculturalism], we have to recognize and even foster particularity. The reproach the first makes to the second is just that it violates the principle of nondiscrimination. The reproach the second makes to the first is that it negates identity by forcing people into a homogenous mold that is untrue to them. This would be bad enough if the mold were itself neutral.... But ... the claim is that the supposedly neutral set of difference-blind principles of the politics of equal dignity is in fact a reflection of one hegemonic culture. (Taylor 1994, 43)

In Mexico, the ambivalence Taylor captured has achieved its full expression. Mexico is an individual-rights nation on paper; but, the era of PRI hegemony also promoted statist corporatism under which unions and peasant groups were alternately co-opted and repressed to maintain tight social control. Strong liberal guarantees were written into the Mexican Constitution in 1917, but were mostly ignored until the 1990s when Mexico's political opening pushed individual rights issues to the fore. The nation engaged in a rather abstract multiculturalist discourse before the Zapatista rebellion (Mattiace 2003, 64–73), but it did not result in the recognition of indigenous peoples' collective rights. After the Zapatista leadership shifted from its class-based argument to a more pro-indigenous-rights discourse,[1] the issues surrounding multiculturalism and a "pro-autonomy" movement drew more intense public attention. This interest peaked again during the 1996 San Andrés Accords and the 2001 constitutional reforms.

The multiculturalist Zapatistas have campaigned in support of ethnocultural autonomy and against globalization. The organization distrusts the government, which, they argue, is inherently biased against them. Indeed, peace talks between the Zapatistas and President Ernesto Zedillo's government (1994–2000) stalled after the president signed an agreement and then did not submit it for congressional ratification. The central tenets of the agreement were the granting of autonomy rights and recognition to Chiapas' indigenous peoples, operationalized as state recognition of internal self-government and economic development initiatives. However, violence broke out in Chiapas when paramilitary groups (vigilantes with ties to local landowners and often to the PRI) tried to remove peasant squatters from lands where there were contested ownership claims. In late 1997, agrarian conflict, religious tensions, and the struggle between Zapatistas and pro-government vigilantes boiled over in Acteal, Chiapas with the massacre of forty-five people by paramilitaries with PRI and state police ties. In the emerging atmosphere of distrust, the already-signed San Andrés Accords languished.

---

[1] The Zapatista discourse also passed through an intermediate stage of "popular nationalism," expressed in the idiom of protest most familiar to Mexicans (see Plutarch 2004, 292).

Campaigning for president during Mexico's watershed 2000 elections, Vicente Fox of the opposition National Action Party (PAN) claimed that he would resolve the Chiapas conflict in "fifteen minutes." After his election, Fox declared a "new dawn" for Chiapas policy and submitted a watered-down version of the San Andrés Accords for congressional approval. The agreement was approved as a constitutional amendment, ratified by the majority of Mexico's state legislatures, and signed into law in 2001. It was viewed by many as a piecemeal effort to patronize indigenous people, however, as rather than granting outright the recognition of indigenous self-government, it left such reforms up to the individual states. Reforms were passed by 22 states, but the states with the largest indigenous populations, including Chiapas and Oaxaca, did not ratify it.

While Oaxaca did not ratify the 2001 constitutional reforms, the state had implemented dramatic indigenous self-governance legislation in the late 1990s. Indigenous rights advocates welcomed recognition of *usos y costumbres* (a traditional method for selecting local leaders through means other than secret ballot elections) by the state as an admission of the virtues of multiculturalism. This process, discussed extensively in Chapter 5, simply recognized practices already in place. Politicians and indigenous leaders alike proclaimed this law was an overdue acknowledgment of indigenous traditions' significance in Oaxacan history, culture, and contemporary life. Some analysts have argued that *usos y costumbres* were legalized in Oaxaca either as a response to Zapatista calls for indigenous autonomy or as a means of perpetuating the PRI's hold over Oaxaca's rural areas after the party's post-1980s electoral decline (Anaya-Muñoz 2002, 192–202). Whatever the reason, the uniform and documented legalization of *usos y costumbres* presents an opportunity to compare de facto multiculturalism in Oaxaca with the more abstract debate over formal autonomy in Chiapas.

Primordialists Versus Instrumentalists: The Empirical Debate

In response to previous generations of primordialist scholars who have argued that ethnic identity is ascribed at birth and remains static, some Latin Americanists are coming to the conclusion that ethnic identities are actually flexible and ever-changing. Some proponents of the view that ethnic identities are malleable are constructivists like Fredrik Barth (1969) and Walker Connor (1994), who still believe that ethnic identity is rooted in strong social, political, and psychological facts. Others are instrumentalists like Michael Hechter (1986) and Paul Brass (1985, 1997), who argue that the makeup of ethnic identity is subjective and based as much on appeals to mobilize as on objective cultural traits or markers. Brass says ethnic elites provoke and foster identity, an idea consistent with other scholars' arguments that identity generation is the product of boundary-drawing exercises and discrimination by outsiders (as well as from within). He argues, "Once it is recognized that the processes of ethnic – and class – identity formation and of intergroup relations always have a dual dimension, of interaction/ competition with external groups and of an internal struggle for control of the group, then the direction for research on ethnicity and on the relationship between ethnic groups and the state are clear" (1985, 33).

In Mexico-based scholarship, revisionist anthropologists like Rus (2002) and political scientists like Trejo (2004) claim that authoritarian state corporatist regimes of the early and mid-20th century granted state benefits to peasants, prompting otherwise disenfranchised indigenous groups to reorganize as peasants and petition the state for resources. State imposed class distinctions rather than indigenous identity emerged as the most salient social cleavage in most areas of rural Latin America, especially as nation-building efforts permeated remote areas in the mid-20th century.

Revisionist scholars have posed a real challenge to static, primordialist views of ethnicity and ethnic groups. Representing the more primordialist position, López y Rivas, for example, defines an ethnic group as a "stable group of people who have in common relatively enduring characteristics of culture (including language) and psychology, as well as a unity of conscience." (López y Rivas 1995, in part quoting Bromley). The 1994 Zapatista rebellion moved what had been a purely scholarly debate into the policy realm. Zapatistas claimed that ethnic identity was fixed and that Chiapas' Mayan-descended communities were rising up against centuries of ethnic discrimination, and demanded that the Mexican government recognize indigenous peoples' particular expressions of citizenship and grant them greater political autonomy. The Zapatistas were part of a trend across the Americas in the early 1990s, from Mexico to Bolivia and Ecuador, that focused on ethnic identity and promoted indigenous rights with a new urgency (Brysk 2000; Van Cott 2000).[2]

While some recent research on ethnicity and the Zapatistas (Inclán 2009; Trejo 2004; Estrada Saavedra 2007) does take a more instrumentalist

---

[2] This connection between the Zapatistas and more contemporary indigenous movements is drawn by international media and politicians. See, for example, "Indigenous people in South America – A political awakening" (*The Economist* 2004) and Alvaro García Linares (2003), a mathematician who is presently Bolivia's vice president.

view of individual identity, much of it focuses exclusively on collective movements as the unit of analysis. Understandably, these scholars study mobilizations rather than individual attitudes and propensities for mobilization. They and other innovative Chiapas scholars (Harvey 1998; Pérez Ruiz 2004) do attempt to consider the relationship between movements, leaders, and followers. They track the causes of political, social, economic, and ethnic movements in order to differentiate the roles of ethnic elites and followers. This approach (consistent with Brass) holds that ethnic appeals by elites have driven the Zapatistas and Mexico's other indigenous social movements.

None of these works, however, consider the silent bystanders, populations who live within the borders of rebel strongholds but do not support the movement (or may even oppose it). Indeed, while the Zapatista rebellion was a famous and public appeal to indigenous and ethnic autonomy, that uprising may not actually be representative of Mexico's indigenous populations. In other words, the flash and fire of violent protest may have created a selection bias in the research. One could ask, in the far more numerous cases where indigenous groups have not mobilized or publicized systematic discrimination, why not?[3] To compliment all the studies about how elites frame issues to catalyze movements, one might ask how potential followers decide whether to cast their lot with these would-be leaders?[4] Instead of always documenting instrumentalism from above, can evidence be amassed to understand the process of instrumentalism from below? (Lucero (2008) attempts a group-level analysis of this kind in his research on the Andean indigenous rights movement.) The survey I conducted allows one to draw conclusions about why individuals mobilized into groups based on an understanding of individual predispositions rather than leaders' rhetoric.

---

[3] Mattiace (2009) asks this important question for the Yucatán, finding that in that heavily indigenous state there has been little in the way of a grassroots Mayan-identity movement, and that state constitution reforms promoting indigenous rights, as enacted in 2007, were top-down instruments to improve the efficiency of the judicial branch, but without explicit efforts to invigorate Maya indigeneity.

[4] Olson pioneered some clever studies on movement participants' side payments and selective incentives. However, if one assumes that ethnic collective actions have any basis at all in objective cultural markers, or even "interior identity and psychic structure, or blood-ties, or chemistry, or soul," (Connor 1994, 204) and seek to engage those who believe that at least some of the movement-propelling passions are real, then there must be more causing the movement than just generic collective action incentives. Such passion would require endogenous primordial motivations or exogenous discrimination, perhaps even repression.

The Case for Indigenous Right Recognition

Despite all the fanfare surrounding the Zapatista uprising, little has actually been done to recognize indigenous peoples' collective rights in Mexico since the 1992 federal constitutional reforms. The Zapatistas certainly drew extensive public attention to their multicultural or pro-autonomy position during the 1996 San Andrés Accords and 2001 federal constitutional reforms. But not much was tangibly gained. In Chiapas, the pro-multicultural movement has been associated strongly with the primordialist position of the Zapatistas and their supporters (such as Díaz-Polanco and López y Rivas). And the Chiapas debate has been polemicized by the Zapatistas' dramatic declarations and the state's intransigent response. In Oaxaca, by contrast, multiculturalism has made more solid inroads, albeit in a haphazard and informal way.

In Oaxaca, the case for multiculturalism, and for *usos y costumbres* in particular, has been that it would make leaders more accountable, give indigenous communities more direct representation, unify these communities and reinforce pride in their traditions, and make distribution of resources more equitable by eliminating interlocutors between indigenous communities and the state. In Chiapas, the movement for multiculturalism was less organic and more strategic. During brainstorming sessions at the San Andrés Dialogues, the Zapatista leadership solicited suggestions from invited participants in four general areas: indigenous rights, democracy and justice, economic development, and women's rights. The first, it turned out, "ended up acquiring greater relevance at the expense of the other initial questions" (Plutarch 2004, 305). The pursuit of indigenous autonomy became central to the cause because it was the issue that galvanized attention.

Usos y costumbres advocates like Jaime Martínez Luna claim that governance through community assemblies, the rule in *usos y costumbres*, is actually accountable to the people's will because decisions and commitments are made publicly; neither voters nor candidates can hide from their words or positions (Martínez Luna interview 2005). Public service is an obligation undertaken by all. Everyone climbs the ladder of public positions (more fully described in Chapter 5). The past works and reputations of candidates for mayor, for example, are known intimately. Many of these candidates have served in the public interest for many years, often receiving no salary but only per diem reimbursements for official travel to Oaxaca City or neighboring communities. The virtues of *comunalicracia*

51

(Martínez Luna's term for indigenous communal democratic government), namely that communal methods of electing leaders and resolving conflict "maintain community cohesion," are echoed by scholars of Chiapas as well (Hernández Castillo 2006, 5).

Local control over the budget and provision of community services is another argument for indigenous autonomy. In the pragmatic perspective of Oaxacan Regino Montes, autonomy should be based on territorial rather than ethnic claims, encompassing the community, the municipality, and the region. At the community level, autonomy would mean taxation authority, greater control over social welfare programs such as *Oportunidades* (later *Progresa*), federal ability to legislate on issues relevant to communal life, and control over natural and communal resources. At the municipal level, autonomy would entail successfully intermediating between the community and the region. (Article 115 of the Mexican Constitution technically granted municipalities greater budgetary authority.) Regional autonomy, according to Regino Montes, would mean greater responsibility for managing indigenous resources, recognition of indigenous law and forms of conflict resolution, and use of indigenous languages and other cultural expressions in education (Regino Montes typescript n.d., 139–143). The Asamblea Nacional Indígena Plural por la Autonomía (ANIPA) and the Servicios al Pueblo Mixe (Regino Montes' non-governmental organization) have called for national proportional representation of indigenous communities in congressional seat allocation as a way to improve Mexico's mixed uninominal/proportional representation system. Devolving decision-making to the community level has been found to make administrators more accountable to the local people who live with the consequences. Communitarian-governance advocates like Martínez Luna (interview 2005) argue that accountability is also enhanced when decisions are made through group debates and authorities "have to face the assembly."

Perhaps the most important argument for indigenous rights is that, as the original stewards of Mexico's natural resources, indigenous people can best maintain the balance between humans and nature. As stated by the ANIPA, a small but articulate indigenous movement that predates the Zapatistas by a decade: "Today we know that this preservation [of ecosystem equilibrium in fragile regions of Mexico] is due to the wise and sustainable forms of utilizing resources, thanks to the communion of indigenous peoples with nature" ("Iniciativa de Decreto por la Creación de las Regiones Autónomos," 1995). Emphasizing indigenous peoples' proximity to and relationship with nature has had a successful recent history in the Americas, at least for numerous groups, starting with Chico Méndes's Brazilian rubber tappers in the 1980s (Keck and Sikkink 1998). In many regards, the ideal of indigenous stewardship of the land, preservation of roots in time and place, and harmony with nature all command respect on their own terms. Not to mention that the indigenous people inhabited the Americas first, and that millions were decimated by disease and the harsh conditions of their enslavement, in many cases, after first contact with the European conquerors.

The Case Against Indigenous Right Recognition

One of the longest-standing and most powerful criticisms of group-based rights is that such systems leave subgroups or individuals vulnerable to discrimination. In the case of *usos y costumbres* (referenced henceforth as UC), for example, which promotes the group rights of indigenous peoples, evidence exists that many UC traditions discriminate against subgroups within indigenous communities. A codification of traditional practices in Oaxaca's initial 412 UC-governed municipalities reveals that 22 percent do not allow participation by women, and 24 percent do not allow participation by citizens living outside of the *cabecera*, or municipal seat (González Oropeza and Martínez Sánchez 2002, 479–808).[5]

In cases of discrimination against women, political calculus rather than tradition seems to be at work. Although intra-indigenous discrimination in Chiapas has not been systematically codified as it has in Oaxaca, there are plenty of examples of its occurrence: the expulsion of thousands of Protestant Chamulas since the 1970s, and the denial of services to citizens of given indigenous and/or political and/or religious groups in San Andrés Larráinzar and Zinacantán (explored in Chapter 6), as well as elsewhere in the state. While political discrimination and repression in Chiapas often has largely non-indigenous sources, religious discrimination is mostly intra-communitarian. In Oaxaca, the discrimination tends to be between linguistic groups or clans (as in the Villa Hidalgo Yalálag and Santa Catarina Minas cases considered in Chapter 6). Either way, the difficulty for legal authorities is that once the state grants autonomy based on a group rights argument, it loses some ability to protect individuals within that group from discrimination.

[5] The reference is to those living outside the municipal center, or *cabecera*. Dwellers living in the hamlet *agencias* often do not receive fair public expenditure shares. In Oaxaca's indigenous communities, they often do not even get a say in who represents them.

The most compelling reason not to grant communitarian rights, according to federal public officials, is that such arrangements are incompatible with national sovereignty and national identity. The federal state is the final word in all matters, so local decisions are nonbinding. The federal electoral court has actually overturned state legislatures' annulments of a few controversial *usos y costumbres* elections, starting with the municipality of Asunción Tlacolulita (see Chapter 5) in 1998. Furthermore, as the Zapatistas have learned, it is extremely difficult to become politically, economically, and culturally autonomous when the population remains dependent on the state.

Almost from the start, the Zapatistas found themselves in conflict with their own natural constituencies. Rural citizens continued to seek economic development aid from Mexico when Zapatista resources (in the form of international assistance) diminished. Citizens needed roads to get goods to market, which conflicted with the Zapatistas' efforts to sabotage road construction to maximize their physical autonomy and thus minimize the Mexican military's ability to contain the Zapatistas through counterinsurgency techniques (Burguete 2004b, 159). Similarly, Zapatista efforts to provide social services, like education, without outside involvement were discredited when anxious parents realized their children would not receive state credit for years spent in insurgent-staffed classrooms (Burguete 2004b, 174–175). As we starting in the next section, the government's modest recognition of indigenous rights as a result of the San Andrés Accords and UC agreements seems to have been part of an effort to incorporate indigenous individuals more fully into the political and economic process, not a move toward allowing real autonomy.

Case Selection and Methods in the Indigenous Attitudes Survey

The empirical questions are threefold. Does Zapatista leadership represent median indigenous attitudes in Chiapas, as it claims to?[6] Does a communitarian worldview predominate among indigenous populations such that they can be readily united, mobilized, and represented under a single banner? Are the Zapatista and allied group leaders the natural interpreters of

[6] Extrapolating from changes in electoral support for the more Zapatista-compatible leftist Party of the Democratic Revolution (PRD) since 1995, Sonnleiter (2001, 57) estimated that the base shifted from about 25,000 (or a quarter of registered voters in a dozen municipalities in the conflict zone) in 1995 to about one-third of that number by 2000. In Chapter 3 of his forthcoming 2011 book, Sonnleiter argues with even greater precision that support for the Zapatistas, measured in willingness to boycott 1995 state elections was only about 3 percent statewide, or 13 percent of Chiapas' indigenous zones (137).

this communitarian cultural frame? I posed a set of related questions to 2,186 indigenous respondents and 3,194 non-indigenous respondents in order to gain insight into these issues. More than half of the indigenous respondents were surveyed in languages other than Spanish. Six-hundred and sixty were interviewed in Oaxacan dialects of Mazateco, Mixe, Mixteco, Zapoteco, and Zapoteco del Valle, and 597 Chiapanacans were interviewed in either Cho'l, Tzeltal, Tzotzil, or Zoque.

Chiapas and Oaxaca are Mexico's poorest states and the two most indigenous (along with Yucatán). They feature contrasting histories of state permeation of traditional communities, as was described in Chapter 2. Chiapas is 28.5 percent indigenous by linguistic criterion; Oaxaca is 47.9 percent indigenous; and Zacatecas (used here as a control site) is 0.3 percent indigenous. Indigenous respondents were intentionally oversampled as a proportion of the total population. Census data guided site selection by indicating where indigenous citizens were concentrated, but the municipalities, statistical tracts, localities, households, and respondents were otherwise selected randomly (but with a replacement rate of at least 20 percent each at the level of locality, household, and respondent).

Defining who should be categorized as indigenous is a complex task. Indigenous identity may be defined by language (which is how Mexico's census has defined it since 1895) or by self-identification (acknowledged by demographers such as Serrano Carreto et al. [2002, 17–20] as an important but problematic complement to the linguistic criterion). After observing less robust response patterns from self-identification[7] and finding linguistic identity to be more consistent with the environmental conditions that scholars have tended to correlate with ethnic identity (such as a shared history and culture, a rural economy, and a remote location that reinforces cultural, social, and biological markers), this study adopted language as the primary form of identification. At least thirty municipal cases per state needed to be surveyed in order to attain the statistical variance useful for learning where *Zapatismo* and UC communitarianism were embraced and where they were rejected. My large-N municipal model is based on a survey of eighty municipalities between the three states.

[7] Respondents were asked whether they considered themselves to be primarily Mexican, Chiapanecan/Oaxacan/Zacatecan, or "part of an indigenous group." There was a 50 percent overlap between the linguistic and self-identified samples, but the linguistic definition was ultimately used as follows: 1) It yielded more robust statistical patterns, implying that it was a better standard by which to measure "indigenousness"; 2) it yielded about 20 percent more respondents and thus greater potential variation in the statistical analysis; and 3) as the Mexican Census standard, this measure allowed for better independent confirmation of results.

A second complex task lies in attributing agency. In the tradition of methodologists who advocate mixed methods, such as Ragin (1987), Lin (1998), and Mahoney and Goertz (2006), this work is undergirded by a large-N causal analysis that emphasizes significant and novel statistical patterns. Following Ragin's approach (1987, 34–68), the "variable-based" data in this chapter will be heavily complemented by a "case-based" approach in succeeding chapters. Although I stop short of formalizing a "method of agreement" design in the tradition of Mill (1970), I do control for contextual variables within a given country by examining how differing historical trajectories in Chiapas and Oaxaca led to widely different sets of grievances and protest outcomes. I rely on case study analyses of the struggle for land in Zapatista Chiapas and the practice of UC in Oaxaca to complement statistical analysis patterns. I conducted extensive field research over six summers to better understand the individualistic attitudes and behaviors apparent in what have previously been interpreted as almost strictly communitarian episodes: land redistribution in Chiapas' Lacandon rainforest after the Zapatista revolt and local elections via customary law in Oaxaca's UC communities. Whereas indigenous rights grievances resonated loudly in Chiapas in 1994, they had little traction in Oaxaca in 2006 (even though indigenous Oaxacan intellectuals figured importantly in the Zapatista quest for autonomy in the 1990s). I argue that these historical trajectories account for much of the variance identified in the probit model for state-level "dummy" variables.

Important caveats are required before extrapolating agency from survey research that measures only latent values and attitudes. First, while surveys try to differentiate between respondents who "strongly agree" with a given statement and those who merely "agree," this tool cannot accurately measure the intensity of respondent preferences or causality. Surveys cannot predict which respondents will join collective actions and which will "strongly agree" from the sideline. Second, when measuring attitudes and testing how they affect other attitudes, it is important to remember that many of the variables are endogenous and cannot be fully separated from the phenomenon in question. Third, when studying the political conditions surrounding collective action (see Inclán's 2008 application of McAdam et al. 1996) it is also important to understand that leaders manipulate (or "frame") their messages based on strategic calculations as well as pure ideological imperatives in order to provoke followers to act. Followers and bystanders then rely upon these frames to shape and inform their attitudes (McCammon 2001; Cress and Snow 2000).

Dependent Variable Construction

In four of the survey questions, I test two sets of attitudes through the construction of three latent variable clusters (listed in Table 3.1) that then measure the degree of a respondent's association with an individualist view of identity versus a collectivist view of identity. In the other four questions (also listed in Table 3.1), I assess whether respondents more readily consider themselves pluralists or communitarians. Each respondent was sorted into one bivariate category on two dimensions based on answers to these eight questions. The objective was to compare indigenous and non-indigenous positions on a two-dimensional model. (This model is similar to the one used by Inglehart and Baker (2000), although they sought to differentiate "modern" and "traditional" worldviews.) The eight questions used to place each respondent along the continuum were selected from twenty eligible questions because they established the most robust cluster analysis extremes (modal clusters) and offered sufficient variance on the categorically dependent variables.

The null hypothesis, tested first at the level of descriptive statistics, is that indigenous respondents will sort into the communitarian modal cluster more frequently than the non-indigenous cohort, which will tend to sort into the pluralist/individualist modal cluster. The premise of the communitarian-pluralist distinction is that if culture is to be viewed as "the structure of meaning through which people give shape to their experience" (Geertz 1973, 312), then people's views about individualism, communal loyalty, and group membership are crucial and tractable components of one's political culture and socialization. The survey results disconfirm this null hypothesis.

The 3,017 respondents from Chiapas and Oaxaca who answered complete questionnaires forming consistent patterns were sorted into one of three categories using latent variable clustering. Two modal clusters were developed by contrasting the response patterns that were generated by responses to the eight key questions (see Table 3.1). Respondents were then sorted into a cluster that was spatially closest to their position, meaning there was a smaller combined distance between their response scatterplots and those of the modal cluster. Conceptually, each modal cluster represents an ideal type, or a pole, and a response continuum stretches between them. Ultimately, 12 percent of surveys were dismissed because respondents logged incomplete, incoherent, or "non-patterning" views. Although multinomial probit analysis was conducted on this so-called

Table 3.1. *Survey Questions Used to Construct Communitarian and Pluralist Clusters*

Cluster Question	Overall Communitarian Response	Communitarian Indigenous Respondents	Communitarian Non-Indigenous Respondents	One-tailed T-test
QS 31 – Mandatory communal work is **not** legal.	37.3%	49.6% disagree	28.9% disagree	56.6
QS 33 – It is better to help collaborate for the good of this place than to pay taxes to the government.	56.8%	69.4% agree	48.3% agree	84.2
QS 36 – The government should always be above the laws or customs of indigenous communities.	55.5%	60.9% disagree	51.8% disagree	81.8
QI 48 – There is poverty in Mexico because individuals do not try enough to get ahead.	38.6%	39.9% disagree	37.7% disagree	58.2
QS71 – The indigenous people are the true stewards of Mexico's land.	58.4%	72.1% agree	49.5% agree	100.0
QI 83 – People have the responsibility of following ideas of the community, and not question them much.	60.2%	69.9% agree	53.6% agree	90.2
QI 85 – One's identity as individual is more important than the groups one belongs to.	22.6%	24.6% disagree	21.2% disagree	39.6
QI 95 – It is more important to teach children a good sense of the history of their people than a good sense of self-confidence.	43.2%	59.6% agree	32.0% agree	63.9

Note: Sample includes 2,186 indigenous[8] and 3,194 non-indigenous respondents (with full analysis conducted on the 4,780 cases with no missing values). For Latent Gold 3.0 latent variable cluster, standard R^2 was 0.866 with a classification log-likelihood of –39645.17. Scaled, the eight questions attained a Cronbach's alpha of .556. The non-response rate for each question was usually below 5 percent, but went as high as 24 percent in one question. Although a five-category Likkert scale response was elicited by each question, the "agree" and "strongly agree" categories, and the "disagree" and "strongly disagree" categories were conflated in the data analysis, as the distinctions were found to be too subtle for some respondents. Hence, the three response categories for each variable were agree, disagree, and the residual (neither agree nor disagree/do not know/no response). Whereas the "raw" scores were correlated with the communitarian modal cluster in the right two columns, left columns were for "unclustered" answers. The modal clusters were as follows: 63.2 percent of the cases overall were sorted into the pluralist cluster, 24.8 percent were sorted into the communitarian cluster, and the remaining 12.0 percent were sorted into the "non-descript" cluster and dropped from subsequent models.

8 The sole linguistically indigenous respondent in Zacatecas was excluded from Table 3.1.

third cluster, it did not pattern coherently and was cut from this analysis for reasons of parsimony.

Independent Variables Tested

Having established a dependent variable based on the dichotomous individual-communitarian modal clusters, I operationalized three possible causes of respondents' positioning on the communitarian continuum. The first is "Ethnic Identity," as per Table 3.2. Since indigenous people are associated with communitarian attitudes, the hypothesis is that non-indigenous respondents are more likely to fit the individualist modal cluster.

Beyond simply using a language-based bivariate (indigenous/non-indigenous) or respondent self-identification, I also tested other indicators of ethnic identity. I included an additional dummy variable for the language in which the survey was administered. Nearly 25 percent of the sample (60 percent of the indigenous language speakers),[9] or 1,321 respondents, were surveyed in languages other than Spanish and were hypothesized to possess more communitarian views. Consistent with Fearon and Laitin (1996), monolingual indigenous speakers were assumed to be the most endogenized to native culture and traditions and less exposed to other perspectives. Another variable tested was the percentage of the population in each hamlet that spoke at least one indigenous language. Finally, for the Chiapas model (Model 1), a dummy was included to gauge the significance of whether the respondent resided in one of the twenty-three Zapatista stronghold communities in 1997. (See appendix for more elaborate definition of these and other variables.)

The second possible cause for respondents' position on the continuum, derived from studies of rural Mexican corporatism (Reyna and Wienart 1977; Guillén 1998; Harvey 1998) and the few works explicitly contrasting indigenous communal-identity development in Chiapas and Oaxaca (Rus 1994; León Pasquel 2001; Stephen 2002), is "Agrarian Structure." One indication of the value of this hypothesis is that communal groups in Chiapas'

---

[9] The survey was translated by linguists into Cho'l, Tzeltal, Tzotzil, and Zoque in the sample from Chiapas, which is 28.5 percent indigenous according to the linguistic criterion. In half the cases, the survey was translated in writing, whereas in the rest it was translated orally, then taped and memorized by the bilingual interviewers. Latent variable modal clusters were constructed to compile attitude variables from survey responses. The data were not weighted, because the objective was to compare two surveyed groups more than to claim representativeness beyond the sample.

Table 3.2. *Summary of Hypothesized Causes of Pluralist Attitudes (Variable Abbreviations are Further Described in Appendix)*

Hypothesis	Operational Indicators	Summary of Findings
Ethnic Identity		
Indigenous respondents are more likely fit communitarian modal cluster *variables*: Pct indig, Survey lang, Indigenous, Chiapas Zapatista	Presence of many linguistically indigenous citizens; conduct of survey in non-Spanish language; indigenous self-identity; whether the respondents were from Zapatista bastions (Chiapas only).	**MOSTLY DISCONFIRMED**
Agrarian Structure		
Respondents with more communally-structured land resources are more likely to fit communitarian modal cluster *variables*: Ejido ratio, Land wealth, Works ag, Chiapas land struggle	Whether peasant lands are held in *ejido* or communal regimes; whether respondent owns sufficient land to provide basic needs; whether respondent works in agriculture; whether municipality was site of extensive land conflicts (Chiapas only).	**STRONGLY CONFIRMED**
Social Capital		
Respondents embedded in more and deeper social networks more likely to fit communitarian modal cluster *variables*: Corporatist, Traditional gov, Oaxaca UC	Whether respondent participates in corporatist groups; whether respondent's municipality observes customary law (Oaxaca only), is a Zapatista stronghold (Chiapas only), or possesses a traditional government parallel to state.	**CONFIRMED**

countryside joined together to fight the state in the mid-20th century, while no such pan-indigenous mentality gripped Oaxaca's traditional "closed corporate communities" (Wolf 2001). By virtue of the Mexican government's benign neglect of indigenous communities in Oaxaca, and the fact that these citizens did not need to band together to petition for *ejido* lands through decades-long protest campaigns as citizens did in Chiapas, it is possible that the Oaxacans actually possess more pluralist attitudes. The hypothesis then is that Oaxaca's indigenous respondents might express less communitarian attitudes than those in Chiapas.

Agrarian and population census data was gathered on the municipal level that detailed the predominate structure of public lands in the targeted rural areas (specifically, whether they were *ejido* cooperatives or autonomous *comunal* lands).[10] Areas with high concentrations of *ejido* dwellers were expected to convey a less individualist orientation than areas with high concentrations of *comunal* land dwellers. Violence was common in Oaxaca, but it tended to occur between communities over boundary disputes that had not been properly settled in the colonial era (Bailón 2002), rather than between peasants and the state (Dennis 1987; Arellanes Meixueiro 1999). Data was also gathered on the individual level about whether respondents own land or work in the agrarian sector (as opposed to industrial or service sectors). In the Chiapas model (Model 1), a dummy was coded for whether the respondent came from one of the twenty-seven municipalities where conflict-resolving land agreements had benefited some five-hundred indigenous families between 1994 and 1998.

The third causal hypothesis, "Social Capital," is derived from Bourdieu's definition of social capital as "the aggregate of the actual or potential resources which are linked to possession of a durable network of more or less institutionalized relationships of mutual acquaintance and recognition – or, in other words, to membership in a group" (Bourdieu 1986, 248). There are four operational indicators of social capital. The first three (greater degree of globalization,[11] higher degree of formal education,[12] and migration from the community over the previous five years,[13]) were expected to positively associate with increased levels of pluralism/individualism. The forth and most important social capital indicator is whether the respondent's local civil society is organized according to traditional governance patterns. A scale was developed that accords one point for each of the following: 1) a *mayordomo* (traditional community

---

[10] All three states possess among Mexico's highest proportions of public lands. In Chiapas, 49 percent of the state's area is occupied by *ejidos* and communal lands (nearly 90 percent *ejidos*); in Oaxaca, 77 percent of the state is divided into these two types (split almost evenly between *ejidos* and *tierras comunales*); and, in Zacatecas, nearly 51 percent of land that is held as *ejidos*.

[11] Globalization was measured by a six-question scale (alpha = 0.589). Questions composing this scale asked whether respondents had ever: 1) lived in another community, 2) been to Mexico City, 3) lived in another country, and whether they had heard of 4) the World Cup, 5) money wiring (remittances), or 6) biodiversity.

[12] Education was coded as a dummy: zero if respondent had not finished primary school and 1 if she had.

[13] Eighteen percent report having migrated within the last five years.

patron) who organizes the annual community fiesta; 2) *trabajo comunitario* (a tradition of required "volunteer" community work, also known in Oaxaca as *tequio* and in Chiapas as *faena*; and 3) *cargos* (voluntary public service in positions of low authority, required for someone wishing to be mayor). The hypothesis is that more traditional forms of governance (not synonymous with ethnic identity[14]) may offer citizens more conflict-resolving options. The presence of these structures, while offering communitarian results, also seems to indicate higher levels of social/political cohesion in a society, which is indicative of more individualist attitudes. Two other dummy variables were measured within this hypothesis: Whether the respondent participates in corporatist state programs, and, in Oaxaca (Model 2), whether the respondent lives in one of the 418 (out 570) municipalities designated as observing *usos y costumbres* (reforms in 1998 increased the number of UC municipalities to 418 from the original 412).

Beyond the dozen variables tested as part of these three hypotheses, nine other variables were also tested as controls. First, several operational indicators of relative deprivation and socioeconomic status were introduced. Each respondent's level of poverty was assessed relative to the overall local poverty level based on the presence of three measures of economic development for each hamlet (as overall percentages): electricity, sewage pipes, and cooking gas. A second measure was derived from the natural log transformation of the total hamlet population on the premise that larger populations would tend toward higher levels of pluralism. Finally, the rate of population change in survey respondents' hamlets between 1990 and 2000 as well as a dummy variable representing whether the respondent had migrated during the last five years were also measured.

A set of operational indicators was also included to measure the propensity for conflict based on group difference. Ethnic, religious, and political heterogeneity were measured among hamlet populations, aggregated at the sub-municipal level using census data and electoral results. (See Appendix for further explanation.) A dummy variable measuring respondents' gender was also included on the premise that gender discrimination may be common in indigenous societies. A four-component conflict scale (alpha = 0.552) was constructed out of individuals' responses to whether they had

---

[14] Correlation between the traditional government index and ethnic identity variables are as follows: 0.483 for overall percentage of the population in each hamlet speaking indigenous languages, 0.317 for those answering the survey in a non-Spanish language, and 0.438 for the scale drawn from self-identification and/or whether the respondent spoke an indigenous language.

experienced conflict based on religious, municipal governance, political party, or resource/environmental differences. A municipal-level indicator of postelectoral conflict was also added as a proxy for broader social and political conflicts (Eisenstadt 2004, 135–143, 293–294).

Discussion of Results

The coefficients reported in Table 3.3 confirm the agrarian structure and social capital hypotheses for all three models and disconfirm the null hypothesis that ethnic identity is an important cause of communitarian attitudes for all but Model 1 (Chiapas).

None of the indigenous identity variables (percent of indigenous language speakers by sub-municipal hamlet and survey administration in a language other than Spanish) are statistically significant in Model 3 (which includes all three states). The survey language and percent indigenous variables are, however, statistically significant at the 0.01 level in Model 1 (Chiapas). Other anomalies in Model 1 include "Chiapas land struggle," which is also significant at the 0.01 level, but in a negative direction (more land struggle makes respondents less communitarian), and "conflict," which is statistically significant at that same level of precision and positively correlated with communitarianism. (In Model 3, the causality with respect to conflict flowed in the opposite direction). These findings may imply that in Chiapas, where intergroup social conflict is much more prevalent and imbued with an ethnic identity frame (as compared to Oaxaca's intragroup conflict), veterans of the land struggle use a communitarian frame to achieve individualist objectives.

Tellingly, whether Chiapas residents live in Zapatista-dominated municipalities (as per the best publicly available data from 1997 shown in Figure 3.2) is not statistically significant as a predictor of respondents' attitude. Similarly, in Oaxaca (Model 2), whether communitarian customary law was formally recognized in a respondent's municipality is not statistically significant. As reported in Table 3.3, within the social capital hypothesis the traditional government operational variable was the single most powerful and carried a counterintuitive negative sign. In other words, respondents from municipalities without traditional social capital organizations clustered much more at the communitarian end of the spectrum. Traditional governance practices correlated with individualism, implying that the impetus to create social capital may be led by strong individuals or caused by strong relations with the state rather than emerge

Table 3.3. *Reporting Split Sample Probit Models (Individualist Cluster is the Base or Reference Category)*

	MODEL 1 Chiapas (N = 1707)			MODEL 2 Oaxaca (N = 1310)			MODEL 3 Three-States (N = 4229)		
	Log Likelihood = −591.2249			Log Likelihood = −215.5114			Log Likelihood = −1540.663		
	Cases Predicted = 85.82%			Cases Predicted = 93.97%			Cases Predicted = 84.25%		
	McFadden's R^2 = 0.386			McFadden's R^2 = 0.447			McFadden's R^2 = 0.403		
	Coef.	Std. Err.	z	Coef.	Std. Err.	z	Coef.	Std. Err.	z
Pct indig**	**.6907967**	**.1982032**	**3.49**	.0304818	.3850292	0.08	.2475431	.1415168	1.75
Survey lang**	**.3043031**	**.1304754**	**2.33**	.0900616	.3776352	0.24	.1886068	.1059584	1.78
Indigenous	−.0820091	.0838619	−0.98	−.2230023	.1301021	−1.71	−.0451574	.0622939	−0.72
Chiapas Zapatista	−.0217371	.090808	−0.24	NA	NA	NA	NA	NA	NA
Ethnic disperse	.0464873	.0656794	0.71	**−1.025074**	**.4541771**	**−2.26**	.0025557	.0261537	0.10
Ejido ratio**	**.0387609**	**.0122273**	**3.17**	**.1041851**	**.0286425**	**3.64**	**.0440151**	**.0071633**	**6.14**
Land wealth**	**−.1152901**	**.0394555**	**−2.92**	.0326777	.0790791	0.41	**−.0530484**	**.0258021**	**−2.06**
Works agriculture **	−.2005512	.1173701	−1.71	.1111632	.1983684	0.56	**−.1543506**	**.0731972**	**−2.11**
Chiapas land struggle**	**−.3349493**	**.1453483**	**−2.30**	NA	NA	NA	NA	NA	NA
Corporatist **	−.058402	.053567	−1.09	.1181471	.0956284	1.24	**−.0874843**	**.0358485**	**−2.44**
Traditional gov**	**−1.018061**	**.0612963**	**−16.61**	**−.9203292**	**.0997983**	**−9.22**	**−.8582413**	**.0365408**	**−23.49**
Oaxaca UC	NA	NA	NA	.3186149	.2344695	1.36	NA	NA	NA
Primary ed?	.1027261	.1176367	0.87	.0793605	.173757	0.46	.011365	.0644698	0.18
Globalize**	−.0404488	.0376573	−1.07	−.0337464	.0588324	−0.57	**−.0432361**	**.0215797**	**−2.00**

Variable									
Population**	.2050125	.0319486	6.42	.1471725	.0754343	1.95	.2095126	.020225	10.36
Chiapas Dummy	NA	NA	NA	NA	NA	NA	.0098277	.0868056	0.11
Pop change**	-.294037	.125279	-2.35	-.1740864	.3736881	-0.47	-.203151	.0920112	-2.21
Gender**	-.164588	.1060498	-1.55	-.1202112	.1510641	-0.80	-.1232305	.0616738	-2.00
Migrant *	.0103906	.1190342	0.09	-.2279942	.1935311	-1.18	-.1314001	.0729349	-1.80
Relative deprive**	-.2030751	.069575	-2.92	.0334481	.1198621	0.28	-.0984846	.048151	-2.05
Elect interact**	-.9000812	.7826224	-1.15	.5438882	1.663141	0.33	-1.573864	.4839855	-3.25
Conflict**	.11429	.0397469	2.88	-.0711223	.0599343	-1.19	-.0780979	.0235483	-3.32
Religion disperse	.0042379	.1063121	0.04	-9.006153	6.275174	-1.44	-.0739567	.0849797	-0.87
Constant	-.5562237	.4651356	-1.20	9.65191	6.534264	1.48	-.1971122	.2808016	-0.70

Note: **Bold** implies that variable is statistically significant at .05 level.

* Means significant at 0.10 level.

** Means significant at 0.01 level.

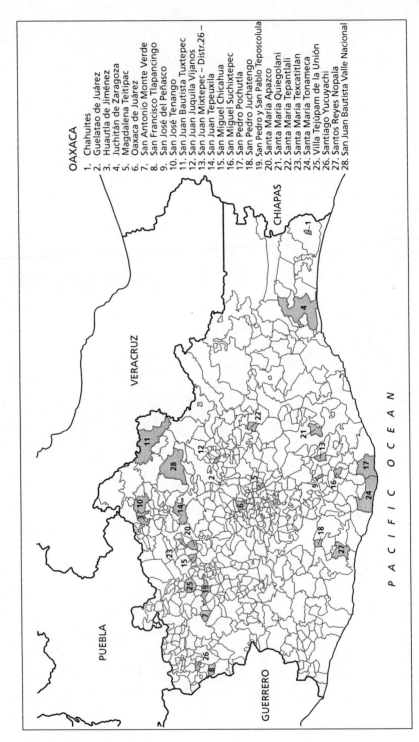

OAXACA

1. Chahuites
2. Guelatao de Juárez
3. Huautla de Jiménez
4. Juchitán de Zaragoza
5. Magdalena Teitipac
6. Oaxaca de Juárez
7. San Antonio Monte Verde
8. San Francisco Tlapancingo
9. San José del Peñasco
10. San José Tenango
11. San Juan Bautista Tuxtepec
12. San Juan Juquila Vijanos
13. San Juan Mixtepec – Distr.26 –
14. San Juan Tepeuxila
15. San Miguel Chicahua
16. San Miguel Suchixtepec
17. San Pedro Pochutla
18. San Pedro Juchatengo
19. San Pedro y San Pablo Teposcolula
20. Santa María Apazco
21. Santa María Quiegolani
22. Santa María Tepantlali
23. Santa María Texcatitlan
24. Santa María Tonameca
25. Villa Tejúpam de la Unión
26. Santiago Yucuyachi
27. Santos Reyes Nopala
28. San Juan Bautista Valle Nacional

Figure 3.1. Oaxaca Municipalities Surveyed.
Map Composed by the Center for Demographic Studies, El Colegio de México.

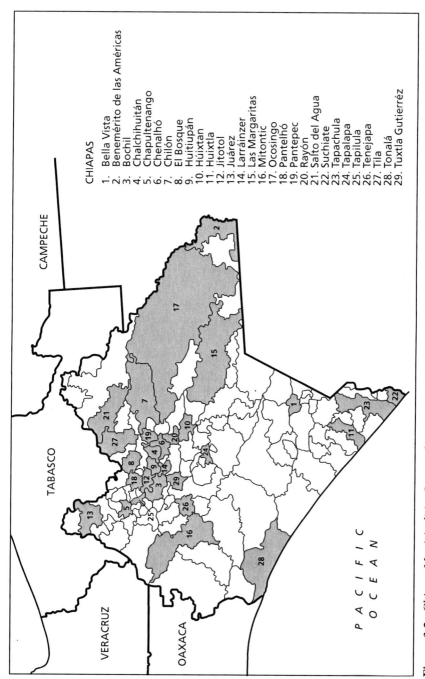

CHIAPAS

1. Bella Vista
2. Benemérito de las Américas
3. Bochil
4. Chalchihuitán
5. Chapultenango
6. Chenalhó
7. Chilón
8. El Bosque
9. Huitiupán
10. Huixtán
11. Huixtla
12. Jitotol
13. Juárez
14. Larráinzer
15. Las Margaritas
16. Mitontic
17. Ocosingo
18. Pantelhó
19. Pantepec
20. Rayón
21. Salto del Agua
22. Suchiate
23. Tapachula
24. Tapalapa
25. Tapilula
26. Tenejapa
27. Tila
28. Tonalá
29. Tuxtla Gutierréz

Figure 3.2. Chiapas Municipalities Surveyed.
Map Composed by the Center for Demographic Studies, El Colegio de México.

67

spontaneously in closed corporate communities. This interpretation is consistent with contemporary efforts by individual indigenous leaders in Chiapas (Hernández Castillo 2002; Burguete 2004a) and Oaxaca (Chance 1986; Aquino Moreschi 2002) to rebuild traditional institutions with historical accuracy and consistent with normative goals.

Agrarian structure is also strongly validated. True to counterintuitive expectations, Oaxacan respondents are less likely to sort into the communitarian cluster than the individualist cluster. Recall from Table 3.1, Oaxacan respondents are 8.64 percent more likely to cluster as communitarians than non-Oaxacans. The significant coefficient from the agrarian structure operational variables (across all three models) is the ratio per municipality of *ejido* dwellers to communal land holders. Respondents from municipalities with higher communal ownership are more likely to cluster as individualists than those with lower communal land ownership. Explanations for these apparently counterintuitive outcomes regarding land tenure institutions may best be understood by looking beyond the labels of communal and *ejido* lands. *Ejido* management requires collective decision making, whereas communal lands do not (Embruz interview 2004, Gijón Cernas interview 2004, Guzman Alcantara interview 2004, Pérez Gómez interview 2004).

Each of the title holders listed on the *ejido* deed has a say in how lands are cultivated, distributed, and whether they may be bought and sold, and *ejido* dwellers are often forced to unite against other *ejidos* in the same municipality or against municipal governments with competing interests. *Ejidos* may also overlap several municipalities, whereas communal holdings more commonly adhere to the political boundaries of a single municipality. Policies governing communal holdings are often set by a single municipal commissioner.[15] This commissioner often parcels out land to either families or individuals, who farm it individually, and buy and sell independently. Furthermore, whereas the struggle to gain *ejido* recognition has been protracted and violent, especially in Chiapas, the recognition of communal lands in Oaxaca often just meant validating colonial-era legal titles. *Ejido* seekers usually based their claims on de facto rights (or squatter occupancy), rather than the de jure land titles invoked by communal land

---

[15] This is a pattern rather than a steadfast rule. Ninety-one percent of Chiapas' municipalities possess more than one *ejido*, but only 15 percent contained more than one communal land holding. In Oaxaca, the only state possessing more communal lands than *ejidos*, 20 percent of municipalities possessed more than one *ejido*, while 29 percent claimed more than one communal land holding (INEGI 2001c).

holders. Confirming this hypothesis, respondents from Chiapas municipalities where negotiations with the state over land titles had occurred in prior years are significantly more individualist.

Many operational indicators are also confirmed. Respondents from more populated areas have stronger positive associations with communitarian attitudes, meaning that the larger the population, the more communitarian the respondent. Although facially counterintuitive, this finding can be understood as a demonstration of the fact that respondents in the largest cities surveyed (the metro areas of Tuxtla Gutierrez [424,579 inhabitants] and Oaxaca City [251,846 inhabitants]) have larger social networks, which lead to more communitarian identities. Where the survey was conducted in several Oaxaca hamlets with fewer than 200 inhabitants, state corporatism may have penetrated heavily (indeed the corporatism variable was significant at the 0.01 level in the three-state model), while more communitarian forces have not. Consistent with the "fight for shares" rationale suggested by Fearon and Laitin (1996), respondents in areas of rapid population growth demonstrate more "zero sum" attitudes and the rate of population change is negatively correlated with communitarianism in Chiapas and the three-state model. In other words, the greater the population growth rate, the more individualist the respondent.

Among demographic and electoral variables, whether the respondent is among the 18 percent of the sample claiming to have migrated over the last five years is of marginal statistical significance in Model 1 only. Respondents' gender was statistically significant at the 0.10 level and negatively correlated with communitarianism in the composite model, but not in Models 1 or 2. Whereas the dispersion of ethnic and religious minorities has little effect on modal cluster classifications, the electoral variable is statistically significant and negative in the three-state model. Thus, respondents in anti-PRI bastions where there is high turnout tend to cluster as individualists.

Respondents who were corporatist peasants (a measure including whether they had voted for the PRI as a component) cluster as individualists. Perhaps the conclusion to be drawn is that citizens with strong connections to the state via membership in social assistance programs or via liberal electoral opposition assume more individualist attitudes. Communitarians tend to interact less with the state, so, perhaps, abstain from voting and hence do not appear as "elect interact" or "corporatist" (as those terms are defined in this chapter's appendix). This would be consistent with the notion that communitarians define identity in opposition to the state and, even more likely, that they tend to abstain from voting at higher rates. The negative sign of the statistically significant corporatism scale (in the social capital hypothesis) reinforces this link between non-PRI electoral support and individualist attitudes, although the correlation is only 0.129 between whether a given respondent lives in a strong opposition area and whether the respondent voted for a party other than the PRI in 2000.

Overall, strong evidence disconfirms most indicators in the ethnic identity hypothesis (except in Chiapas) and strongly confirms the "agrarian structure" and "social capital" hypotheses. The most provocative result is that the higher the proportion of *ejido* land holders to communal land holders in a village (both measured as a percentage of overall hamlet populations), the more likely a respondent is to hold communitarian attitudes. Indeed, the most communitarian respondents were rural dwellers in non-indigenous Zacatecas, where public lands are overwhelmingly divided into *ejidos*. Only 20–30 percent of the municipalities in Chiapas and Oaxaca possess more than one *ejido* within their boundaries, whereas nearly 90 percent of municipalities in Zacatecas possess multiple *ejidos*. More ethnographic research is needed to draw out the implications of differences in land tenure structure on political and economic development, but these findings are highly suggestive. Interpreting the coefficients that were significant (and the many that were not) offers an important departure point for the ethnographic validation of my hypotheses in subsequent chapters.

The limited salience of the ethnic identity hypothesis lends credence to the constructivist position (between primordialists and subjectivists/instrumentalists) that ethnic identity is partially manipulated by or subject to the influence of other hypotheses' indicators. This claim has been argued in the literature, but rarely, if ever, using an extensive survey, and never considering land tenure institutions as a cause of identity. But in rural areas, what variable could have a greater role on the formation of group identities?

The results are provocative, suggesting lines of follow-up research for ethnographic studies. First, if ethnic identity is not immutably fixed but rather fluid and somewhat subject to activation and deactivation, can social demands particular to an ethnic group even exist? Second, if the social demands made by the Zapatistas and other Latin American indigenous movements (such as in Bolivia) are really universal demands for economic justice and development, why has couching these struggles as "ethnic" led to successful mobilization?

Conclusions

Survey respondents in Chiapas hold more communitarian views than those in Oaxaca. While much of this variance is explained by socioeconomic variables, much is also explained by whether respondents live in rural areas and whether they live on *ejidos* or communal land farms. Stark differences between pluralists and communalists are identified through the latent attitude clusters, but the distinctions do not correspond to a division between indigenous and non-indigenous Mexicans. It seems that individuals consciously choose Indian identities in some circumstances and class-based identities in others.

The macro-historical processes underlying group solidarity in Chiapas and individualism in Oaxaca underscore the micro-institutional differences in each state's land tenure structure. Rural dwellers in Chiapas made the transition from corporatist subjects to democratic (or quasi-democratic) citizens as a result of solidarity, collective action, and the formation of region-wide social networks surrounding the Zapatista movement. This contrasts markedly with political development in Oaxaca, where colonial legal deeds to entire villages gave citizens control and a sense of political autonomy that allowed for individually-based property rights and community relations.

Overall, during the 2002–2003 period when the survey was conducted, Zapatista communitarianism was not reflective of the attitudes of most indigenous respondents in Chiapas. On the strength of these findings, I infer that the median indigenous attitude in Chiapas is more individual-rights oriented than commonly projected in academic studies, policy debates, and media renderings and that a large gap exists between the opinions of indigenous citizens (whether silent bystanders, free-riders, or pro- or anti-Zapatistas) and the communitarian leaders who claim to speak for them.

Having established that individualistic and communitarian attitudes are correlated with patterns of indigenous land tenure and political history, as well as with ethnic identity, it is now possible to understand how these attitudes manifest themselves. The next chapters explore concrete cases of negotiation between the state and indigenous citizens, focusing on how both collective and individual incentives guide behavior. Going beyond leaders' scripted communitarianism to describe cases of individual agency and collective action will provide a more nuanced picture of these events and help show the power of indigenous actors.

Appendix

Descriptive Statistics for Independent Variables

(4,229 three-state case-sample)

Variable	Mean	Std. Dev.	Min	Max
DV Communitarian	.2991	.4579	0	1

Hypothesis 1 – Ethnic Identity

Pct indig (municipal)	.3793	.4199	0	1
Survey lang	.2225	.4160	0	1
Indigenous (individual)	.6356	.7765	0	2

Hypothesis 2 – Agrarian Structure

Ejido ratio	.9804	5.6766	–9.4665	8.0946
Land wealth	1.0690	1.2370	0	3
Works agriculture	.4363	.4960	0	1
Chiapas dummy	.4036	.4907	0	1
Corporatist	.9764	.8786	0	3
Chiapas Zapatista (Chiapas)	.2999	.4583	0	1
Chiapas land struggle (Chiapas)	.1849	.3883	0	1

Hypothesis 3 – Social Capital

Traditional gov	1.5583	.9796	0	3
Globalize	2.1863	1.5318	0	6
Primary ed	.2977	.4573	0	1
Oaxaca UC (Oaxaca)	.5300	.4990	0	1

Control Variables

Population (n log)	7.8525	1.9755	3.9512	12.9589
Pop change	.0706	.3920	-3.92105	.8098
Gender	1.4994	.5001	1	2
Migrant	.1896	.3921	0	1
Relative deprive	.4077	.6508	-2.7367	3
Elect interact	.2511	.0935	.0334	.4594
Conflict	1.2285	1.1882	0	6.5
Religious disperse	1.2189	.4124	1.0000	2.8907
Ethnic disperse	1.4567	1.1267	0	6

Derivation of Independent Variables

Ejido ratio – This is the natural log transformation of the percentage of the municipal-level population who are *ejido* dwellers, divided by the percentage who are communal land holders (0 denominators converted to 0.001) taken from the agrarian census (INEGI 2001b).

Land wealth – This is a two-point scale measuring the respondent's level of landholding, according one point each for the following: 1) whether respondent possesses any land; 2) whether this land produces "lots" for autoconsumption; and 3) whether this land produces "lots" for sale on the market.

Works agriculture – Dummy variable equaling 1 if survey respondent worked in agricultural sector and 0 otherwise.

Population – This is a natural log transformation of the municipal level population as given by the 2000 census (INEGI 2001a).

Pop change – This is the percentage change in hamlet or submunicipal population between 1990 and 2000 (INEGI 2001a and CEDEMUN 2003).

Gender – Dummy variable that equals 2 if survey respondent was a woman and 1 if a man.

Migrant – Dummy variable that equals 1 if survey respondent had migrated and returned in previous five years, and 0 otherwise.

Primary ed – Dummy variable that equals 1 if survey respondent had finished primary school and 0 otherwise.

Relative deprive – The three indicators comprising the individual and locale indices were possession of: 1) electricity; 2) a sewage system; and 3) gas (rather than wood) for cooking. Respondents possessing all three have a poverty scale of 3; those possessing none have a poverty scale of 0. Relative deprivation was lowest at 3, meaning that the individual respondent has all three amenities, whereas the average locality member has none. The highest level of deprivation was –2.737, meaning the respondent has none of the amenities, but that most members of the community have all three (INEGI 2001a; INEGI 2002).

Elect interact – Average percentage of votes cast for non-PRI candidates (measured at the municipal level) in 1997 and 2003 midterm congressional races multiplied by average participation rate across the two federal elections measured at the municipal level (IFE 2004).

Chiapas – Dummy variable that equals 1 if survey respondent was in Chiapas and 0 otherwise.

Oaxaca – Dummy variable that equals 1 if survey respondent was in Oaxaca and 0 otherwise.

Globalize – Levels of globalization were measured by a six-question "Awareness of Outside" scale (alpha = 0.589). The questions composing this scale inquired as to whether respondents had ever lived in another community, been to Mexico City, lived in another country, and whether they had heard of the World Cup, money wiring (remittances), or biodiversity.

Conflict – This variable was constructed by adding two components: 1) a four-component conflict scale (alpha = 0.552) constructed out of individual responses, granting one point each if respondents had experienced religious, municipal governance, political party, or resource/environmental conflicts; and 2) an average measure of municipal-level postelectoral conflict severity (coded from 0 to 3) over the four local electoral cycles between 1989 and 2003 (found to be a useful proxy for other types of social and political conflicts (Eisenstadt 2004, 130–162)).

Traditional gov – This is a three-point scale measuring the respondent's assessment of the degree of traditional organization of his/her community, according one point each for the following: 1 if a *mayordomo* (traditional community patron) organizes the annual community fiesta, 1 if there exists *trabajo comunitario*, a tradition of required "volunteer" community work (also known in Oaxaca as *tequio* and as *faena* in Chiapas), and 1 if voluntary public service in positions of low authority are required for someone wishing to be mayor.

Religious disperse – This is a measurement of religious dispersion to assess "effective number of religions" beyond the majority religion. (Catholicism is observed by 79 percent of the survey respondents.) The formula, derived from the Molinar Index (Molinar 1991) that measures the effective number of political parties, is:

$$Effective\ Number\ of\ Religions = 1 + N \left(\frac{\left[\sum_{i=1}^{n} Pi^2 \right] - P_1^2}{\left[\sum_{i=1}^{n} Pi^2 \right]} \right)$$

Where:

$$N = \left(\frac{1}{\left[\sum_{i=1}^{n} Pi^2 \right]} \right)$$

Pi is the percentage of the population represented by each religion and P_1 is the percentage of the population represented by the largest religion using data from 2000 census at hamlet or submunicipal level (INEGI 2001a; INEGI 2002).

Corporatist – This is a three-point scale measuring the respondent's level of corporatism, according one point each for whether the respondent meets each of the following criteria: 1) member of state corporatist productive groups; 2) receives social program assistance from the state; and 3) voted for the PRI in the watershed 2000 presidential election.

Pct Indig – This is the percentage of indigenous language speakers by hamlet or sub-municipal community, as assessed by the 2000 census (INEGI 2001a; INEGI 2002).

Survey lang – This is a dummy variable that equals 1 if survey was conducted in a language other than Spanish, and 0 if it was conducted in Spanish.

Indigenous – This is a two-point scale measuring the respondent's level of indigenous identity, according one point each for the following: 1) whether respondents consider themselves primarily to be: Mexican, Chiapanecan/Oaxacan/Zacatecan, or "part of an indigenous group" (those choosing indigenous group scored 1, whereas other answers scored 0); and 2) whether the respondent spoke an indigenous language.

Ethnic disperse – This is a measurement of ethnic group dispersion to assess "effective number of ethnicities" beyond the largest ethnic minority in a given locality. The formula, derived from the Molinar Index (Molinar 1991) to measure the effective number of political parties, is:

$$\text{Effective Number of Ethnic Groups} = 1 + N\left(\frac{\left[\sum_{i=1}^{n} Pi^2\right] - P_1^2}{\left[\sum_{i=1}^{n} Pi^2\right]}\right)$$

Where:

$$N = \left(\frac{1}{\left[\sum_{i=1}^{n} Pi^2\right]}\right)$$

Pi is the percentage of the population represented by each ethnic group and P_1 is the percentage of the population represented by the largest ethnic group measured by linguistic group using data from 2000 census at hamlet or sub-municipal level (INEGI 2001a; INEGI 2002).

Chiapas Zapatista – Dummy variable that equals 1 if survey respondent was in one of the twenty-three Zapatista communities in 1997, and 0 if not. The pro-Zapatista communities surveyed (as assessed in 1997 per Figure 4.3 on pages 92–93) as are: Bochil, San Pedro Chenaló, Chilón, El Bosque, Huitiupán, San Andrés Larrainzar, Las Margariats, Ocosingo, Pantelhó, Salto del Agua, and Tila. Benémerito de las Americas, formed before 2000 out of the southeastern border of Ocosingo, was also counted as a municipality with some Zapatista presence.

Chiapas land struggle – Dummy variable that equals 1 if survey respondent was in one of the twenty-seven municipalities where land agreements to resolve conflicts benefited more than five-hundred people between 1994 and 1998 (Villafuerte Solís et al. 1999, 370–372).

Oaxaca UC – This dummy variable is positive for those among the 418 (out of Oaxaca's total of 570) municipalities that legalized UC in 1995.

4

Agrarian Conflict, Armed Rebellion, and the Struggle for Rights in Chiapas' Lacandon Jungle

No one seems to know exactly why, in 1971, sixty-six Lacandons in the Mexican rainforest were granted more than 614,321 hectares (61,400 km² or nearly 2,400 square miles) of communal land when they had only petitioned for 10,000. Perhaps they should have realized it was too good to be true. After President Echeverría made the grant, his successor, President José López Portillo (1976–1982), regranted a small portion of the Lacandon communal lands to 1,452 petitioners from Chol and Tzeltal indigenous groups who had been encouraged by his government to migrate from the highlands of central Chiapas to the eastern Lacandon lowlands. In 1978, the López Portillo government yet again regranted the Lacandon communal lands, this time declaring that more than half of the land (331,000 hectares) was to become the Montes Azules Biosphere and the Yachilán, Chankin, Bonampak, and Lacantún national parks and protected areas. Tens of thousands of Tzeltales and Choles agreed to concentrate their populations in two urban settlements within the conservation area and Lacandon communal lands. The Lacandon communal assembly members (the original sixty-six grantees), seeing no other means of avoiding being overpowered by the Tzeltal and Chol demographic boom, agreed to allow non-Lacandon members into the communal lands assembly. They insisted, however, that the president always be a Lacandon and that Lacandons always constitute a majority of the assembly to dilute the presence of the Tzeltales and Choles.

Mexico's largest communal land holding by far, larger than some Mexican states and Mexico's legendary pre-revolutionary *latifundias*,[1] the

---

[1] The original Lacandon Communal Lands zone occupied 6,140 km². By comparison, Tlaxcala, Mexico's smallest state, is 3,914 km². The Lacandon tract is larger than the nation of Luxembourg (2,586 km²), several island nations, and most of Mexico's notorious

Lacandon communal lands grant has been the subject of hundreds of legal challenges. Before 2005, claims had been filed by Lacandon, Chol, and Tzeltal indigenous groups, seventy-one private citizens with unique legal deeds, sixty-nine *ejido* and/or *communal* land recipients (some with claims pre-dating the Lacandon grant and some with regifted land claims), and fifty-six groups of squatters, some of whom had been planting and harvesting Lacandon land for decades (Secretariat of Agrarian Reform 2005a). Political and social claims to the land had also been made by several groups, including the Zapatista National Liberation Army (EZLN), which established its most important base camp there well before the group's 1994 public emergence. Countervailing claims were also filed by human rights groups, political parties, peasant unions, and international environmental groups seeking to preserve the Montes Azules Biosphere as one of the most pristine rainforest habitats in the Western Hemisphere. As Figures 4.1 and 4.2 vividly illustrate, of the original 614,321 hectares, legal counterclaims were made by individuals on 29 percent (176,000 hectares) and by federal environmental protection agencies on 38 percent (almost 232,000 hectares). Informal claims by conflicting groups were filed on even more of the area.

This great mishmash of overlapping public and private land involving large- and medium-scale farmers, peasants, indigenous groups, environmentalists, and political movements from across the ideological spectrum rendered the conflict over the Lacandon area Mexico's most complicated agrarian crisis (Salazar González 2003; Ascencio Franco 2008 provides an extensive recounting of the antecedents and the conflict).[2] During the Fox administration, the Lacandon communal lands were targeted as one of Mexico's fourteen agrarian conflict "trouble spots." Many officials put it at the very top of that list. Nestled on Mexico's border with Guatemala and at the center of the EZLN insurgency's sphere of influence, instability in that area is a potential threat to Mexico's domestic and international security.

> pre-revolutionary *latifundias* (according to Bazant, the Coahuila land claim of Emérito de la Garza was about 6,000 km², and the Sonora claim of Cornell Greene was 5,000 km² [1975, 126]). The most opulent land tracts were probably the Luis Terrazas *haciendas* in Chihuahua, said to be at least four times the size of these other holdings. Silva Herzog (1960, 20) wrote that Terrazas probably owned the most land of anyone "in any country at any time."
>
> [2] The national security element of the crisis has drawn the most official attention. According to media reports, it was declared the most delicate of the "red flag" agrarian conflicts in 2003–2004 because "the possibility of a violent confrontation persists and armed groups, drug and arms traffickers have all been found there" (Guillén, Ochoa, and Martín 2003).

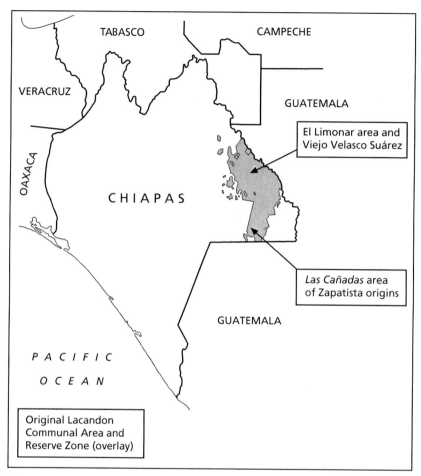

TABASCO   CAMPECHE

VERACRUZ

GUATEMALA

El Limonar area and
Viejo Velasco Suárez

OAXACA

CHIAPAS

Las Cañadas area
of Zapatista origins

GUATEMALA

PACIFIC

OCEAN

Original Lacandon
Communal Area and
Reserve Zone (overlay)

Figure 4.1. Map of Chiapas Showing Lacandon Communal Land Zone Claims.

So why *did* President Echeverría make sixty-six Lacandons the legal owners of more land than even the most notorious *hacenderos* in northern Mexico, whose conspicuous consumption in the face of great poverty helped launch the Mexican Revolution?[3] And why didn't Echeverría or his successors ensure that the land was properly titled and granted to a single

---

[3] Rumors still abound that Echeverría's generosity may have been based on personal motives. Jan De Vos (2002b, 97), perhaps the foremost anthropologist on the Lacandon region, reports that the charismatic pro-Lacandon activist, Trudi Duby, who advocated for decades in favor of a Lacandon reservation or homeland, met with Echeverría and her friend and Chiapas governor Manuel Velasco Suarez just one year before Echeverría's 1971 declaration. The implication, also mentioned by other Chiapas literati, is that Echeverría may have had a fondness for Duby.

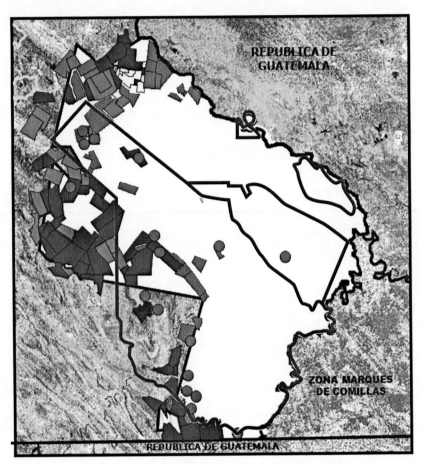

Figure 4.2. Map of Lacandon Area Showing Land Claims (2005).
Map of Lacandon Communal Lands (dark border) showing scores of contested land claims in little polygons concentrated on the left side, and a light trace overlay showing the areas designated also as the Montes Azules Biosphere Reserve. The lower left portion of the Lacandon Communal Lands border, dotted by polygon claims, is the canyonlands where the Zapatista movement first emerged.

Source: Office of the Secretariat for Agrarian Reform, Chiapas Special Representative, with thanks to Marta Cecilia Díaz Gordillo and Fermin Ledesma Domínguez.

group? While the answers offered here are speculative, they do support the argument that the Chiapas conflict is more clearly about land tenure than ethnic identity and autonomy.[4] Pedro Díaz Solís, one of the Chol

[4] The Zapatistas' original pronouncements were about agrarian rights rather than indigenous rights, but the movement changed its focus over time. Scholars like Reyes (1992),

leaders in the Lacandon, said that he and many other dispossessed Chol colonists decided to seek legal remedies by petitioning the government for land titles. "Those who did not [pursue legal channels] went with the clerics, and eventually went on to become Zapatistas.... The mistreatment of ethnic groups was not the issue. The issue was other than that. It was the problem of the land" (2005 interview).

This chapter further develops the connection between land and *Zapatismo*, between land tenure institutions and communitarianism. The survey results demonstrate that *ejidatarios* (*ejido* dwellers, primarily in Chiapas) are more collectivist in their outlook, while *comuneros* (those with rights to communal lands, primarily in Oaxaca) are more individualistic. I use the Lacandon land case to demonstrate how a mix of individual and communitarian motivations contributed to the rise of the Zapatistas. Evidence of this pluralist/communitarian duality is seen in the decades-long conflict in Lacandon. The chapter concludes by arguing that the higher levels of communitarianism observed in Chiapas may be partially due to the history of collective mobilization around the Lacandon land. Oaxaca's land conflicts have always had a much stronger intraethnic dimension because they tend to center on the proper legal boundaries between individual tracts of group-owned land.

The lands at issue in the Lacandon case were a model of Chiapas' *ejido* land tenure regime. They were settled recently, mostly in the 20th century, and were not the ancestral homes of the inhabitants, as is more typically the case in Oaxaca. The Gordian knot that is the Lacandon conflict is composed of many smaller land struggles that were created by the Mexican state when it granted the same land to several different owners and then tried to backpedal by negotiating partial agreements with agrarian unions, peasants, religious groups, civil society organizations, insurgencies, social movements, and government agencies. These groups shared a common objective and a virulent animosity toward the Mexican government. The Lacandon conflict sparked an "us-versus-them" mentality that the Zapatistas capitalized on beautifully. The EZLN gave Mexico's indigenous peasants new language for framing rights claims, but did not fundamentally reconstruct identity on a broad scale. The insurgency simply gave land

---

Harvey (1998), Collier and Quaratiello (1999), and Villafuerte Solís et al. (1999) have documented the agrarian roots of the Zapatista rebellion. These scholars' meticulous work has been insufficiently represented in the broad-ranging, contemporary discourse on Zapatista demands for indigenous rights and autonomy.

petitioners another option besides continuing to play their state-assigned role as corporatist peasants.

The central objective of this chapter is to demonstrate that, contrary to claims by the Zapatista leadership, Chiapas' indigenous communities historically have been more united by socio-economic and land interests than by ethnic identity. Building on the statistical models presented in Chapter 3, this chapter uses those statistical findings to inform this study of the Lacandon agrarian conflict. Without discounting the presence of communitarian worldviews, I construct plausible individualistic explanations for the actions taken by groups and individuals. In the next chapter, I will offer individualistic explanations for outcomes in Oaxaca's customary law disputes, again to complement the more conventional communitarian story. Together, these chapters add qualitative evidence to the statistical evidence already offered that in rural southern Mexico, ethnicity alone was less important in shaping peoples' attitudes than whether the dominant land tenure institutions were the "communitarian" state-penetrated *ejidos* of Chiapas or the more "individualist" communal lands of Oaxaca.

Insurgents, Peasants, Clerics, Bureaucrats, and the Zero-Sum Struggle for Lacandon Lands

There are by now as many answers to the question of why Echeverría made the original land grant as there are petitioners. One descendant of the original sixty-six title holders answered, simply, "It was just the right thing to do" (Chambor Yuk interview 2005). Former Chiapas Special Representative for Agrarian Reform Martha Cecilia Díaz Gordillo added two additional explanations (2005 interview). First, she argued that Echeverría, whose administration also created the Montes Azules ecological reserve, sought to legitimize Mexico's government as an advocate for the environment and indigenous rights. This was especially vital after the military's crackdown on student protesters in 1968 (when Echeverría was Secretary of the Interior under President Gustavo Díaz Ordaz), killing dozens of people and tarnishing Mexico's international image. Second, and consistent with other accounts (Benjamin 1996, 236; Collier with Quaratiello 1999, 50), Díaz Gordillo suggested that the federal government sought to create loyal interlocutors to mediate between the local labor force and private logging interests.

It is curious, though, that the land was allocated via *tierras comunales* rather than through the *ejido*-granting mechanism. The federal Agrarian Affairs

Attorney General's Chiapas representative, Arturo Marquez Mendoza, confirmed that whereas the mechanism for establishing communal lands (*tierras comunales*) involved the submission of a primordial land claim by a cohesive indigenous community (the pattern prevalent in Oaxaca), the sixty-six Lacandon petitioners possessed no such title. However, Marquez Mendoza suggested that the federal government may not have wanted to grant *ejido* land because such an allocation would formally involve granting over 9,000 hectares per petitioner, inviting direct comparisons to the notorious large-scale *latifundia* holdings that were supposedly expropriated during the Mexican Revolution. Communal lands had the benefit of being granted in one indivisible and, hopefully, more politically palatable lump. Establishing *ejido* claims also requires extensive title checks and other legal proceedings, whereas establishing *tierras comunales* is a more streamlined process because private citizens with claims to property in the expropriated area only have six months to file claims before the legal title is granted to the title-holding *comuneros* (Marquez interview 2005).

The competing legitimate land claims in the Lacandon communal land zone created by the government's own double dealings ultimately had little to do with ancestral ethnic identity and more to do with economic interest. Indeed, at the time the Lacandon communal land zone was formally recognized in 1972, only a few hundred Lacandons occupied the area whereas thousands of Choles and Tzeltales had returned to the jungles after being forcibly relocated by the Spanish conquerors hundreds of years earlier. By 1980, according to De Vos (2002a, 355), the estimated 456 Lacandon residents of the disputed area and its surroundings (more than double the disputed territory) comprised a mere 0.5 percent of the 91,229 people living there (118,517 by INEGI estimates). There were, however, 41,874 Tzeltales, 12,681 Tojolabales, 8,210 Choles, and 27,369 *mestizos* in the area, mostly encouraged to relocate from Mexico's northern states in a federal effort to colonize the jungle. According to De Vos, the Lacandon land transfer was little more than a "smoke screen" rushed into place to redirect attention from the launching of a state-owned lumber company, the *Compania Forestal de La Lacandona, S.A.* (De Vos 2002b, 108, 113).

If designing a system to mediate between the new company and local workers was part of the government's motivation, had it succeeded, the new regional economic structure would have been consistent with efforts throughout Chiapas (and rural Mexico) to channel peasant demands for economic development through corporatist structures (such as a lumber company) and, in indigenous regions, to undertake a policy of assimilation known as *indigenismo*. According to Rus:

The Cárdenistas and their successors reached inside the native communities [in highlands Chiapas], not only changing leaders but rearranging the governments, creating new offices to deal with labor and agrarian matters at the same time they were granting vast new powers to the officials charged with maintaining relations with the party and state.... To some extent, the result of this process – the centralization of political and economic power within communities and the tying of that power to the state – resembles the *caciquismo*, or "bossism," that characterizes Mexican rural society in general. (Rus 1994, 267)

In the more remote Lacandon region, corporatist arrangements were less developed and the state's permeation less thorough. Even in the early 1980s, the church was still the main political institution in those areas.

As previously mentioned, President Cárdenas quintupled the number of state land grants compared to his eight immediate post-Revolutionary predecessors, from 70 between 1917 and 1934 to over 300 between 1934 and 1940. Only half were actually executed during his term (Villafuerte et al. 1999, 349 and Table 4.1).

While the Lacandon communal lands present an extreme case, presidential decrees often double- and triple-granted the same land, leading to a notorious backlog in actual titling in a government ceremony that invoked the legacy of the Mexican Revolution. By this logic, the president and his party, in a grandiose act of corporatism showing how he cares for the people, bestows land upon the adoring masses but forgets to tell his cartographers. It was an act befitting kings and which displayed the power of Mexico's president and the PRI, and the importance of staying in their good graces. And social upheaval and desperation on the part of the PRI's authoritarian government prompted presidents to "gift" even more lands in the 1960s and 1970s, but while implementing even fewer transfers from the state to *ejidatarios*. As evidenced in Table 4.1, presidents Díaz Ordaz and Echeverría together delivered an average of only 38 percent of all the land they pledged. Fourteen percent of all the hectares pledged as *ejidos* and *tierras comunales* via presidential decree had still not been delivered even by the conclusion of President Zedillo's term in 2000.

The huge backlog, particularly in Chiapas, coupled with the 1992 law ending agrarian transfers, prompted peasants to look for advocates. This quest for representation coincided with the disenchantment of new Chol and Tzeltal migrants under the weight of demographic and economic strains. These migrants sought to air their grievances and turned to the few

Table 4.1. *Land Redistributions by Presidential Decree, 1918–1992 (and beyond)*

President	Hectares Pledged by National Presidential Decree	Pledges Executed at Nacional Level	Percentage of Land Delivered
Before Cárdenas	128,673	92,628	72
Lázaro Cárdenas	434,062	241,457	56 .
Manuel Avila Camacho	333,380	204,467	61
Miguel Alemán Velasco	206,648	382,447	185
Adolfo Ruíz Cortines	512,411	407,089	79
Adolfo López Mateos	340,327	373,973	110
Gustavo Díaz Ordáz	959,011	245,693	26
Luis Echeverría Alvarez	880,516	459,176	52
José López Portillo	220,114	359,187	163
Miguel de la Madrid H.	457,950	483,246	106
Carlos Salinas Gortari	204,346	772,301	378
Ernesto Zedillo	203,087	54,093	27
Vicente Fox	Not Known	Not Known	Not Known
Without Date	15,983*	10,989*	Not Known
TOTAL	4,896,509	4,186,746	86

* "at least" the given quantity of hectares, but perhaps more.
Source: Calculations based on Villafuerte Solís, et al. (1999, 349).

social service providers who did reach out to them in the remote jungles. With the state and its corporatist structures absent from the jungle, first the Protestant and Catholic churches,[5] and then, ultimately, the Zapatistas sought to fill this void.

Evolving Frames of Agrarian Contestation and the Rise of the Zapatistas

Whereas some authors emphasize the influence of the Catholic Church's left-wing ideology on the Zapatistas, Trejo focuses on the church's competition with Protestant Evangelicals as an explanation for the close relationship between the Catholics and Zapatistas. Losing increasing numbers of Protestant converts[6] prompted the leftist-Catholic prescription for social

---

[5] Trejo (2004, 140–145) provocatively argues that incursions by Protestant ministries, which had selected Latin America as a potential area for expansion, prompted a Catholic reprisal and forced the Catholic Church to tailor more relevant social service offerings.

[6] The Protestant missionaries in rural southern Mexico (including Chiapas) studied indigenous languages (through a specialized summer institute of linguistics), translated biblical passages into Spanish, promoted bilingual education, and established rural clinics and farm cooperatives (Trejo 2004, 139–140).

change, personified by Bishop Samuel Ruíz's liberation theology. Indeed, in an effort to win back these wayward sheep, the Catholic Church not only made doctrinaire appeals, but also began to offer social services and advocate forcefully on behalf of remote and destitute peasants. Replicating the Protestant model, socially aware catechists started religious doctrine study groups; launched cooperatives for the production, transport, and marketing of agricultural goods; constituted community-run banks; and helped facilitate agrarian movements to petition for land (Trejo 2004, 144–147). Analysis of available literature led Trejo to propose that "these skillful leaders [the first Zapatista recruits], centrally positioned in communal social networks, were the catechists and deacons" (2004, 230). In other words, even religious leaders seem to have appealed first to constituents' needs as individuals and to a communitarian spiritualism second.

 These nascent social movements, established before the Zapatista uprising, emerged as natural liaisons between the state and peasants. For example, the faction of the *Union de Uniones* known as the *Quiptic Ta Lecubtesel* (formed by Dominican catechists and deacons as well as local peasant leaders[7]) sought government recognition of twenty-six member *ejido* titles inside what would later become the Lacandon communal lands. Started by Tzeltales who lived in the Lacandon region and sought to keep the federal government from executing an order to survey and demarcate the Lacandon area after the original 1971 grant, the *Quiptic* convinced the federal government that demonstrations staged by Chiapas landowners to receive federal compensation for nonexistent land invasions had reached fraudulent extremes and managed to convince the federal government to shut down this loophole (Harvey 1998, 160). In retaliation, and with backing from the governor, large landowners conducted a string of violent evictions throughout Chiapas, burning down homes and destroying crops. The *Quiptic* peasants responded by launching extended demonstrations, and their title claims were recognized in a 1984 redemarcation of the Lacandon communal land area by President de la Madrid. But the federal Secretariat for Agrarian Reform (SRA) "held up implementation of the accords, and further delays were caused by the loss of relevant documents when the SRA building in Mexico City was destroyed by the earthquakes of September 1985" (Harvey 1998, 161). The patchwork quilt of property

---

[7] According to Trejo (2004, 224–225), the group was formed immediately after Chiapas liberation theologist Bishop Samuel Ruíz's 1974 Indigenous Congress and used the network of statewide social activists the bishop helped develop.

rights in the rainforest was further complicated by repeat demarcations and governmental delay.

Harvey argues that the delay was at least partly political in that the twenty-six *ejidos* belonged to an independent organization and the federal government's offer of resolution required the *ejido*-seeking peasants to join the CNC. Rather than becoming part of the CNC, however, the *Quiptic ejidatarios* argued before the SEDUE (the Secretariat of Urban Development and the Environment) that there would be less overall rainforest deforestation if they were granted sufficient credits, farm machines, and other inputs to maximize production of lands already under cultivation (Harvey 1998, 162) rather than move onto new land. They advocated for keeping the land and for serving as their own interlocutors with the government (thereby undercutting the PRI-state's official corporatist CNC peasant union).

The SEDUE, formed in 1986, was apparently anxious to demonstrate the government's environmental sensitivities and agreed to grant these definitive titles to the *Quiptics*. Previously, the *Quiptics* had been denied agrarian input subsidies and they had been regarded legally as squatters in the Lacandon communal land zone. In 1988, they were granted titles. Newly inaugurated President Salinas presided over his first titling ceremony there in early 1989, in the heart of Zapatista country, where just five years later rebels would dramatically undermine the president's authority. The early 1980s saw the the *Unión de Uniones* split over the *ejido* titling controversy into a broad pro-state coalition, the ARIC *Unión de Uniones*, and a dissident ARIC that preferred extralegal tactics. This split and the discontent it generated were credited with fomenting support for the Zapatistas (Harvey 1998, 164), who started organizing as early as 1983.

As mentioned previously, two federal policies are probably the most proximately responsible for the rise of the Zapatistas: 1) acquiescence to the Chiapas' state legislatures granting of loopholes to benefit the landed gentry, and 2) the 1992 reform of Article 27, which ended land reform throughout Mexico. In the face of this state-sponsored effort by Chiapas' regional elites to preserve the status quo and the end of the federal land dispute process that had been in place for more than a half century, Chiapas' peasants needed a new approach.

President Carlos Salinas' tried to paper over this brewing unrest. He ratified the 1989 International Labour Organization Convention 169, "the most progressive legislation on Indian rights in the world" (Mattiace 2003, 92), which guaranteed indigenous peoples' right to participate in decisions affecting them and to establish their own development priorities. His government's enthusiastic support for the declaration probably owed much to Salinas's desire to co-opt domestic indigenous activists during the lead-up to the 1992 quincentennial of Columbus's "discovery" of America (Mattiace 2003, 93). In 1990, Salinas also proposed an amendment to Article 4 of the Mexican Constitution, acknowledging the plural composition of the Mexican nation and, hence, abandoning *indigenista* policies of assimilation. However, according to Mattiace (2003, 95), the location of Article 4 within Chapter 1 of the document ("Of Individual Guarantees") limited the potential utility of the amendment as a legal argument for genuine indigenous autonomy. International precedent for claims to indigenous territorial and self-rule had already been set by ILO 169, and the Mexican federal government had at least indicated support in the abstract. Mexico's indigenous rights movement was still nascent at the time, but potential support for it was already growing beneath the surface.

Broad Zapatista-Induced Land Negotiations to De-escalate Conflict: Political Cover for Peasants Throughout the Region

The Zapatistas' originally called for a class-based revolution. Ethnic identity was not even part of their discourse. Tojolabal activist Margarito Ruíz confirmed that "Marcos' original speeches said nothing about indigenous rights. We had to talk to him" (Interview 2004). Certainly, the reform of Article 27 ending Mexico's seventy-year land redistribution program played a big role in encouraging the Zapatistas to approach things from an ethnic perspective as well. As peasants, Mexico's rural dwellers had diminishingly little to gain from the state after the 1992 conclusion of land reform. However, no obstacles existed to pursuing stewardship of the land (and including nature reserves and national parks, as well as farmlands and pastures). In any event, even after the Zapatistas adopted their ethnic frame and rhetoric, they were still very much involved with the economic and agrarian issues in the Lacandon region. The threat they posed to civil order gave the Zapatistas a good deal of leverage, and their existence essentially cowed the state into negotiating directly with their constituents over land disputes.

The first of these land negotiations between the state and dispossessed peasants with implicit or explicit Zapatista ties occurred from 1995 to 1997 and resulted in a statewide land bonanza that redistributed 240,000 hectares, more than 6 percent of the state's land area. The second ran from 2003 to 2007 and concerned a land redistribution only one-seventh as large (resulting in the redistribution of 43,821 hectares) but involved the Lacandon tinderbox directly. An analysis of these two cases provides a very clear illustration of how the individual incentives of private property seekers interacted with the stated communitarian imperatives of protecting autonomous areas and communal lands.

As argued in Chapter 2, non-Zapatista land-seeking groups donned the balaclava face masks in a few cases, and the threatening rhetoric in many others, and demanded a piece of the action. Like many of the urban youths of Mexico City, who found in Marcos a rebel for their generation and conveyed this with a chant "We are all Marcos!," there were many Marcos' in the Chiapas countryside. In fact, demands by a dozen insistent groups ensured that, even though the federal government could no longer formally redistribute land, a mechanism had to be found for redistributing it anyway.

Interest groups in Tila, for example, which is in northern Chiapas, far from the Zapatista epicenter, were not necessarily loyal to Marcos and his balaclava-clad insurgents in the jungle, but they certainly seized upon the political opportunities presented by the uprising in the canyons of the Lacandon (Agudo Sanchíz (2010, 240–289). There, dispossessed peasants who had acted as defenders of the PRI-aligned land barons in the past assumed a pro-Zapatista position after rumors of the rebellion reached the northern backlands and hopes for its redistributive potential. Groups of peasants in Tila quite strategically exploited the political moment. They adopted their own peculiar *Zapatismo* (Agudo Sanchíz 2010, 273) and, on the strength of that claim, took over lands they had been contesting for decades. Calling themselves the First of January Ejido (named after the Zapatistas' debut date), they eventually won title to those lands (Agudo Sanchíz 2010, 266). Another group, the El Limar group, also of Tila, took a more moderate position.

Like most squatters and land petitioners, the El Limar petitioners sought to own their land in the form of an *ejido* rather than as private property, "given the continuing ideological weight of that figure [the *ejido*] as part of a legal and administrative framework with which many of them had grown familiar based on their prior struggles and agrarian demands" (Agudo Sanchíz 2010, 264). The Mexican government, having formally ended distribution of *ejidos* in 1992, still faced continuous pressure from population growth (and Zapatista-imposed political strains) to declare new *ejidos* in many parts of Chiapas. With dramatic population increases and a finite amount of land to distribute, the private property resulting from *ejido* titling, certification, and sell-offs was being inherited by fewer sons (and even fewer daughters). While *ejido* membership rosters were subject to communal approval, most families had been able to keep most of their family members on the list. However, market transactions tended to concentrate title-holding, especially since many Chiapas communities deeded the entire land holding to one son, as had been practice for hundreds of years (Burguete interview 2007).

The demographic strains and increasingly concentrated land holdings, even among groups which had not traditionally been *hacienda* owners, forced the federal government to reinstate *ejido* distribution as a social conflict "safety valve" and easer of demographic pressures, albeit through ad hoc mechanisms not supported by the constitution. And petitioners such as those in late 1990s El Limar continued to demand lands as *ejidos*, which they associated with Emiliano Zapata, the Mexican Revolution's humble but heroic peasant general who launched the country's original land reform and inspired his namesakes, the contemporary Zapatistas.

To this end, an inter-ministerial commission was established between the federal SRA and the Attorney General for Agrarian Concerns, the Chiapas' state government, and the federal agrarian registry (National Agrarian Registry or RAN) to conduct below-the-radar land redistributions. The SRA brought federal funds and spearheaded the technical aspects of the deliberations, while the Attorney General for Agrarian Concerns provided the census information and titling status of lands in question. The Chiapas state government provided access to state services and specific information about the areas in question. The RAN checked names of squatters seeking land against a list of preexisting *ejido* members to ensure that peasants already listed as *ejido* members were not making repeat claims. In the wake of the Zapatista uprising, the Mexican government had granted the official peasant union (CNC) three-fourths of the area to be redistributed (Villafuerte et al. 1999, 156, fn 3). So, a land trust was also created by the federal Secretary of Agrarian Reform, the Attorney General for Agrarian Concerns, and Chiapas' Secretary of the Interior to buy land from private owners in Zapatista-occupied areas in *las cañadas* (or "the canyons," the contested western edge of the Lacandon) and grant cash indemnities to help the former landowners relocate.

These land redistribution strategies, used mostly between 1994 and 1996 (but continuing through 2005), sought to defuse tensions quietly, squatter group by squatter group, through ad hoc negotiations that would not technically violate the letter of the 1992 federal reform. In the end, over 6 percent of Chiapas' territory was redistributed via these extra-judicial means.

Consistent with the Mexican PRI-state's strategy of co-optation, however, much more of that land was given to PRI supporters than opponents. Roughly 70 percent of the land bought for reallocation was given to pro-regime *campesino* groups (Villafuerte et al. 1999, 195, 196 and Ruíz interview); twenty percent was given to squatters from Chiapas' independent *campesino* groups not complicit with state corporatism (and whose movements were radicalizing under Zapatista cover); and one-tenth of the redistribution was in Zapatista-occupied areas (Luna Luján interviews 2002, 2004, 2005).[8] After this seeming slight of the Zapatistas relative to PRI-affiliated peasants, however, the federal government then tried to defuse the Zapatista conflict by loaning an additional 65,000 hectares to Zapatista squatters (Luna Luján interview 2002). The state government's informal land reform has been credited with diminishing the land tenure element of Chiapas' rural conflict.

Several other reforms were also credited by longtime Chiapas watchers like Luna Luján, a former CIOAC activist and PRD leader recruited into the Chiapas government in 2000 to help negotiate agrarian disputes (interviews 2002, 2004, 2005). First, state government policy forbid Chiapas police to pack small arms in conflict areas. Second, state services providers were encouraged to extend those services (health and education among them) to Zapatista-controlled areas where many citizens, increasingly disappointed with the insurgency's meagre services, sought state assistance. And third, the state government established informal but regular communications with the Zapatista leadership through the Secretary of Indigenous Affairs initially, and also through the Chiapas Governor's Commission for Reconciliation of the Communities in Conflict which became the full-service office for intermediation with the Zapatistas, conflict refugees, and Zapatista opponents living in Zapatista-held areas. In addition to these broader efforts to de-escalate tensions, several land use negotiations were launched by the state, including in Chiapas' and likely Mexico's most intractable dispute, the Lacandon land conflict.

A Case of Zapatista-Induced Land Negotiation: The Lacandon Challenge

State perceptions of a Zapatista threat prompted some additional investment in Chiapas' rural hinterlands, and the insurgents were able to offer

---

[8] The precise allocation of lands among pro-Zapatistas, neutral third-party squatters, and anti-Zapatista organizers within the Zapatista-occupied areas was unavailable.

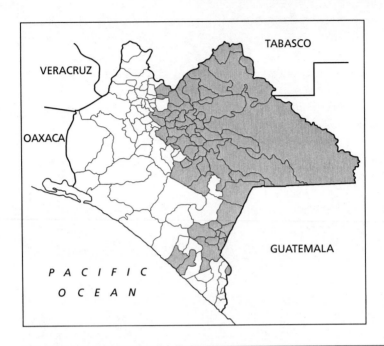

"Official" Municipality	Autonomous Municipality Name
Ocosingo	Libertad de los Pueblos Mayas, cabecera del ejido Santa Rosa
Las Margaritas	San Pedro Michoacán, cabecera en La Realidad
Las Margaritas and Trinitaria	Tierra and Libertad, cabecera en Amparo Agua Tinta
Altamirano and Chanal	17 de noviembre, cabecera en Morelia
Comitán and Las Margaritas	Miguel Hidalgo and Costilla, cabecera en Justo Sierra
Ocosingo	Ernesto Che Guevara, cabecera en Moisés Gandhi
Ocosingo	1° de enero, cabecera en Sibajá
Ocosingo	Cabañas, cabecera en Tushkijá
Ocosingo	Maya, cabecera en Amador Hernández
Ocosingo	Francisco Gómez, cabecera en el ejido La Garrucha
Ocosingo	Ricardo Flores Magón, cabecera en el ejido Taniperlas
Ocosingo	San Manuel, cabecera en la ranchería San Antonio
Ocosingo	San Salvador, cabecera en el ejido Zapata
Huitiupán	Huitiupán
Simojovel	Simojovel
Sabanilla	Sabanilla
Palenque	Vicente Guerrero
Palenque and Chilón	Trabajo
Salto de Agua	Francisco Villa
Tila and Salto de Agua	Independencia
Tila, Yajalón and Tumbalá	Benito Juárez
Tumbalá and Chilón	La Paz
Ocosingo	José Ma. Morelos and Pavón, cabecera en Quetzalcóatl

San Andrés Larráinzar	San Andrés Sacam'chen de los Pobres
El Bosque	San Juan de la Libertad
San Pedro Chenalhó	San Pedro Chenalhó
Pantelhó and Sitalá	Santa Catarina
Bochil	Bochil
Zinacantán	Zinacantán
San Pedro Chenalhó	Magdalena de la Paz, cabecera en Magdalenas, Polhó
San Juan Cancuc.	San Juan Kankujk
Nicolás Ruiz	Nicolás Ruiz

Figure 4.3. Autonomous Municipalities and Their Corresponding "Official" Municipalities, circa 1997. Shaded areas represent zones of high Zapatista influence.
Source: García Torres, Ana Esther, Esmeralda López Armenta y Alma Nava Martínez (1999) "Municipio Autónomo de Polhó" en *Revista Chiapas No. 8,* Año 1999. México: ERA-Instituto de Investigaciones Económicas. http://www.ezln. org/revistachiapas/No8/ch8garcia-nava.html [accessed June 16, 2006]. Note that this is a pro-Zapatista estimation for 1997, representing perhaps the high tide mark of Zapatista influence.

some social services to supporters, at least while the influx of international donations lasted. (See Figure 4.3 for Zapatistas' rendering of their sphere of influence in 1997.) But the Zapatista military's supply needs had started to conflict with their philosophy of promoting indigenous rights. According to Lacandon activist Chambor Yuk, the insurgents poached indigenous peasants' cows in the Tumbala area and resisted state efforts to pave a road in the Chancala areain 2003, even though local citizens desperately needed that road to get produce to market.[9] The Zapatistas apparently hid the paving machine to halt the job, and then demanded 15 percent of the paving fund as a tax before they would release the machine (Chambor Yuk interview 2005). Even federal government officials now acknowledge that the Zapatistas successfully pressured the state to resolve some agrarian conflicts, but goodwill on the ground was slowly diminishing, as evidenced by the unfinished paving job and other stories throughout areas of Zapatista influence underscoring the contradictions between the movement's general objectives of local autonomy and self-government and its immediate strategic needs of maintaining troops and

[9] Burguete (2004b, 159) notes that, in general, the construction of roads has been a great cause of tension between Zapatistas and non-Zapatistas throughout the zone of conflict. Regarded by the Zapatistas as acts of counterinsurgency to prevent military movements against them, many community dwellers viewed new roads as essential infrastructure for getting their agricultural goods to market.

supplies, even if they had to conscript these from increasingly uncooperative villagers and townspeople.[10]

And the Zapatista movement did not have the power to force a resolution to the Lacandon land conflict. A very different dynamic was at play, of course, in the Lacandon than in the rest of Chiapas. This was not a situation where the Zapatista could lead land invasions, displace middle- and upper-class ranchers and private landowners, and open the gates for peasant squatters. Rather, the Lacandon conflict pitted tens of thousands of poor migrant Chol and Tzeltal peasants against hundreds of also poor (but land-rich) Lacandones inside the reserve (see Figure 4.4). There were no "good guys" and "bad guys" for Marcos to frame in his clever writings. The conflict pitted thousands of poor indigenous peasants against a few rich ones, but who had the advantage of having settled there first, even if critics accused them of being carpetbaggers originally from the Caribbean, and perhaps more poignantly, of having benefitted from PRI- state cronyism and of becoming insensitive large landowner *latifundistas* themselves.

After President Echeverría's 1971 decree granting the land to sixty-six Lacandones was usurped (without retraction or amendment) by the 1978 decree granting *comunero* status to 1,452 Lacandon, Tzeltal, and Chol residents, the area's population almost quintupled from 118,517 in 1980 to 493,797 in 2000 (INEGI data cited by the SRA). Further complicating the boundary demarcation, the Montes Azules Biosphere national conservation area was established in 1978. Despite its protected status, migrants continued to move into the Montes Azules Biosphere, which by 1990 was home to more than 9,000 people. Several hundred people voluntarily left the communities of Nueva Argentina and Rudolfo Figueroa in the Montes Azules Biosphere area in 2000 with promises that they would be provided eighty hectares per family outside of the protected area. Many of them returned a year later, however, disillusioned with the government's failure to deliver on its promises (Martín Pérez 2004).

Discord arose between federal agencies as the SRA prioritized solving land disputes and the environmental protection agency prioritized evicting squatters from national park lands (Ascencio Franco 2008, 54–57). After the SRA gained coordination responsibilities and decided to grant financial

---

[10] Repeated attempts in 2002, 2003, and 2004 to interview Zapatista representatives failed. The Zapatistas are widely known to only have received sympathetic scholars they had previously vetted.

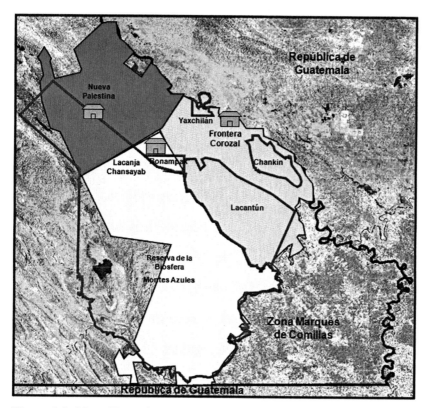

Figure 4.4. Map of Lacandon Area Showing Ethnic Group Divisions (2005). The dark shaded area centered on the town of Nueva Palestina is the Tzeltal zone, the medium shaded area containing Frontera Corozal designates the Chol area, and the white area including Lacanja Chansayabab indicates where the Lacandon group is concentrated. The gray overlay represents environmentally protected lands.

Source: Office of the Secretariat for Agrarian Reform, Chiapas Special Representative, with thanks to Marta Cecilia Díaz Gordillo and Fermin Ledesma Domínguez.

indemnities to allow for resettlement of parties in conflict rather than merely evict them, differences in how the various indigenous groups calculated their self-interest became apparent. According to Ascencio Franco (2008, 130): "[T]he Tzeltales sell if the expropriation indemnity suits them, the Lacandon press to recover their lands, and the Choles, between the other two, are inclined to recover what they can, taking a moderate attitude."

In late 2002, Ignacio Campillo, the attorney general for environmental protection (PROFEPA), expelled twenty-seven Chol citizens from the settlement of Arroyo San Pablo after repeated voluntary relocations

95

failed.[11] Without any hint of interethnic solidarity, Lacandon Communal Lands Commissioner Alfonso Chankín, organized a group of Lacandon to ensure that government authorities expelled the Chol "invaders," stating: "We're old, we're not young, and people think that the Lacandon are idiots, but they're going to see that we're not ... May they see on television that the Lacandons are not the ones who are destroying our forest. That's a lie. We want to participate, so that people can hear our voice and that we're worried" (Guillén and Almazán 2002). The Choles were never granted the twenty hectares per family in the nearby municipality of Palenque that they were promised because the owners of that land refused to sell to the government. The twenty-seven dispossessed Chol peasants were ultimately repatriated in Montes Azules in May 2003, after a visiting Conservation International delegation denounced the government's action and argued that the Choles had not degraded the forest. Rather, the international agency claimed that third party Montes Azules squatters had actually been the ones responsible for the 2,000 hectares of deforestation over the last two years (Becerril 2003; International Service for Peace 2003).

The Lacandon continued to demand the removal of the 1,425 mostly indigenous families occupying Montes Azule lands, more than half of whom were identified as squatters by the government (Guillén 2003), and many of whom, such as those in the Nuevo San Rafael area, were Zapatistas. "We will not permit expulsion or resettlement," said one Zapatista squatter. "We will not be complicit with government strategies to 'divide us, lie to us, and repress us'" (Martín Pérez 2004). Given the complex ethno-social makeup of the area, the various demands of the interest groups involved, the ineffectiveness of federal government relocation efforts, and the unwillingness of many groups to even have a dialogue, by 2003, the situation appeared hopeless.

In 2004, after an ill-fated effort by SEDUE to expel residents from 38 percent of the common lands occupied in the Montes Azules National Park, the SRA formally replaced SEDUE and PROFEPA as lead negotiator. Despite facing resistance, they relocated nearly three hundred biosphere dwellers to new homes outside the biosphere, reclaiming 7,103 hectares of land (SRA 2005). The SRA was more conciliatory and approached the

---

[11] Campillo had earlier listed the Montes Azules Biosphere region as one of Mexico's nine areas of environmental ungovernability and one of the two highest priorities (after the Sea of California whale reserve). He said he would accept military participation to expel the peasants, and media accounts (Bellinghausen 2002) linked the expulsions to the government's desire to fortify foreign investment in the area and develop a transportation and infrastructure corridor from Puebla, Mexico, to Panama.

situation homestead by homestead rather than en masse. Also, it relied on resettled peasants to convey to others via word of mouth that the government had kept its promises this time regarding the delivery of new homes on the public service grid (i.e., with running water and electricity) and parcels of workable land (Ledesma interview 2007). The broader issue of whether the communal stakeholders vested in the Lacandon common land zone would be willing to part with the 10 percent of their land outside the Montes Azules boundaries that had become hopelessly occupied squatter territory was still unresolved. But the SRA's special agent in Chiapas was hoping to buy back that land and distribute it among the occupying groups.

Ethnic Identity, Individual Rights, and the Lacandon Communal Lands

By 2005, the original sixty-six Lacandon communal land stakeholders (referred to below as *comuneros*) had increased in number to 1,452 (after Chol and Tzeltal homesteaders were added in the late 1970s) and then to 1,678 (after the Lacandons got one more roster extension in response to the addition of the Choles and Tzeltales). One possible benefit of the oft-criticized 1992 reform to Article 27 of the constitution was that it offered the hope of definitively demarcating legal land boundaries and resolving title disputes once and for all. (This process of boundary demarcation was called PROCEDE and was administered by the Attorney General for Agrarian Concerns.) Authorities initially hoped to conclude the process in the rest of Chiapas before reconciling the multiple claims and related conflicts in the Lacandon. But, opposition to the surveying and legalization efforts in many communities prompted the government to settle for less ambitious goals.[12] By 2006, only 62 percent of Chiapas' *ejidos* and communal lands were demarcated[13] and discussions continued among the Lacandon

---

[12] As of 2005, only about 60 percent of Chiapas' 2,034 social properties (*ejidos* and *tierras comunales*), had assented to PROCEDE (Marquez Mendoza interview 2005). The Chiapas delegate from the Attorney General for Agrarian Concerns argued that some of the socially held lands were still awaiting legal titles, some experienced social conflicts that precluded surveying efforts, and some residents did not want to participate. While stakeholders often argued whether the regularization of boundaries would pressure people to sell their lands, Marquez Mendoza says that while it might allow *ejidatarios* (but not *comuneros*) to sell land to outsiders, certifying land through PROCEDE was just a definitive means of guaranteeing property rights, which in *ejidos* are passed from generation to generation. See http://www.ran.gob.mx/archivos/estadisticas/avance_procede.pdf

[13] Data from correspondence with Chiapas' office of National Agrarian Registry (June 2007).

comuneros, private property holders, and squatters in the Lacandon over how to find a definitive solution.

While no quick fix was imminent, by late 2005, authorities had resolved roughly 10 percent of the claims in the Lacandon by offering peasants voluntary relocation assistance (SRA 2005). As part of the SRA's goal of resolving more than a dozen "red light" agrarian conflicts nationwide by compensating petitioners with competing land claims, SRA authorities sought to persuade the *comuneros* to allow the Attorney General Agrarian concerns to survey the Lacandon communal land zone. The government wanted to establish the current outer boundaries of the Lacandon area. So much land had changed hands since the original 614,321-hectare grant had been made, the government needed to establish a new baseline from which proper compensation could be divided among the Lacandones, Tzeltales, and Choles.

The pan-indigenous ethnic identity so vociferously promoted by the Zapatista was not in evidence at the Lacandon negotiations. The Lacandon men, who still use traditional garb, chose to distinguish themselves by having waist-length hair and wearing traditional knee-length cotton shirts (author observation of September 26, 2005 meeting). The formerly polygamous (observers say this tradition has mostly been discontinued) and nomadic Lacandon found themselves somewhat alienated from the traditionally monogamous and sedentary Choles and Tzeltales. Cultural differences and diverging strategic interests trumped any pan-ethnic solidarity in negotiations among the three groups.

Discussions among the 1,678 indigenous men with land rights on assignation of financial indemnities in exchange for conceding Lacandon communal lands to decades-long squatters did not convey a harmonious communitarian ethos (Solís Rios interview 2005). The Lacandon, who accounted for only about 13 percent of the 1,678 votes in the *comunero* land stakeholder assembly, wanted compensation to be allocated evenly among all three ethnic groups (each one receiving one-third of the expected US $30 million compensation). The Choles (36 percent) and the Tzeltales (51 percent) wanted compensation allocated on an individual basis (for *comuneros* only), which would entitle them to more per person and as a whole group. The divisions between the groups were based purely on rational economic calculations, rather than communitarianism, illustrating the tenuousness of the Zapatista claim of a common indigenous identity when applied to concrete conditions. See Table 4.2 for possible allocations under each formula.

Table 4.2. *Distribution of Land Indemnities under Different Compensation Schemes*

Group (Number of Assembly Members in Parentheses) N=1678	SCHEME A By Ethnic Group – Compensation per Assembly Member (in pesos)	SCHEME B By Comunero – Compensation per Assembly Member (in pesos)	By Lacandon Dweller – Compensation per *Tierra Comunal* Resident (in pesos)
Lacandon (225)	50,000	**17,900**	61
Tzeltales (852)	11,800	**17,900**	61
Choles (601)	16,700	**17,900**	61
Residents Not Members of Assembly (492,200)	0	**0**	61

Note: The bolded Column B was the one decided upon for compensating *comuneros*. The righthand column is entirely hypothetical, because compensating all legal Lacandon dwellers, or all Lacandon dwellers, the purely egalitarian option, was never even considered. They are given as hypothetical options only.

Source: Secretariat for Agrarian Reform, Chiapas Special Representative.

In addition to differences over how to allocate compensation, the indigenous communal land stakeholders also differed in their support for the ability to trade property rights claims for indemnities (Solís Rios interview 2005). The critical fact that distinguished supporters and nonsupporters was whether they owned small businesses (taxi or boat transport concessions, neighborhood stores, eco-tourism services) that might face increased competition from other start-up businesses that could be launched with money received through indemnification claims. Many of the *comuneros* had benefited from the SRA's initial December 2004 indemnity for the Loma Bonita and Trece de Septiembre areas of the Lacandon communal land zone (at a rate of US $2 million, or some $1,500 per person, as per Table 4.2), and they did not want to jeopardize the relative success of their post-2004 business start-ups by supporting the issuance of one-time cash payments some ten times that size to potential competitors. Between 2005 and 2007, thirty negotiations were held. In the end, each of the 1,678 *comuneros* (0.3 percent of the Lacandon region's total population) received 242,769,889 pesos, more than US $20,000 each (SRA "Asuntos Concluidos 2003–2007" internal document 2008). This was an incredible windfall in a region where almost 40 percent of the population has inadequate nutrition, 42 percent of the indigenous population reports earning no income, and another 42 percent say they earn less than five dollars per day (International Service for Peace 2003).

The SRA spent three years disaggregating Mexico's worst land conflict into manageable pieces and resolving the issues one by one, but many observers worry that the government's purchase of squatter-occupied lands may not have settled the underlying problem: the lack of any comprehensive economic development plan for the region. After all, unlike the many rural Mexican areas that are being depopulated by migration to Mexico's cities and the United States, the population of eastern Chiapas is actually increasing. That demographic reality poses challenges as diminishing tracts of unclaimed land must be divided among more people. Some argue that children left out of the chain of inheritance (all but the oldest or youngest son, depending on the specific indigenous group) will have no means of acquiring land and will be driven to launch new land invasion movements (Burguete and Goméz Gómez 2008, Martínez Coria interview 2008). According to Ramón Martínez Coria, director of an NGO, without further extensive land transfers, the only vehicles for mobility in rural Chiapas will be immigration, drug trafficking (on the rise over the last several years), and postsecondary education (also steadily increasing) (interview 2008).

Establishing government trusts to buy land from owners who have lost the use of their land to squatters and then granting that land to those squatters with historic claims (however compelling) may also serve simply to reward land occupation and lawlessness (Frias interview 2006; Ledesma interview 2005). The case of Viejo Velasco Suárez provides a partial illustration. In early 2006, six families were relocated from the Viejo Velasco Suárez area, part of the Lacandon communal lands, to the municipality of Palenque. The Chiapas government spent US $30,000 to purchase the new land for the families. In July 2006, several masked individuals invaded the former settlement, now back in the hands of the Lacandon communal lands assembly, saying they were Zapatista supporters who had returned to reclaim the land. "Perverse incentives exist," said Ricardo Frias, a government biologist whose agency forcibly relocated occupants of Montes Azules Biosphere reserve lands. "[It's a problem] when you treat invaders like people with grievances, offering them stimulus for invading, by giving them a house, land, and money." Even though most of what the Viejo Velasco Suárez invaders knew of the Zapatistas came "only from the newspapers of 1994, putting on that shirt gives them an advantage in negotiations" (Frias interview 2006).

Viejo Velasco Suáréz is part of a larger group of twenty-eight Lacandon communities called El Limonar, which bargained with the SRA collectively rather than *ejido* by *ejido*. But their collaboration was more the result of prisoner's dilemma calculations than an all-for-one mobilization. According to SRA records ("Diagnóstico Agrario – Región Desempeno-Valle Santo Domingo," 2005, 14), the Tzeltal and Chol communities in El Limonar, themselves consisting of a wide range of interests (see Figures 4.1 and 4.2), refused to negotiate directly with the Lacandon communal lands assembly, refused to accept any resolution short of full regularization of lands, and refused to accept the topographic and census maps drawn by technical authorities who had entered El Limonar to update their documents without their permission (and had subsequently been missing for days). Adding to the negotiation logjam, none of the El Limonar settlements would negotiate separately. They insisted on negotiating only as a single block.

One of the El Limonar negotiators, Tzeltal activist Antonio Jiménez Moreno, explained that the communities distrusted the government, which had expelled them from their pre-1971 homes and sided with the Lacandon when the Lacandon burned down Tzeltal homes and crops in efforts to chase them from the Lacandon communal lands:

We decided that with papers or without papers, the land was going to continue to be ours. We agreed that we would be removed dead, but not alive. We were from different parties, different social groups, different religions, different ethnic groups – languages, that is – but because of the violence against us we united, but only on the subject of the land. And that continues to be the point we share in common. In electoral, religious and social questions, everyone organizes apart. But in things agrarian, we are but one. (Jiménez Moreno interview, 2007)

Another of the Tzeltal negotiators, Samuel Sánchez López, also argued that suspicions about the intentions of state and federal surveyors sent to delineate the edges of the Lacandon communal land area in the spring of 2005 justified taking thirty of them hostage for two days (Sánchez López interview 2007). Jiménez Moreno said that belligerence toward the government was understandable because the Lacandon people had the legal rights and "we [the Tzeltal] had the rights of antiquity" (interview 2007). The group agreed to come back to the negotiating table a year later and was successful in winning permanent rights to the valley where they live.

Conclusion: How the Jungle Camouflaged Individual Interests as Communal Movements

This chapter has presented a little-known story of the greatest concrete material gain from the Zapatista movement: the redistribution of over

6 percent of Chiapas' land, despite the formal end of agrarian reform. In addition to giving hundreds of thousands of hectares to landless peasants, the Chiapas government was also pressured to loan tens of thousands of hectares to Zapatista squatters (Luna Luján interview 2002). The Chiapas state government managed to achieve all this without technically contradicting federal policy by lending 4,000 pesos per hectare to the legal land owner who then put the land up as collateral and defaulted on the loan. These post-Zapatista insurgency informal land deals have been credited with diminishing the conflicts over land tenure in Chiapas, although in the 21st century, demographic pressures are building once again. In addition to the state government's land tenure concessions, the Zapatistas also sparked an increase in federal social spending in Chiapas.

Of course, copycat groups exploited the government fears by donning balaclava masks and claiming land for themselves. Landowners were also said to have taken advantage of the opportunity to dump fallow or unproductive lands on the state for distribution' to landless squatters. And, the intractable Lacandon land dispute was not totally resolved. But the pragmatism of the Lacandon *comuneros*, at least in their dealings with outsiders, allowed the SRA to make progress toward resolving the long-standing agrarian and social conflict created by the federal government's nonsensical regranting of the Lacandon communal lands.

Many groups had taken up the cause of land reform in the decades leading up to the Zapatistas' emergence. Chiapas was ripe for rebellion, in a sense, given the number of social movements in the 1970s and 1980s made up of peasant land petitioners and squatters with legitimate, but complicated, land claims. Many of these groups were violently repressed by the authoritarian state when they undertook collective actions (Trejo 2004) to try to force the state to create new *ejidos*. When the opportunity came, members of these groups either joined or sympathized with the Zapatistas. Even those who continued to follow statist legal strategies for registering grievances (as opposed to the Zapatista pursuit of change through insurgency and other extralegal means) benefited from the political climate created by the Zapatistas.

Supporters of the Zapatistas have clearly been drawn to the group out of individual self-interest as well as communal loyalties. While indigenous autonomy has been the Zapatistas' main objective and has been taken up by many in the academic community as the root of Zapatista support, it is actually the insurgency's material achievements that have kept the group alive despite nearly two decades of stalemate and frustration. Indigenous autonomy, weakly recognized in the 2001 constitutional reforms, has had no practical effects at all. The evidence presented in this chapter makes a case against the common interpretation that Mexico's rural indigenous populations changed from peasants to Indians when the Zapatista rebellion burst on to the scene. Rather, their identity has remained fairly constant. They are both peasants and Indians, and, like most strategic actors, they favor one identity over the other according to the demands of a given situation.

This strategic recourse to ethnic identity is especially apparent regarding the Lacandon, Choles, and Tzeltales in their negotiations over the Lacandon rainforest communal lands. The state's failure to establish and guarantee property rights created political opportunities that were seized upon by the Lacandon and their allies to claim a large amount of land. But the demographic, social, and religious strains posed by the federally encouraged migrations of other groups to that area led to a zero-sum negotiation and pitted indigenous groups against each other, even as the Zapatista leadership was heralding Chiapas' pan-indigenous identity as a basis for establishing autonomous homeland administrative bases (discussed further in Chapter 6). The mix of material and ethnic motivations that governed the negotiations disconfirms the stylized story of a purely ethnic uprising and highlights the complexity of the relationships in those jungle canyons. Moving forward, the question in the Lacandon, and elsewhere in present-day Chiapas, is how long such disproportionate national and international attention can be given to the region's problems absent urgent threats by the Zapatistas, whose capacity to pressure the federal government has dwindled with the movement over the last decade.

Reinforcing the findings from the survey analysis presented in Chapter 3, intra-indigenous conflicts were much more prevalent during the 2003–2007 Lacandon agrarian conflict negotiations than most portrayals of the Zapatista movement would suggest. But, consistent with the political histories presented in Chapter 2, it is clear that poor resource distribution and repeated repression by governing elites created a uniquely toxic situation in Chiapas for all indigenous people (and other peasants). Indeed, despite the demonstration here that individual material interests were pursued and defended vigorously by social movement adherents, insurgents, and even bystanders, the movements themselves were essentially communitarian and adhered to communitarian rights agendas. No such communal solidarity existed among the indigenous communities in Oaxaca, whose intra-group conflicts will be described in Chapter 5.

5

Customary Practices, Women's Rights, and Multicultural Elections in Oaxaca

Indigenous rights movements in Bolivia, Ecuador, and Mexico have drawn a huge amount of attention over the last decade. They have led to the ousting of presidents in both Andean nations, and Mexico's EZLN has won land concessions and forced indigenous rights issues prominently onto Mexico's public policy agenda. The movements have precipitated more drastic change in Bolivia and Ecuador than in Mexico, where only discrete legal changes have been made to recognize indigenous customary laws. This chapter evaluates new evidence on the scope limitations of *usos y costumbres* recognition (the selection of local leaders via traditional election practices rather than through parties and ballots) in Mexico's Oaxaca state, and puts these practices into the context of the broader normative debate over multiculturalism and pluralism. *Usos y costumbres* is practiced in a number of places in Mexico, as well as in other Latin American nations with strong indigenous rights movements. But Oaxaca may be alone in that *usos y costumbres* has been widespread and consistently practiced over a considerable time period in hundreds of municipalities.

The central objective of this chapter is to demonstrate that, as in Chiapas, Oaxaca's indigenous communities have been united as much by their socioeconomic and land tenure status as by their ethnic identity. Building on the statistical models presented earlier, this chapter provides a narrative study of customary law practices in Oaxaca. Without disavowing communitarian worldviews, this chapter, like the last, seeks to construct plausible explanations for actions based on individual agency, focusing particularly on actions in the name of *usos y costumbres* that result in gender discrimination. The empirical evidence presented here and in the previous chapter suggests that political action in rural southern Mexico has been driven by individual incentives as well as by communitarian ethnic imperatives.

The very definition of what constitutes *usos y costumbres* practices is often debated. Indeed, ambiguities surrounding this practice have led victims of unfavorable *usos y costumbres* judgments to argue that customary law is so loosely defined that it empowers traditional-style chieftains to exercise their will arbitrarily under the guise of communitarian decision making. If this allegation is true, individual political motivations are clearly taking precedence over ethnic group solidarity.

In the sections that follow, I discuss the debate on the history and causes of *usos y costumbres* (UC) recognition and consider the normative debate about UC and its virtues. I describe several controversial elections that have occurred under UC and focus attention on claims of gender discrimination. (These are easier to document than ethnic or religious discrimination because of the basic immutability of gender.) I then tease out and analyze the individualistic and communitarian considerations at play in these *usos y costumbres* conflicts.

UC and the Broader Debate on Indigenous Autonomy in Mexico

A normative debate exists over whether to legally recognize existing cultural differences and strengthen group identities, or to view culture as basically conditional and incorporate the rights of individuals to maximize their potential. The Mexican Constitution includes impressive language about individual and group rights, although until the 1990s it went largely untested. At that time, individual rights started to gain importance in a gradual strengthening of the human rights ombudsmen, electoral institutions, and then the judiciary. Also, while labor law in Mexico had traditionally been strong in that it protected the PRI-state's corporatist pillars, a preliminary debate over multiculturalism arose as perhaps the first vital group rights discussion in democratizing Mexico apart from labor law. Nothing extremely substantive came of it, but this new debate about multicultural rights laid the groundwork for what was to come: the Zapatista uprising. Their multicultural, pro-group rights, antiglobalization, and antigovernment rhetoric generated tremendous debate in Mexico and around the world about the meaning of multiculturalism in a liberal democracy.

Within this context of national discussion punctuated by the Zapatista insurgency but without any real legal expression, the Oaxaca state government took a firm stance in 1995. Of course, the decision to recognize *usos y costumbres* was not entirely about recognizing indigenous communities' rights to self-determination. There were almost certainly other political considerations involved. Some analysts have argued that *usos y costumbres* was legalized in Oaxaca in order to prevent an imagined Zapatista-led contagion of indigenous uprisings. Others have suggested it was a way for the PRI to perpetuate its monopolistic hold over Oaxaca's rural areas in the face of the party's national decline in the late 1980s. Anaya-Muñoz (2002) and Recondo (2006) have made a cogent argument that even though a consensus existed among Oaxacan state officials and PRI partisans that something had to be done about the Zapatista rebellion, the immediate cause of *usos y costumbres* electoral reform was that in August 1995 the PRI in Oaxaca experienced the most precipitous decline ever in their winning margin in state legislative elections.[1] While state legislators said the law was intended to keep indigenous municipal elections "free" from party involvement and promote indigenous representational purity, it was designed in such a way to keep them free of every political party but the PRI (Anaya-Muñoz 2002, 192–202; Recondo 2006, 8–18).

The legalization of *usos y costumbres* offers a rare opportunity to compare outcomes in municipalities that adopted traditional customs with outcomes in those that did not. Specifically, I compare the degree of electoral conflict in UC versus non-UC municipalities. Among the conclusions it is possible to draw from this data is that UC municipalities do experience more conflict around elections than non-UC communities, but the conflicts are not markedly more severe than those in non-UC municipalities. It seems that UC customs imbue local government institutions with more credibility and foster ethnic pride. At the same time, UC practices disenfranchise women and residents living in hamlets or communities outside the municipal seat. Drawing on data from my 2008 Survey of Oaxaca, Mexico, Customary Law Municipalities[2], I show that UC municipalities tend to have a very active citizenry and encourage participation, but also exclude individuals. Upon presenting these empirical findings, I draw the normative conclusion that customary practices must be brought into line with international human rights norms.

Before focusing on the set of municipalities where UC recognition increased conflicts, it bears mention that in a large set of cases, UC

---

[1] PRI votes declined from a 94 percent share in 1980 local elections, to 91 percent in 1983 and 92 percent in 1986, and then dipped precipitously to 74 percent in 1992. The PRI's vote share continued to drop dramatically in the mid- and late 1990s to the 40–50 percent range (Anaya-Muñoz 2002, 170).

[2] This survey was conducted also with Moisés Jaime Bailón Corres, Michael S. Danielson, Cipriano Flores Cruz, and Carlos Sorroza, as part of a collaboration between American University and the Benito Juárez Autonomous University of Oaxaca (UABJO).

106

recognition seems to have actually decreased conflict. In some cases, those where UC is practiced by consensus in a harmonious manner, the reforms seem to have decreased *overall* municipal unrest, increased respect for long-standing traditional practices, and even reduced partisan involvement in the electoral process. Although the PRI did stay involved in communities where it had gained footholds, as described later in this chapter, many municipalities remained relatively free from partisan influence with regard to local elections.[3]

Furthermore, a previous study of postelectoral conflicts in Oaxaca found that there were fewer conflicts in more heavily indigenous communities, defined by the percentage of indigenous language speakers (Eisenstadt and Ríos 2010). Ethnographic studies have shown that in cases, like the Oaxacan town of Santiago Ixtayutla, where UC recognition legitimized authentic customs, UC empowered groups of citizens (supported by the Catholic Church and NGOs) to rise up against traditional *caciques* within their own communities and establish communitarian general assemblies. In these cases, an elitist council-of-elders approach to selecting leaders was overthrown in favor of an open general assembly (Recondo 2007, 391–393). Hernández-Díaz and Juan Martínez (2007, 291) have reported on several communities that have "demonstrated the flexibility of the UC electoral system to adjust to the new circumstances of political struggle" and demographic changes. UC has not, however, been universally successful in its goals of diminishing conflict, keeping parties out, and fostering an ancient communitarian ideal.

As identified by Eisenstadt and Ríos (2010), the problem seems to be that communities were not sorted into UC and non-UC groupings based on ethnic composition of the municipalities based on linguistic distributions, or some other proxy for community identities. Rather, politicians have acknowledged – off the record – having sorted municipalities into UC and non-UC groupings according to a political logic based on which communities the political parties (mostly the PRI, but in negotiation with the other parties with legislative representation) wanted to preserve as party bastions and which they were willing to "sacrifice" to UC. Indeed,

---

[3] Overall, 92 percent of municipal authority members surveyed said that it was "never" necessary to be proposed by a political party to be elected as a member of the municipal government. Also, when asked, 70 percent of mayors said they were not members of a political party. The community of Guelatao de Juárez was cited as one where no parties had strongholds in local races. However, even in such municipalities, parties did try to mobilize for state and national elections, and hence could not be excluded entirely.

a study of linguistic characteristics of UC versus non-UC municipalities shows that dozens of UC municipalities are not constituted by a majority of indigenous language speakers, whereas indigenous languages predominate in several non-UC communities (Eisenstadt and Ríos 2010, 14). We will return to indications that political – as well as ethnic identity – criteria were used to designate UC municipalities, but first we consider the normative benefits derived from this unique experiment in multicultural rights recognition.

The Longstanding Case for Usos y Costumbres

After the federal government's negotiations with the Zapatistas stalemated in the mid-1990s, subnational multicultural policies became one way for the government to defuse tensions. When PAN candidate Vicente Fox came to power in 2000 and declared a "new dawn" in Chiapas, he submitted a watered-down version of the San Andrés Accords that was approved by congress and ratified by the majority of Mexico's state legislatures. As previously discussed, states with the largest indigenous populations, including Chiapas and Oaxaca, did not ratify it because of the controversy over giving indigenous groups concrete rights over resources such as the subsoil. Bailón Corres estimates that only one-third of Mexico's states have updated their laws to comply with these federal indigenous rights requirements (2009, 9). He blames both Mexico City policy elites who "have left the indigenous issue aside and do not consider it a national priority, and also the groups within the indigenous community who, not seeing their proposals reflected in the 2001 law, practically constrained other indigenous movements and organizations in the states" (Bailón Corres 2009, 9).

The truncated San Andrés peace process coincided with efforts by policy makers in Oaxaca in 1995 to legalize UC. Regardless of the larger political interests being served, indigenous leaders rallied around the new law, which was seen as legitimizing their cultural practices and representing a crucial first step toward giving them authority over the land they had occupied for centuries. It was a moderate but very real concession by the state to the cause of indigenous group rights.

UC advocates like Jaime Martínez Luna, a longtime Oaxacan activist, claim that governance through UC community assemblies, *comunalicracia*, as he calls it, increases accountability because all decisions and positions have to be defended publicly. According to advocates, electoral assemblies (which are held instead of secret ballot elections) are an effective means of

Table 5.1. *Scope of Issues Discussed at UC Electoral Assemblies*

Topic	Missing N (out of 404)	Always	Sometimes	Never
Evaluation of prior administration	72	21.4%	17.2%	61.4%
Setting of agenda for incoming local government	83	14.6	13.4	72.0
Criticism of diverse groups or people	90	19.7	23.2	57.0
Discussion regarding type of people who should form new government	71	49.8	15.6	34.5
Proposed candidate slates for new government	69	69.0	7.8	23.3

Source: 2008 Survey of Oaxaca, Mexico Customary Law Municipalities. Directed by Moisés Jaime Bailón Corres, Michael S. Danielson, Todd A. Eisenstadt, and Carlos Sorroza and sponsored by Higher Education in Development (HED), the United States Agency for International Development (USAID), and the Benito Juárez Autonomous University of Oaxaca (UABJO).

vetting candidates, even though they may not draw out the specific platforms of incoming governments in the traditional sense (see Table 5.1).

UC is also said reinforce other Oaxaca indigenous traditions such as the system of *cargos* and the *tequio* that lead to tangible public goods. *Cargos* are public positions that all citizens (or, in many communities, just men) are expected to fill.[4] *Tequio* is short-term volunteer work to complete a specific goal such as paving a road or building a school. Although the precise form these traditions take varies from community to community, they are vital communal endeavors that benefit the entire community and succeed only when all citizens are culturally (not legally) compelled to contribute. Under a system of *cargos*, public service is an obligation. All citizens (or, as is often the case, all men) must offer service on a rotating basis,[5] every

---

[4] Some UC advocates (such as Flores Cruz and Méndez 2005 interviews) argue that women play an important role by handling family finances and social/political relations while their husbands are away giving cargo service in the municipal seat or *cabecera*.

[5] In some communities, migrants tapped by the municipal religious and/or civil authorities (often called the Council of Elders) must return to serve or be banished. Increasingly, however, migrants to the U.S. are allowed to "buy" the services of someone local to fulfill their *cargo*. This trend is accelerating the decline of this custom and increasingly allowing women to offer *cargos* as "acting" heads of household (Alcántara Guzmán interview 2004).

several years, and with increasing responsibilities as they get older. Roles include serving as *topil* (village sheriff), errand runner, church caretaker, *mayordomo* (sponsor of patron saint feast days), and mayor. This system, which also varies slightly by municipality, means that the community knows its mayor intimately and the mayor knows all the basic institutions and their functions. *Usos y costumbres* reinforces *cargos* because it recognizes the experience of men who have given a lifetime of service. *Tequio* likewise offers an enormous community benefit, if it is properly supported. This system of voluntarism has been essential to providing community enhancements in poor areas where local governments can contribute, for example, the cement and basketball hoops, but not the labor to build courts.

Before UC was formally recognized, elections in Oaxaca were haphazard and undemocratic affairs. Local authorities would select leaders via UC and then have to legitimize those selections by registering the winners as unchallenged PRI candidates (Recondo 2001, 94; Velásquez 2000, 96–98). But political representation by this local candidate was not guaranteed because the unicameral state legislature routinely dismissed duly elected mayors and replaced them with gubernatorial appointees from a pool of politically acceptable local PRI loyalists. Starting in the 1970s and 1980s, opposition party candidates, frustrated by election rigging and corrupt vote tallying, protested their losses and demanded the creation of multiparty municipal councils as an alternative to the appointment of interim mayors. Under this system, at least they were assured of holding some position. By the early 1990s, conflicts occurred in more than 10 percent of local elections (Table 5.2).[6]

UC was intended to diminish the frequency and intensity of these conflicts and, thereby, cut back on the state's involvement in naming interim governments and municipal councils. This practice had begun to take up an inordinate amount of the state legislature's time and attention. In 1992, 48 percent of the 116 decrees issued by the Oaxaca State Legislature addressed the composition of new municipal governments (Oaxaca State Legislature Decree Book 1993). UC recognition seemed like a means of improving local representation without much of a cost to the grassroots groups which had been short-changed by the authoritarian political boss system.

Another argument made in favor of UC recognition was that it might break the patronage stranglehold the PRI had over rural Mexico, where

---

[6] While still rife with conflict, preliminary data from 2008 local elections in Oaxaca indicates that postelectoral conflicts have diminished slightly from previous cycles.

Table 5.2. Oaxaca's and Mexico's Post-electoral Conflicts, 1989–2007, by Local Election Cycle

Category of Elections	Number (%) 1989–1991	Number (%) 1992–1994	Number (%) 1995–1997	Number (%) 1998–2000	Number (%) 2001–2003	Number (%) 2004–2006	Number (%) 2007–2009
Oaxaca Parties	47 (8%)	76 (13%)	50 (33%)	29 (19%)	21 (14%)	25 (16%)	26 (17%)
Oaxaca *usos y costumbres*	N/D	N/D	22 (5%)	32 (8%)	42 (10%)	44 (11%)	40 (10%)
Oaxaca Total	47 (8%)	76 (13%)	72 (13%)	61 (11%)	63 (11%)	69 (12%)	66 (12%)
Mexico-wide Total	369 (15%)	389 (16%)	257 (11%)	180 (7%)	170 (7%)	Data Incomplete	Data Incomplete

Notes: The total number of municipalities from which percentages were extracted has changed because of constant addition and redistricting of municipalities. The total number of municipalities nationwide was 2,389 for 1989 to 1991; 2,395 for 1992–1994; 2,418 for 1995–1997; 2,427 for 1988–2000; 2,435 for 2001–2005, and 2,455 after 2005. Similarly, the total number of UC municipalities in Oaxaca in 1995 was 412, whereas since 1998, this number increased to 418. Since the number of municipalities in Oaxaca has remained constant at 570, the increase in UC municipalities diminished the number of municipalities holding standard party-based elections from 158 in 1995 to 152 for 1998 and after. Percentages rounded to the nearest whole number; intensities are rounded to the nearest tenth.

Multiple opposition party mobilizations in one municipality were rare, but when they occurred we entered only the mobilization by the higher vote getter among the runner-up parties credited with the conflict, as that party was considered to be the main postelectoral contender (and usually there was a large margin between second- and third-place finishers). Just as electoral contention was either PRI-PAN or PRI-PRD but almost never PAN-PRI-PRD (at least not until the late 1990s); postelectoral contention also followed this pattern during the period under study.

As per Eisenstadt 2004 (135–140), with conflation of the four categories into three, postelectoral conflict intensity was coded as follows: 3 for conflicts resulting in deaths, 2 for conflicts producing serious injuries and/or building occupations (or other manifestations) lasting longer than one event, and 1 for single-iteration (one-day) mobilizations.

Source: Database assembled by the author, Viridiana Ríos, and Michael S. Danielson, and coded from Oaxaca Electoral Institute data and from continuous coding of national (*La Jornada, Reforma*) and local (*Noticias – Voz e Imagen de Oaxaca*) press accounts between 1989 and 2004. Other sources for Mexico-wide sample are given in Eisenstadt (2004, 296). Intensity levels for all conflicts except 2007–2009 are given in Eisenstadt (2007b).

votes were routinely traded for a few sheets of roof laminate or cans of food. Before legalization of *usos y costumbres*, votes would be harvested by local *caciques*, or chieftains, who were affiliated with the PRI and rewarded accordingly for loyal service. Prior to the economic crisis of the mid-1980s, the PRI had actually established a patronage supply network to respond to the thousands of requests from local affiliate groups. Nationally, the PRI's patronage supply network included 778 union stores, 155 butcher shops, thirty-five consumer cooperatives, fifteen bakeries, fifteen supply depots, and one pharmacy (González Compeán, and Lomeli 2000, 533).

This grip was increasingly important to the PRI as it started facing real electoral competition in local races in the late 1980s. Oaxaca was known as a bastion of PRI support and provided a strategic reserve of votes, so-called green votes, that could be easily mobilized (or falsified) in Mexico's rural hinterlands. Turnout in Oaxaca was often dubiously high and suspiciously one-sided, like in the heavily contested 1988 federal elections. (It is possible that that election was actually won by PRD founder Cuauhtémoc Cárdenas, although the PRI's Carlos Salinas was ultimately inaugurated.) In that contest, 87 Oaxaca electoral precincts granted 100 percent of their 40,664 votes to the PRI (Aziz Nassif and Horcasitas 1990, 166). This was a particularly unlikely event, given that it was a tight, three-way election. Official returns granted Salinas a 20-point margin of victory (51 percent Salinas to 31 percent Cárdenas) and credible allegations of fraud were widespread. While savvy and organized opponents, particularly PAN lawyers (dubbed "parachutists" because they were dropped in from Mexico City [Eisenstadt 2004, 181 fn 17]), contested PRI fraud in critical races. Mexico's small, rural communities were largely ignored. It was possible for the PRI to maintain hegemony in these areas and claim to have received all municipal votes cast.[7]

Direct recognition of UC in 1995 has weakened the PRI's hold in that rural communities can now undertake local elections and make decisions without direct intervention. But, UC could not completely dismantle the strong corporatist ties that have permeated Oaxaca's peasant associations[8]

---

[7] This circumstance did not hold in 2010, as allegations of authoritarianism, an apparent unwillingness to distribute patronage, and the left-right coalition against his centrist platform overwhelmed Governor Ruíz and his party. While the PRI's political machine is still powerful in Oaxaca, Governor Gabino Cue may start to actively dismantle the PRI's generations-long hold on local politics.

[8] The National Peasant Confederation (CNC), headed until recently by Senator Heladio Ramírez López, a former PRI Oaxaca governor, is still more powerful in Oaxaca than

or the end practice of local *caciques* buying votes for the PRI in state races with fertilizer, school supplies, or canned food. The PRI can still channel desperately needed resources to indigenous communities in order to co-opt votes or repress dissent.[9] And political parties still control nearly all discretionary spending because local taxation authority is minimal. But UC has changed the dynamic. "If a person never offered *tequio* and becomes mayor, how do they expect us to obey them?" said one Oaxacan interviewee. "This [a non-UC system] breaks the ties of legitimacy which are based on reciprocity and respect for authority" (Guerra Pulido 2000, 78).

New Evidence Against Usos y Costumbres

Along with compelling arguments in favor of *usos y costumbres* practices, relatively new evidence suggests that there may be some costs as well. While the 1995 law acknowledged the group-based rights of a victimized and oppressed minority, some UC traditions themselves victimize and oppress minority groups within indigenous communities. A codification of traditional leader selection practices in the initial 412 UC municipalities (Ríos 2006, 36) revealed that 18 percent allow no participation by women whatsoever, and 21 percent systematically forbid the participation of citizens living outside of the *cabecera*, or municipal seat, where most decision are made (see Table 5.3).[10] Unofficial reports suggest that women are not permitted to vote in 70 percent of Oaxaca's hundreds of UC assemblies (Tapia 2010).[11] Our 2008 Survey of Oaxaca, Mexico,

elsewhere. As one Oaxaca PRI leader said matter-of-factly, "Whenever an uncontrolled mobilization happens, I call the head of the peasant confederation (Cortés López interview)."

[9] The PRI infiltrated dozens of UC municipalities over decades. Three municipalities openly accepted that the means of selecting new leaders was designed by the PRI, and more than forty acknowledged that the PRI openly participated in certifying the winner (see Table 5.3). More than 160 admitted that even before UC was legalized, the custom was routinely practiced as a sort of definitive primary. The leader was selected by assembly, a Council of Elders, or via another customary method. The winner registered with the PRI (and/or other parties starting in the 1990s) to be formally "elected" via the party ticket, even though s/he was the sole candidate and the outcome of the election was a foregone conclusion (Aquino Centeno and Velásquez Cepeda 1997).

[10] The reference is to those living outside the municipal center, or *cabecera*. Dwellers in the hamlet *agencias* often do not receive fair public expenditure shares. Members of Oaxaca's indigenous communities, often do not even get a say in who represents them.

[11] The vote is not secret in 81 percent of the 418 municipalities. Information was not available for 8 percent of municipalities.

Table 5.3. *Participation in Customary Governance Institutions*

Direct Participation by Different Groups	Tequio	Religious Post	Fiesta Organizer	Posts in Civil Govt.
Men in Population "Seat"	95.5%	n/a	95.8	96.8%
Women in Population "Seat"	60.9	n/a	86.1	42.8
Men in *Agencia* Hamlets	30.2	n/a	32.4	31.7
Women in *Agencia* Hamlets	20.5	n/a	28.7	13.4
Non-Catholics	88.3	47.3	47.8	89.2
Migrants	22.5	27.8	31.2	29.4

Note: Total N-404 although the valid N varies from question to question. This table reflects only surveys where answer was affirmative not negative or "don't know."

Source: 2008 Survey of Oaxaca, Mexico Customary Law Municipalities. Directed by Moisés Jaime Bailón Corres, Michael S. Danielson, Todd A. Eisenstadt, and Carlos Sorroza and sponsored by Higher Education in Development (HED), the United States Agency for International Development (USAID) and the Benito Juárez Autonomous University of Oaxaca (UABJO).

Customary Law Municipalities showed that discrimination was even more pervasive than previously known from the 1995 *usos y costumbres* catalogue (Aquino Centeno and Velásquez Cepeda 1997). Chi-square tests confirm strong, positive relationships between the following: 1) postelectoral conflict and UC and 2) electoral disenfranchisement and postelectoral conflict.[12]

Individual rights violations caused by the UC system have thus far not been remedied by state or federal electoral authorities. The federal government is the final arbiter of elections; Local decisions are nonbinding.[13] In the few cases where the federal electoral court (TEPJF) has demonstrated

---

[12] Disenfranchisment was computed on a zero-to-three scale, with one point given for each of the following: if women were not allowed to vote, if the election process revealed each individuals' vote to others, and if citizens from *agencias* were not allowed to vote. Chi-square and Cramer's V tests relating the postelectoral conflict scale (zero to three, with one point per conflict in the 1998, 2001, and 2004 local elections) to disenfranchisement, and postelectoral conflicts to *usos y costumbres* were statistically significant at the .05 level. As expected, a very strong and statistically significant relationship was found to exist between *usos y costumbres* and disenfranchisement, and these two variables possess a correlation of 0.693. These calculations were based on disenfranchisement data for 522 of Oaxaca's 570 municipalities (8.4 percent of cases were missing).

[13] Reforms to Oaxaca's state law were approved by the state legislature in 2008, allowing the possibility – for the first time – that UC elections might also involve electoral court complaints, but there was, as of 2010, still no implementing legislation or rules to bring electoral court mediation/regulation of UC into effect (Oaxaca Electoral Institute 2009 (169-173)).

that it will favor the constitutional rights of citizens over local traditions, thereby limiting indigenous autonomy (Morales Canales 2008), there has been no effort by judicial authorities to actually enforce these verdicts. In Asunción Tlacolulita, for example, the TEPJF overturned the state legislature's routine annulment of a controversial election when two individuals argued that their rights had been violated by the annulment. The TEPJF ordered the Oaxaca Electoral Institute to do "whatever was necessary" to reconcile the factions in the political dispute, including hold a special election to solve the crisis (Electoral Tribunal 2001, xix). The special election was never held, however, and subsequent UC elections, although more peaceful, continued to exclude "women, some young people, neighbors from the hamlet *agencia* of San Juan Alotepec, and local citizens who lived outside the community" (Services for an Alternative Education 2002, 20; Services for an Alternative Education 2005, 14–20).

The success of UC in promoting harmonious local governance may be overly romanticized. Those seeking to end legal recognition of UC argue that, in addition to discriminating against minorities, the system allows local communities to emphasize hierarchy at the expense of meritocracy. Young people with university educations rarely return to their UC villages, say detractors like López López (interview 1998), because they will have to spend up to one-third of their time serving in generalist *cargos* positions rather than using their professional training; In extreme cases, young accountants and lawyers serve as errand runners for semiliterate or illiterate mayors who are unable to fill out municipal expenditure spreadsheets or interpret local ordinances but who spent decades scaling the *cargos* hierarchy. The traditional view of community service as voluntary also may be impractical. Authorities in some communities are beginning to receive payment for service; Otherwise, they are forced to migrate to seasonal fruit-picking jobs in Sinaloa and Baja California. They can better support their families as undocumented workers in US agriculture, construction, or service sectors than they can through subsistence farming and volunteer public service in Oaxaca.[14]

The idea that UC will diminish postelectoral conflict is also not borne out by empirical evidence. Since recognition in 1995, the number of post-electoral conflicts (contestation of the results by losers through protests and

---

[14] Nationwide, remittances from migrants to the United States served as the primary income source for over 1.6 million households (Sarabia and Galán) by 2005. The 2000 census estimated that 2.6 percent of Oaxaca's men over 18 had migrated to the U.S., but this estimate is thought to severely underreport the true number.

mobilizations) in Oaxaca's UC communities has actually doubled overall. Nationally, the percentage of contested elections diminished over the same electoral cycles. In Oaxaca, postelectoral conflict in municipalities with party-based elections fell from a rate of 33 percent in 1995 to 17 percent in 2007. In UC communities, that rate started at 5 percent in 1995 and doubled to 10 percent in 2003 and 2007 (see Table 5.2). Oaxaca's postelectoral conflicts, while not as numerous as those in Chiapas (which had an average conflict rate of 24 percent over five recent electoral cycles), were much more severe, resulting in dozens of deaths (Eisenstadt 2004).[15] In Oaxaca, 39 people died in postelectoral conflicts between 1989 and 2003. By contrast, there were 18 postelectoral conflict fatalities in Chiapas over those fifteen years and 196 nationwide. The overall intensity of conflicts in UC municipalities (explained in Table 5.2) was 2.3 on a scale of zero to three (zero meaning no conflict and three meaning conflict with mortalities), which is about the same as for Oaxaca's party-based municipalities.[16] However, more than 11 percent of Oaxaca's conflicts (counting UC and party-based elections) reached severity level three, whereas fewer than 8 percent of conflicts nationwide were that severe.

Finally, UC recognition has not substantially loosened the PRI's monopoly in Oaxaca. Stories abound of local partisans appropriating party ticket colors for their supposedly nonpartisan leader selection processes or of PRI operatives recruiting voters in local elections (Recondo 2006). And although parties need to continue to operate if UC municipalities are to influence statewide and national races where customary law does not apply, UC may be dampening indigenous participation in these non-UC elections. Recent studies by Benton (2006) and Goodman and Hiskey (2008) show that turnout in national elections is lower among voters from UC municipalities, which, like most of Oaxaca's municipalities, seem to also be growing independent of the PRI.

Perhaps even more important is the inability or unwillingness of Oaxaca state courts to judicially intercede in UC controversies. In the absence of

---

[15] According to former Governor José Murat (as quoted by Flores Cruz interview 2005), "Postelectoral conflicts in Oaxaca are measured by the number of cadavers they produce."

[16] These averages fall between severity level 2 (multiple-event mobilizations lasting less than one month) and 3 (conflicts producing serious injuries and/or building occupations or other manifestations lasting longer than one month). As per Eisenstadt 2004 (135–140), with conflation of the four categories into three, postelectoral conflict intensity was coded as follows: 3 for conflicts resulting in deaths, 2 for conflicts producing serious injuries and/or building occupations (or other manifestations) lasting longer than one event, and 1 for single-iteration (one-day) mobilizations.

judicial challenges, Oaxaca's unicameral state legislature (in partnership with the governor) has been able to manipulate UC election outcomes. The state legislature has dissolved hundreds of Oaxaca's 570 municipal governments over the last five years on grounds of "ungovernability."[17] However, unlike during the PRI's heyday, when the legislature (often at the governor's bequest) allowed at least some opposition participation on appointed interim city councils (albeit in secondary roles), the beleaguered party, which narrowly defeated a left-right coalition of the PRD and PAN in the 2004 gubernatorial race and finally lost the governorship in 2010, increasingly used the state legislature to dissolve local governments and substitute non-elected administrators directly responsible to the governor.

By seizing the opportunity disorder presented to send armies of administrators into dozens of UC municipalities between 2001 and 2004 (Cruz López interview), the PRI was able to consolidate support in key areas prior to the closely contested gubernatorial race in 2004. That same strategy fell short in 2010, however, as Governor Ruíz's authoritarianism led Oaxacans to elect a non-PRI governor for the first time since before World War II. More shocking, perhaps, have been the PRI's efforts to directly intervene in customary elections. In more than one-third of allegedly pure UC municipalities, the PRI participated in deciding how customary elections would transpire, candidate selection and registration, and/or election organization and certification, according to the 1997 catalogue of elections in Oaxaca's 418 UC municipalities (Auino Centeno and Velásquez Cepeda 1997). Indeed, analysts are watching closely to see how quickly change at the gubernatorial level trickles down to Oaxaca's localities.

From *Asunción Tlacolulita* to *Santa María Quiegolani*: *Gender Discrimination in* Usos y Costumbres

It is instructive to take a closer look at the case of Asunción Tlacolulita because it is illustrative of the costs of institutionalizing *usos y costumbres*. The 2000 verdict in this case established the important precedent that federal electoral law supersedes *usos y costumbres*, although the municipality arguably presented the country's most important legal challenge to that ruling to date. The case also underscores the dynamic nature of cultural

---

[17] Governor José Murat (1998–2004) suspended 140 municipal governments, as many as thirty at a time (Del Collado 2003), ensuring PRI dominance. He also punished mayors in even the poorest communities who could not find sizable enough campaign contributions to support the PRI in their paltry budgets.

norms and shows why caution should be taken before strictly codifying cultural practices in the name of multiculturalism.

Even though only approximately 10 percent of Asunción Tlacolulita's residents were considered indigenous (the majority were Zapotec Spanish-speakers), the town's population center was joined for the purposes of constructing a municipality with a neighboring outlying hamlet where residents spoke Chontal. The municipality (the municipal seat and hamlet together) was ratified as among the 412 of Oaxaca's municipalities where UC elections would occur. In general, the village had fewer conflicts between indigenous and non-indigenous citizens than much of rural Oaxaca, where it was not uncommon for indigenous communities to speak no Spanish at all.[18] Residents said political conflicts in Asunción Tlacolulita had to do more with power and PRI patronage than clashes between linguistic groups or cultures.

In 1998, dozens of women invaded the all-male community assembly in the rural town, calling attention to the discrimination common in *usos y costumbres* practices. Several women said they had come to vote for a left-leaning opponent of the long-standing local PRI political boss. They wanted to promote representation of new groups, including women from non-PRI families. One of the female leaders of the movement, tortilla factory worker Anastasia Zenón Flores, stated that the women had to attend the plebiscite "to defend our rights. We have seen that in many places women have even held public offices. We are taken for ignorants, but [the] human rights [activists] have always told us we have the same rights as men (interview 2004)." The women argued, furthermore, that UC was a myth constructed to perpetuate PRI's one-party rule over indigenous Mexico. They said that UC practices were designed to advantage those already in power and that the procedures unfairly denied women the right to participate in local politics. Indeed, the PRI had been threatened in recent party-led elections. However, Cipriano Flores Cruz, director of Oaxaca's electoral institute (IEE) during the Tlacolulita conflict, remembers it differently – more as a struggle between the PRI and PRD for control rather than as a struggle for women's rights (2004 interview).

UC conflicts are supposed to be submitted to a special mediator in the IEE rather than to the state courts (where party-based election conflicts are resolved). But no strict laws exist governing the mediation process; There

---

[18] Overall, slightly more than one-third of Oaxaca's citizens speak indigenous languages, and one-quarter of these do not speak Spanish (National Institute for Federalism and Municipal Development, 2003).

is only a partial list of suggested norms around UC traditions that was developed and catalogued by anthropologists. The Asunción Tlacolulita case went first to IEE mediation, but ended up being heard in the federal election court (TEPJF), Mexico's highest court for adjudicating postelectoral disputes. The immediate issue was the intractable conflict after the election which precluded anyone from taking office. This stemmed from several disgruntled groups, which broke across party lines (despite the formal inexistence of parties), including the PRD-supporting women and the traditional power broker clans led by PRI-supporting men. In the end, the federal court invalidated the 1998 local election in Asunción Tlacolulita, siding with the disenfranchised women and other PRD supporters, and invalidating the claim of victory by the ruling group. The verdict was part of the electoral court's establishment of final jurisdiction over what had been intransigent postelectoral conflicts over the previous decade that had claimed nearly 200 lives.[19] Despite the ruling handed down in far away Mexico City insisting that a new election be held, no action was taken to rerun the election or reform UC's discriminatory practices in Asunción Tlacolulita. Having won their battle, the women withdrew from public participation in the 2001 and 2004 local elections. "We have decided not to go to the assembly now because things have quieted down," Zenón Flores explained. "But if things get difficult again, we will be back " (2004 interview).

According to Flores Cruz (2004 interview), the movement had not come out of "the collective conscience of the women, but rather the actions of an activist teacher from the PRD who got some women the vote in an assembly. The teacher left, and there was no more conflict." Florez Cruz added that Tlacolulita had a history of radical political activism. While the feminist rights activists of Tlacolulita refused to reduce their movement to the teachings of one teacher (Zenón Flores interview 2004), the town was known for its history of activism on the left. After the Communist Party was relegalized nationwide in 1977, the town defied the PRI in subsequent elections and become one of Mexico's only municipalities ever governed by the Communist Party. But whether it was launched by a heroic tortilla maker or PRD rights advocate, the millennial movement for representation was clearly not launched by primordial collective indigenous

[19] These conflict-related fatalities occurred in Oaxaca with much greater frequency than in the rest of the country. Twenty percent of fatalities occurred in a state containing only 3.5 percent of Mexico's roughly 97 million people (database compiled by Danielson, Eisenstadt, and Ríos and cited in Eisenstadt [2004, 293–295]).

rights interests. It was created by self-interested individuals with political agendas. Contrary to long-standing traditions, dozens of women wanted a direct and individual say in how their community was governed.

An even more dramatic case of gender discrimination arose in 2007 when Eufrosina Cruz was told after winning a mayoral election in which only men could vote that women were also ineligible to run for office. Denied the mayorship of tiny Santa María Quiegolani by her challenger, who allegedly ripped up her ballots after stating that women could not stand for election there, Eufrosina Cruz staged public protests across Mexico during much of 2008. In an interview (2008), Cruz claimed that the system had been manipulated by an individual *cacique* seeking to retain power for his political group, and that the state electoral institute's director for resolving *usos y costumbres* conflicts, Jorge Cruz Alcántara, added the final insult, telling her, "My daughter, let it go. In three years, I'll advise you [for the next election]. Why are you persisting? Wait three years, if you want, and I'll be your advisor. Are you single? I'll invite you for a coffee, *morenita* [dark-skinned one]" (Izquierdo 2006).[20]

Eufrosina Cruz might have benefited from a good lawyer. She did not file a complaint to the federal electoral court in Mexico City within the requisite few days after the election, and thus her later complaint was inadmissible. To make matters worse, Oaxaca human rights officials confirm that Eufrosina Cruz had been formally banished from community in the summer of 2008 (Cruz Iriarte interview 2008). Whatever the legal status of her case, Cruz believes that *usos y costumbres* election procedures were discriminatory based on gender. President Calderón and the PAN made Cruz a cause célèbre in their fight against UC, nominating Cruz for a congressional seat as part of the party's proportional representation list. In 2010, Eufrosina Cruz, was elected to represent her people after all, in the lower chamber of the Mexican Congress. But she still cannot return to her village where she was banished for causing shame by discrediting the traditional system.

---

[20] The state electoral institute under Flores Cruz, who led implementation of UC in Oaxaca between 1996 and 1999, was widely regarded as one of Oaxaca's more transparent institutions. It became inaccessible after Governor José Murat Casab replaced Flores Cruz with José Luis Echeverría Morales soon after his election in 1998. At Echeverría's electoral institute, researchers were denied access to public documents, like the outcome of postelectoral negotiation cases. The research library was reduced in size and then restricted from public access, and officials stopped granting information or even interviews (author's observation).

In general, women have been discouraged in large and small ways from participating in political life in UC communities. In 2009, Beatriz Leyva Beltrán, a teacher and PRD activist, was killed for challenging the decisions of municipal authorities in San Pedro Jicayán in Oaxaca's Mixe region.[21] In Capulalpam de Mendez, Municipal Treasurer Olga Toro said: "To suppress [women's] active participation, anytime a woman attempted to speak, the men would make disruptive noise by vigorously shaking a cup or a can filled with pebbles" (Danielson and Eisenstadt 2009, 171). Although this practice has stopped, Toro says the antagonism it created means that she is still the only woman who participates regularly in municipal community assemblies.

All of these examples, and the broader pattern they reflect, have a predictable impact on the number of women officeholders in UC communities. According to Zafra (2009), five women were elected mayor from all 418 UC municipalities in the 2001 elections (ten women were elected mayor from all of Oaxaca's 570 municipalities statewide), and only one finished her term (Zafra 2009, 66–67). In 2004, only one woman was elected mayor via *usos y costumbres* (eight women were elected mayor state-wide) (Zafra 2009, 68). In 2007, three women were elected mayor via *usos y costumbres*, and fourteen women mayors were elected overall (Zafra 2009, 70). Zafra argues (2009, 63–64) that *usos y costumbres* elections are rife with interest-group politics, but that these groups can be even more tactically and personally aggressive toward women candidates: "The obstacles faced by women are legal, cultural, and relating to communal organization ... The lack of normative figures [laws] to assure and defend women's participation causes electoral institutions to do very little ... Furthermore, they [women candidates] face fierce opposition from interest groups, which, to avoid losing control, will use any means necessary to impede access by women to political competition and winning seats, especially local ones." So much for communal harmony, at least in many municipalities where women pose any threat to the male-dominant status quo.

A systematic study of discrimination under *usos y costumbres* did partially confirm the long-held view that UC institutions discriminate against women (Danielson and Eisenstadt 2009). However, it also revealed that in municipalities that do tolerate service by women in leadership roles,

---

[21] Mexico's Attorney General instructed Oaxacan authorities to investigate Leyva's death in June 2009, and the National Human Rights Commission issued a similar proclamation about an investigation being needed to see if there had been any political "cover up" of Leyva's death (Zafra 2009, 10).

women actually participate in elections. In other words, while discriminatory practices discourage female participation, if you remove the discrimination, women jump into the fray. Such open policies are not the norm, however, and women constitute only 20 percent of Oaxaca electoral rolls overall. When women are permitted to hold offices, more often than not, they are assigned to school or health committees that address the needs of children and families (Velásquez Cepeda 2003, 27), as opposed to the budget committee or village security detail. The Mexican government has recognized the central role of women in family life by delivering *Oportunidades/ Progresa* federal welfare aid directly to women rather than men. (Research is needed to assess whether such transfers may improve women's leadership roles in traditional communities.) According to Velásquez Cepeda (2003, 28), 80 percent of women who do serve in official positions face significant challenges, ranging from "simply not being taken into account in any internal decisionmaking, to personal conflicts in which they are delegitimized, criticized, and discriminated against by a member of the local government or the mayor, to fatigue caused by family tasks or work."

Of course, women's rights have routinely been ignored in much of Mexico (Danielson and Eisenstadt 2009), Latin America (Deere 2006), and around the world (Inglehart and Norris 2004). In Chiapas, Subcommander Marcos acknowledged that female participation in the Clandestine Revolutionary Indigenous Committees in 2004 was between 33 and 40 percent, but that women constituted less than 1 percent of the membership of the Good Government boards and autonomous governing councils (Marcos cited in Lewis, 2008, 182). This begs the question, what is the status of women's rights claims in a multicultural rights movement such as the one launched by the Zapatistas.

A few scholars such as Hernández Castillo (2006) argue that women's individual rights must be subsumed under the movement's universal communitarian vision.

Disqualifying these proposals [of indigenous women's norms, including communitarianism, equilibrium, respect, dualism, and multifaceted vision] because they do not depart from our perspective of equality or because they do not assume our preoccupation with sexual or reproductive rights or because we think differently in urban and *mestizo* areas, is to reproduce the mechanisms of silencing and exclusion of [women in] political movements marked by patriarchal perspectives. (Hernández Castillo 2006a, 16)

While those steeped in the liberal tradition may have difficulty comprehending tolerance, and even justification, for gender discrimination, such advocates raise a valid question. Hernández Castillo acknowledges that patriarchal movements silence and exclude women and implies a normative judgment that this is not right. However, she also advocates forcefully for multicultural relativism in the preceding phrases, creating a tension between the two. Are women's rights universal? If so, should state authorities force citizens to recognize them? Many observers note, perhaps from a Western human rights orientation, that even where women have formal rights to civic participation, these rights are often ignored or compromised (Rodriguez 2006, 62–63; Lewis 2008, 182).

Explaining the Increase in Postelectoral Conflicts under Usos y Costumbres

While the number of postelectoral conflicts diminished drastically across Mexico during the first decade after UC recognition (Table 5.3), the number of conflicts in Oaxaca remained nearly constant. The total number of conflicts in local elections in Oaxaca during the three cycles before UC recognition in 1995 (1989, 1992, and 1995) was 195; the total for the three cycles after UC recognition (1998, 2001, and 2004) was 193. This aggregation masks two distinct patterns: conflict rates actually dropped by half in areas with party-based elections and nearly doubled in UC municipalities (Table 5.2).

The increase in postelectoral conflicts under UC may be due in part to a selection bias. UC was recognized in order to defuse tensions in Oaxaca's indigenous communities because they tend to be some of the state's most remote, rural, and discordant communities (Dennis 1987; Díaz Montes 1992). Hence, these municipalities may have been the most conflict prone regardless of *usos y costumbres*. But this would not explain the degree of conflict in communities that Ríos (2006) dubbed "false *usos y costumbres*." As many as 46 percent of UC municipalities are non-indigenous by linguistic criteria, and less than 30 percent of the population speaks an indigenous language in 191 UC municipalities, according to 2000 census data.[22] The lack of correspondence between majority indigenous populations and the adoption of UC suggests that cold political calculus rather than ethnic identity drove some communities to make the change.

[22] Conversely, in 13 percent (20 out of 152) of non-*usos y costumbres* municipalities, 80–100 percent of the population speaks an indigenous language.

123

Consistent with this interpretation, Anaya-Muñoz (2002) and Recondo (2006) argue that "impure" UC municipalities simply obeyed a partisan logic. The PRI regarded UC as a way to keep other parties out of their critical local fiefdoms. The PRI played a role in the selection process in 21 percent of UC municipalities in 1995 when these systems were being codified into a baseline catalogue of *usos y costumbres* norms (Aquino Centeno and Velásquez Cepeda 1997). The PRI-majority legislature also approved the law, and the state Electoral Council designated which municipalities would be *usos y costumbres*. And, with a PRI governor in Oaxaca City, there was no check in place.

The process by which municipalities are classified as UC or party-driven is rife with inconsistency. The relevant passage of Article IV of the electoral law states vaguely that UC is applicable in communities that have developed community assemblies or other collective forms of local leader selection, or those which "by their own decision" decide to opt for such a system. In other words, "the possibility of 'inventing' UC fits within the realm of choices" (Guerra Pulido 2000, 37). The ability to create an indigenous party, or some party representative of local interests, and petition to change from customary law to party-based elections was also an option.[23]

It may also be that tensions in UC communities have risen because both the level of competition and the stakes in local contests have risen. When local municipalities were given the authority to allocate more of their own budgets, local elections started to have real meaning (Fox 2002, 108). Former state electoral institute director Flores Cruz agrees that many of Oaxaca's worst conflicts since 1995 have been about resource distribution. Municipal seats receive state funds and decide how to distribute them, while outlying *agencia* hamlets have little say in the distribution of those resources or in the selection of municipal leaders (interview 2004).[24] Of course, this increase in municipal-level budgetary discretion was a national reform, and postelectoral conflicts diminished markedly in Mexico's other thirty-one states over the same time period. But in Oaxaca, residents of the

[23] Unlike the Andean nations' indigenous right movements (see Madrid 2005 and Van Cott 2003), Mexico's indigenous rights movement has not produced viable indigenous political parties. In Oaxaca, the Partido Unidad Popular (PUP), claiming to be the state's "indigenous party," ran a candidate in the 2004 governor's race, but has not publicly mentioned fielding candidates in local races.

[24] Municipal reforms in the 1980s started decentralizing Mexico's budget authority, giving municipal governments (or at least *cabeceras* or "municipal seats") unprecedented authority over spending (see Fox 2002). Local governments still have little taxation authority, so federal and state disbursements are the major source of local funds.

state's 731 outlying *agencias* (each associated with one of the 570 municipal seats which generally take the lion's share of all federal transfers for themselves) filed over 200 complaints alleging they had been shorted in federal resource distribution in 2003 alone (Hernández-Díaz and Juan Martínez 2007, 180). To these authors, "these contradictions between communities within a municipality have found articulation in the electoral process which they use to pressure to have their demands attended to, or if they are customary law [UC] communities, demand participation in the process whereby their municipal authorities are elected (162)."

It is necessary, therefore, to consider causes of postelectoral conflict unique to Oaxaca. One may be that Oaxaca's political system provides the least accountability and least transparency of possibly any state in Mexico.[25] In addition, under the UC system, conflict is now the norm and the accepted process by which local actors can gain state acquiescence. While the electoral courts have jurisdiction over party-based elections, *usos y costumbres* elections are mediated on an ad hoc basis. As Graciela Ángeles Carreño said, in reference to Santa Catarina Minas's turbulent 2001 election (described in the next chapter), "The electoral institute lawyers and director of UC came in the middle of a heated conflict to tell us that UC was whatever we wanted it to be" (interview 2009).

Opposition party activists (Moreno Alcántara interview 1998; Cruz López interview 2004) and election authorities (Jiménez Pacheco interview 1998) all acknowledge the fluidity of postelectoral negotiations under current UC legislation and emphasize that the ability to mobilize supporters carries more weight than formal legal procedures. This lack of legal structure has forced election losers to wage their battle in the streets, knowing that, short of an appeal reaching the federal courts, a strong legal case does not matter, and that even federal appeals remain unimplemented. Mass mobilization and political finesse can lead to bargaining table victories. In the words of one former Oaxaca government mediator, "Winning and losing elections used to be absolute; now it's relative" (López López 1998

---

[25] Oaxaca was among the last of Mexico's states to elect a non-PRI governor and was the last of Mexico's thirty-two states to allow state legislators-elect to ratify their own elections. To this day, the legislature publishes no regular *Diario de Debates* proceedings. In other words, no public record exists of legislative activity, and finding out who supported the dozens of dissolutions of victorious municipal governments in the postelectoral horse-trading requires connections with the often-absent *oficialia mayor* and his assistant. These low-level administrators effectivly control all access to state legislative pronouncements, initiatives, and decrees (author observation 2004).

interview). Building on this logic, UC created incentives for disgruntled candidates or groups to mobilize, sow discord, create tension, and force the state to intervene, all outside the formal strictures of vote tallies and electoral courts. The lack of clear mechanisms to resolve postelectoral disputes only encourages groups to ratchet up their level of civil disobedience. Far from being a communitarian enterprise, elections under *usos y costumbres* are power grabs by individuals and special interests.

On the flip side, there is evidence that *usos y costumbres* reduced tensions in communities where there had been protracted struggles over whether to use liberal partisan voting methods or traditional customs (Eisenstadt and Ríos (2010)). Subordinating the partisan and bureaucratic interests to stronger customary laws may have restored community harmony in such cases, just as *usos y costumbres* advocates had hoped (Regino Montes n.d.). However, in *mestizo* communities where indigenous practices may never have been followed, *usos y costumbres* recognition did not relegate partisan and bureaucratic institutions to the sidelines. Particularly in areas of discrimination against individuals – be they women seeking representation for their views or hamlet *agencias* seeking federal resource "pass throughs" from municipal seats, UC may have actually helped further concentrate power in traditional hands and allow coercive block voting at the expense of participatory governance.

If this negative picture of manipulation by partisan interests is accurate, even if just in some UC municipalities, then the outcomes of *usos y costumbres* elections are foregone conclusions. And, on the rare occasions when local elites do not get the results they wanted, Oaxaca's unaccountable legislature can dissolve municipal governments and name interim city councils, or the unaccountable governor can send an emissary to take charge. Disgruntled UC losers have very little legal recourse. They can appeal to the federal electoral court. But only rarely, has the court ruled that a UC election discriminated against prospective voters and needed to be conducted again and to date no such verdict has been implemented. State authorities summarily ignore such federal verdicts as the one in Tlacolulita. And several other *usos y costumbres* cases have languished in the federal electoral court since then. Unlike activist courts, such as Colombia's, which – as we consider in Chapter 7 – have generated jurisprudence after jurisprudence delineating the fine line between individual and communitarian rights, while taking multiculturalism seriously (Sánchez Botero 2010), federal courts in Mexico have ruled on few multiculturalism cases and established no consistent normative position on related matters (Martínez interview 2008).

For decades, Oaxacans enjoyed a kind of de facto autonomy that was the envy of their brutally repressed neighbors in Chiapas. But formal codification of custom may have actually made these traditional practices vulnerable to co-optation and manipulation by the *mestizo* Spanish-speaking majority in a wide set of cases. Indigenous Oaxacans in these UC municipalities may have actually lost the very autonomy they were trying to augment. Oaxaca Governor José Murat (1998–2004), for example, regularly weighed in on UC elections during his tenure, dissolving scores of municipal governments (through legislative action) and sending agents to cull votes for statewide races and even, in well over 100 cases, to govern directly on a mandate from the governor rather than from the people.

Conclusion: Splitting Normative Differences on the Individual-Communitarian Divide

In her essay celebrating cultural differences and decrying the discrimination against women existent in so many cultural practices, Seyla Benhabib concludes that democratic civil society may be better served by "modifying our understandings of culture; rejecting cultural holism, and by having more faith in the capacity of ordinary political actors to renegotiate their own narratives of identity and difference through multicultural encounters ..." (2002, 104). Discrimination against women (and other minorities) has been acknowledged, even by advocates of customary law, as the "Achilles' heel" of *usos y costumbres* (Aguilar interview 2005). Universal participation should be institutionalized to allow women and other victims of discrimination to guard against manipulation by political bosses, and perhaps these are feasible reforms. UC advocates like Aguilár (interview 2005), Aquino Maldonado (interview 2009), and Flores Cruz (interview 2005) argue that it is imperative to improve UC rather than giving up, and that in discussing only the controversial cases of UC implementation, analysts miss the scores of cases where UC has diminished conflict. Indigenous political institutions do seem to enjoy more credibility and be more readily heeded than those imposed from outside. While the lack of a judicial authority to adjudicate disputes in a consistent and enforceable manner is deplorable, a regime of more inclusionary *usos y costumbres* with new institutions to formally resolve disputes may yield positive results. More importantly, it may be a more explicit recognition of the dynamic nature of cultural practices. It would allow traditional practices to move past their existing limitations and become part of (not erased by) the modern world (Velásquez Cepeda 2004; Hernández Castillo 2002).

More research is needed before definitive judgments can be made about whether UC systems are beyond repair. It is necessary to understand the causes underlying the rise in postelectoral conflicts in UC communities while conflict has diminished dramatically throughout the rest of Mexico. Research must also be conducted to ascertain whether individual citizens (including those victimized by *usos y costumbres* discrimination) want UC; whether more transparent institutions could help Oaxacans move disputes from town plazas to courtrooms; and whether improved education and other training could empower Oaxacans to take more control of their own direction. Moving forward it is important to decide whether UC should be restricted to majority indigenous communities. While there is a desire to protect rural communities from predatory *caciques* and outside interested parties who are simply seeking to use UC for their own political advantage, it might be a mistake to be too dogmatic about the idea of UC being a purely indigenous affair. After all, cultural practices, like the people who adopt them, are constantly changing. Recognizing the dynamic nature of multiculturalism may be imperative to its success.

Regarding the struggle between individual and communitarian rights, I have argued that discrimination against individuals and groups, especially with regard to gender, is a real cost of pursuing multicultural rights in general and UC in particular. However, having made the point that UC discriminate against individuals, in the next chapter I try to reframe these practices, focusing on the adaptive nature of UC and how the flexibility of this system has in some instances actually helped diminish conflict. I will also begin to try to reconcile individual and communitarian views of rights. It is valuable to understand how groups utilize communitarian frames to achieve both individual and group goals. And in real time, citizens do not choose just one identity or another; They assume multiple identities simultaneously and in true constructivist fashion, they constant adapt their identities to circumstances and necessities.

6

From Balaclavas to Baseball Caps

THE MANY HATS OF "REAL WORLD" INDIGENOUS IDENTITIES

Zinacantán was a closed and conservative indigenous community when Professor Evon Vogt negotiated entry for students with the Harvard Chiapas Project in the 1950s. This became one of anthropology's most "singularly successful" efforts ever to "describe the inside of native culture" (Rus 2002, 240). Fifty year later, aggrieved citizens of the same Tzotzil municipality were among those who most effectively took up the Zapatistas cause and rallied under the banner of indigenous rights. But they weren't advocating class warfare: the region is actually one of Chiapas's most capitalistic by virtue of its booming trade in greenhouse flowers. And they weren't demanding political or economic autonomy: the proximate cause of citizen unrest was that they received too few state resources. They joined the Zapatistas because joining the Zapatistas worked. It drew attention to their grievances and forced the government to respond. Far from the conflict in the Lacandon jungles that was discussed in Chapter 4, this small but well-networked group of Zinacantán Zapatistas essentially seized upon the Zapatista identity. They became citizens of an imagined collective and adopted a novel identity in order to find a new means of protesting harsh treatment by the state. They joined a communalistic group rights organization for partly individualistic and instrumental reasons. Such is the duality of everyday indigenous ethnicity in southern Mexico.

In December 2003, Zinacantán's first PRD-led state government shut off running water to the impoverished Jechvó community in Zinacantán. Tensions had grown over the winter between that hamlet community and the much more prosperous municipal seat of Zinacantán, until thousands of masked Zapatistas were dispatched from the Oventik "Good Government" Junta to march in Jechvó in April 2004 in support of the waterless local residents. The Zapatistas' show of support emboldened local Zapatista sympathizers, many of whom did not have a history of participation in the insurgency[1] but had seized upon the symbolic value of being considered part of the larger movement. Like other second-generation Zapatistas in Chiapas's central highlands communities, these citizens were grasping for new, more resonant means of expressing grievances against the municipal and state governments.

Unlike the first-generation Zapatista uprising, which concerned the extravagant failures of federal and state agrarian policies and the landed elite's decades-long effort to maintain dramatically unequal wealth distribution through repression and co-optation, the second-generation of Zapatista conflicts, such as the one in Zinacantán, concerned the nonexistent or inadequate provision of services, political corruption, and local authoritarianism. As just a group of peasants protesting the shut-off of their water, the Zinacantáns were powerless. But as Zapatistas, they were members of an international movement with a history of taking action and getting results. They could suddenly portray themselves as part of a powerful network that had to be reckoned with.

In addition to simply being necessary for survival, water has been shown to have a special life-giving meaning for indigenous citizens in Zinacantán (Burguete 2000, 72–77). This made water withholding a fairly easy and credible issue to ethnicize, and thereby connect to the larger Zapatista movement.

Ironically, the goal of these second-wave indigenous Zapatista protesters was to hold the Zinacantán local government (and unresponsive state agencies) accountable and to force them to reintegrate the township into the public service grid. This is in stark contrast to the aims of the first-wave protesters who sought separation from the same services; autonomy from the government's paternalistic provision of services. First-generation Zapatista protesters had actually refused to cooperate with the state by withholding payment for electricity and obstructing passage of government service vehicles. The Zinacantán Zapatistas' declaration of autonomy, contrarily, was meant as a threat to local PRD authorities. It was a call for service providers to stop taking them for granted and to better integrate them into the service grid. The fact that the second-generation

---

[1] There had been little overt Zapatista activism in Zinacantán during the early years of the Zapatista rebellion, despite its relative proximity to the movement's Oventik administrative headquarters in the nearby municipality of San Andrés Larrainzar and the heavily populated autonomous hamlet of Pohlo in the nearby Chenalhó municipality.

Zapatistas' objectives conflicted directly with the organization's original goals caused schisms and confusion. Ultimately, utilization of the Zapatista "brand" empowered the locals in Jechvó, but probably at the expense of the original Zapatistas.

During the zenith of the first-generation Zapatistas' military might in the mid-1990s, a rash of so-called third-party protests had been launched by masked opportunists around Chiapas, claiming to be part of the Zapatista insurgency in order to rob, plunder, and sometimes gain resonance also for the expression of legitimate grievances, of which there were many. They used the Zapatista cover to engender fear and inoculate themselves against persecution. Even analysts sympathetic to the Zapatistas acknowledge that the federal protections afforded in the 1996 San Andrés Accords were broad enough to shield these Zapatista-wannabes from prosecution. After the dramatic 2000 elections, a very different kind of second-generation social protester, like those in the poor outskirts of Zinacantán, started using the shield of *Zapatismo* to help them wage finite, local struggles around subsistence issues and social service provision. Rebellions by these reimagined Zapatistas occurred all over Chiapas' highlands and jungles at the turn of the milennium. In Salto de Agua and Tila they refused to pay property taxes; in Tumbala and Nicholas Ruiz they refused to pay electrical bills; in Sabanilla and Chenalho they refused to perform customary community work (*tequio*, but in highlands Chiapas called *faena*); and in Aldama and San Andrés Larráinzar they started a shadow Zapatista government (González Esponda interview 2007).

Benedict Anderson first used the phrase "imagined communities" in reference to the new forms of nationalism driven by the advent of book publishing (edited by Hutchinson and Smith 1994, 91–94). The interplay between this printing technology, capitalism, and linguistic diversity opened opportunities for Protestant European capitalists in the 16th century to develop a redesigned nationalist identity. However, as the Zapatistas demonstrated, the processes Anderson identified are no longer limited by geographic proximity or defined by political boundaries. The Zapatistas are only among the most recent in a long line of groups who have forged group identities out of propagated images and aspirations. But perhaps even more important than the new nationalism or ethnic identities themselves is how these can serve the needs of individuals and groups.

What connected these second-generation Zapatista movements to Subcommander Marcos's original Zapatistas was the tenor of their symbolic appeals, their strained relationship with the government, and the fact that the original movement needed this infusion of fresh adherents. By the time they established the Good Government Councils in 2003, the original group, the rebels from the Lacandon's canyonlands, were in precipitous decline. Perhaps the founders recognized that *Zapatismo* had to evolve or perish. So, the original leadership sent emissaries to these new outposts, selectively, to lend credence to those groups seeking to trade on the Zapatista reputation for effective collective action.[2]

Analyst Hernández Castillo (2006, 119) has argued that the Zinacantán confrontation was the result of a cynical attempt by some indigenous leaders: "Long-standing indigenous *cacicazgos* [political bosses] have recently recycled themselves by switching partners – linking themselves with the PRD" because that center-left party had finally come to power. This may explain elites' behavior, but it does not explain the motives of movement followers who developed new identities as "imaginary Zapatistas."

This chapter explores the divide between first- and second-wave Zapatistas and considers the Zinacantán Zapatistas' appropriation of the Zapatista social movement's ethos to achieve ends not imagined by the original Zapatistas. I also consider recent changes in Oaxaca's *usos y costumbres*, particularly how immigration has altered the practice at the municipal level. I argue that southern Mexico's indigenous communities, while predisposed to the objectives of *Zapatismo*, temper that identity with a commitment to being a citizen of the state. This dual approach ensures them of having access to both the Zapatistas' "innovative repertoires of contention" (McAdam, Tarrow, and Tilly 2001, 138) and the resources and recourses granted to citizens.

After having emphasized the differences between individualistic and communitarian political behavior among indigenous groups for much of the book, I now try to show how indigenous communities reconcile

---

[2] Several attempts to interview Zapatistas about a host of issues, including which copycat groups they supported which they disavowed, were thwarted. After a morning of screenings and interviews at a Ché Guevarra-muraled gift shop at Oventik headquarters, I did get permission in July 2004 to travel to the Pohló autonomous community. I made it past the first checkpoint on foot and entered the Zapatista community. I was then taken by masked handlers to the village eatery, where I was left to wait while the Zapatistas sought to confirm my "permission." I wandered outside and saw an abandoned Red Cross clinic, an inactive elementary school, and several Italian-speaking tourists, but I was not permitted to walk freely and my questions were never answered. I eventually left the secured area and got a ride back to San Cristóbal de las Casas (field notes July 29, 2004). It is widely known that the Zapatista ruling hierarchy has managed to maintain great discipline to ensure that researchers without Zapatista "approval" do not get interviews (see for example Lewis 2008).

these divergent approaches. The theoretical dichotomy between individual and communitarian rights breaks down in the real world. Drawing on examples from both Chiapas and Oaxaca, I argue that whatever the apparent inconsistencies in identifying both as state-legitimizing citizens and state-defying Zapatistas, indigenous-majority communities have tended to choose both. This has been especially true since the evolution of *Zapatismo* from a "detached identity" (in the parlance of McAdam, Tarrow, and Tilly 2001, 133–135) requiring certain obligations, sacrifices, and a real willingness to resort to violence, to a political identity, a brand, that connotes bold defiance, disciplined determination, and global alliance-building saavy. Interestingly, the new *Zapatismo* may have a more lasting legacy. It offers a true means for indigenous citizens to effectively synthesize their communitarian and individualistic impulses.

Zapatismo Redux: Imaginary Rebels in Zinacantán and Beyond

Population growth, economic globalization, and political discord had been straining Zinacantán for decades before the showdown over water rights. Cancian (1992, 171–174) describes how monetization of the economy and the growth of alternative means of establishing social status diminished the importance of *cargos* during the 1970s. As in Oaxaca, governmental decentralization of resource flows in the 1970s and especially the 1980s politicized the municipality. The growing cadre of truck drivers and flower growers involved in the greenhouse flower trade were able to channel resources like water to Zinacantán's affluent communities, while residents of the poor hamlets on the steep hills outside the town's central valley (*agencias*, or *parajes*, as they are known in Chiapas) endured their relative deprivation in silence, at least until their inconformity found a suitable and creative frame.

But their move toward the Zapatistas' camp was not immediate. In 1994, just days after the Zapatistas took over nearby San Cristóbal de las Casas, a meeting was held in Zinacantán where support was expressed, according to Camacho and Lomelí (2004) for "our brother Zapatistas, but not for their methods," referring to the use of violence. When it was revealed that there were a few original Zapatistas in Zinacantán, they received a tepid welcome. It was "concluded that we could live together without problems."

Over time, however, some members of the indigenous communities in Zinacantán began to look for new leadership and a sense of hope. As class differences and government responsiveness deepened between the poor *parajes* and the municipality's bustling central town, several families of Jechvó area residents (including some in the destitute Pasté hamlet) told local officials in December 2003 that they were joining the Zapatistas but would continue to participate in community affairs (Pérez Hernández interview 2004). These sympathetic accounts say that the PRD-led government responded by "forcing" voluntary service on the Jechvó Zapatistas and padlocking their water well. The march organized by the Zapatistas in April 2004, and which apparently included some original Zapatistas, made for good political theater as supporters carried buckets of water into Jechvó from surrounding areas. The conflict was based on the tension between periphery and center rather than on ethnic identities, as 80 percent of Pasté's 3,400 residents spoke indigenous languages, which is similar to the rate among Zinacantán's 29,800 residents as a whole, according to 2000 census data. The tensions came to a head during Easter week 2004.

Zinacantán officials do acknowledge making a strategic error by closing their offices and leaving town on April 10, 2004, for the Easter holiday, which was also the 85th anniversary of Emiliano Zapata's death (Reyes Aguilar interview 2007; Jimenez Pérez interview 2004). Zapatistas from around the state brought potable water to the Pasté neighborhood, which stirred resentment among anti-Zapatista residents, and a tussle occurred in a corner store where some visitors apparently took items without paying (Reyes Aguilar interview 2007). The ensuing conflagration left thirty-five people wounded, forced 500 people to flee their homes, and widened the breach between the Zapatistas and the rest of Zinacantán. It also signaled a larger break between the Chiapas PRD and the Zapatistas, although the relationship had been strained since Subcommander Marcos called on the Zapatistas not to vote in the 1995 municipal elections and likely cost the PRD several mayorships. The Zinacantán melee also exacerbated tensions between the dominant PRI and the upstart PRD, which had been bad for years.

Indeed, municipal officials had continued to argue through the late 1990s that coexistence between the PRD and the EZLN was possible, on the grounds that "the Zapatistas vindicated indigenous life, and the legal way of doing that [recognizing indigeneity] was through the PRD" (Reyes Aguilar interview 2007). But the creation of the Councils of Good Government in 2003 ended any tacit collaboration between the parties. According to Zinacantán officials (Reyes Aguilar interview 2007; Jimenez Pérez interview 2004), the Zapatista leadership was responsible for the rupture because their new system required citizens in zones of influence to channel all matters through their council rather than the municipal government. "That kind of order [from the formal Zapatista hierarchy], without going into too many details, painfully divided Zinacantán," said Reyes Aguilar. "There was no particular problem [that incited the break], but the EZLN here broke relations with the government because they [the Zapatistas] were a hierarchy following orders."

The Zapatistas stopped contributing to Zinacantán's frequent religious fiestas. According to the town's public works manager at the time, Reyes Aguilar (interview 2007), the feeling was, "If they [the Zapatistas] were not going to participate in religious fiestas, we were going to retire [public services from their neighborhoods]. One can lose one's identity and traditions. Our traditions are what distinguish Zinacantán and give it life. They are also what outsiders come to see." Accounts of various officials differ over whether the local government retaliated against Zapatista noncompliance regarding religious fiesta donations or whether it was the Zapatista sympathizers who launched the ill will against the local government of Zinacantán. Either way, the roots of the tensions went back at least to the mid-1990s.

Even back in 1995, several PRIístas were expelled from the party on accusations of corruption and switched to the PRD, which was increasingly viable as Chiapas' second party in a democratizing system. These new PRD recruits established "parallel" local governments in Pasté, Nachig, and Apaz (Camacho and Lomelí 2004), and – based on their strength in the paraje hamlets - won the Zinacantán local election of 2001. However, the PRD administration actually had to take over city hall by force because the PRI refused to evacuate municipal offices after their loss. In March 2003, vengeful PRI supporters stormed city hall, killed two people, and usurped control of the government. With the PRI rebels at city hall and the PRD officials governing from their homes, the Jechvó confrontation – when it emerged - was impossible to manage effectively. And divisions had nothing to do with differences between different groups of the Tzotzil speakers who constituted nearly 100 percent of the municipal population. It was matter between political parties and clans, class differences between water-requiring export florists and poor neighbors, and between the parajes and the town center. The Zinacantán conflict evolved into one involving Zapatistas too, but that was only years after it emerged, and the Zapatistas were, for the most part, figurative devil's advocates invoked in this chilly highlands town by small farmers, merchants, and construction workers in baseball caps rather than fatigued and balaclava-clad military professionals from steamy Lacandon jungles.

The Zapatistas of Zinacantán and Other Extensions of the Movement

The Zapatistas who came from elsewhere in Chiapas to march in Zinacantán on April 10, 2004, wore their famous masks, but the identities of the Jechvó protesters were well known. To Burguete (2004), the presence of outsiders was a means of concretizing opposition to state corporatism and showing they were a force to be reckoned with. *Zapatismo* gave second-generation practitioners like those in Zinacantán the opportunity to protest the fact that "the government's program amounts to a *lamina* [an aluminum laminate siding or roofing panel] (Burguete 2004 interview)" and that services, inasmuch as they existed, were paternalistically bestowed by the state government and international donors, leaving little decision-making autonomy to local residents. Instead of just refusing to pay their electric bills to the price-gouging state monopoly, hundreds of thousands of consumers could invoke *Zapatismo* and suddenly be part of a larger and more ideologically credible movement (Burguete 2004 interview). Indeed, the motives of these 21st-century Zapatistas were much different from those of the Zapatista wannabes of the mid-1990s who appropriated the Zapatista name merely to spread fear of an organized threat much larger than actually existed. Of course, the new Zapatistas did share one thing with those third-party parasites: upon declaring their loyalty to the Zapatistas, they were considered political refugees under the 1996 San Andrés Accords and protected from state persecution.

While the Accords were not enacted nationally, as pledged by President Zedillo, to foster indigenous autonomy, the Mexican government did honor the amnesty provisions of the agreement by maintaining a strong military presence in the area, but without provoking further confrontations. Zapatistas far and wide, new and old, credible and slightly less so, all received free passage. The Chiapas state government sought to "starve" certain municipalities of services, redraw municipal maps in a manner that would diminish the Zapatista presence, and as of 1998, have state police violently dismantle Zapatista autonomous communities. However the governor responsible, Roberto Albores Guillén was forced by the PRI to resign two years into his projected six-year term, and his brutal reversion to the "bad old days" of state violence against peasants, well-documented in the media, helped lead to the historic 2000 victory of Pablo Salazar's unlikely PAN-PRD left-right coalition candidacy.

Against this backdrop of violence alternating with uneasy coexistence between government authorities and the Zapatistas, some combination of the movement's ideological purity and the physical protection it offered seemed to spark a 21st-century rebirth. From the tricycle taxi drivers in the coastal town of Huixtla (Luna Luján 2004 interview) hundreds of miles from any of the Zapatistas' original battlegrounds, to separate churches for Zapatista-affiliated congregants in the newly districted highlands town of Aldama complete with parallel patron saint processions in Aldama by the Zapatistas and the non-Zapatista "official" government-affiliated groups, a loosely reimagined form of *Zapatismo* flourished early in the new millennium (Sánchez Pérez interview).[3] By 2004, nearly one-third of Chiapas' 800,000 electricity users were refusing to pay their electric bills and invoking the Zapatistas as inspiration (the actual movement had by that time dwindled to no more than a few thousand active militants). Many of these protestors, whose electric bills added up to nearly US $20 million, continued to resist even when the government started shutting down services (Villafuerte Solís and Montero Solano 2006, 194).

In San Andrés Larráinzar, the epicenter of the Zapatistas' Good Government Council administration (also called *caracol* administration in Spanish), two parallel governments have existed since 1995, one administered by the Zapatistas and the other by the PRD. This phenomenon traces its roots to Subcommander Marcos's call for citizens of Chiapas not to participate in the 1995 state elections. In San Andrés Larráinzar, all but thirty-one PRD supporters refused to vote at that time, whereas 2,891 PRI supporters went to the urns. Since these formal elections were simply ratifying a decision already made by the town assembly, which had selected the PRD candidate, the outgoing administration still gave the town's symbolic "staff of command" to the PRD mayor-elect.[4] But because of the Zapatistas' efforts to sabotage the process, enough votes were cast against

---

[3] Lomi estimated in 2005 that one-third of Chiapas' three million residents were Zapatista sympathizers, but offered no basis for that estimate. Our survey found that only 15 percent of Chiapanecans rated the Zapatistas as trustworthy. This rate is more consistent with other estimates like the one provided by Sonnleiter (2001).

[4] Many of Chiapas' indigenous towns, especially in the state's central highlands where communities have been able to partially regroup after diasporas, practice *usos y costumbres*. However, unlike in Oaxaca, these practices are not legal (i.e. recognized by the state), hence they are recorded only in oral tradition and not rigorously tracked. The systematic study of customary law practices in Chiapas at present offers a great challenge, whereas state recognition in Oaxaca has brought many more opportunities for methodologically sound research.

ratification of the PRD mayor to throw the outcome into doubt. The PRI was quick to step in and defend its own candidate.

According to Aguilar Hernández et al. (2010, 378–379), the PRI mayor received the town's all-important federal funds subsidy from the PRI-led federal government and managed to construct a second city hall. The Zapatista-allied PRD members charged rents for the moving trucks formerly owned by the town government, and also charged San Andrés Larráinzar's minimal local taxes, such as on kiosk "stands" at the Saturday central market. To this day, the "PRI government" controls the civil register, causing many young Zapatistas to not even have registered birth certificates. But the "PRD and Zapatista government" controls the town bus and have taken over the school. Authorities describe relations between the two "parallel" governments as civil (for example, the Zapatistas let the elected authorities use the bus, and the elected authorities allow the PRD/Zapatistas to collect mail and resources delivered to them via city hall). State and federal government authorities allow the existence of multiple authorities because, in Larráinzar and Aldama, if not in Zinacantán, coexistence has allowed both sides to "save face" without confrontation and avoid escalation. However, unlike nearby Zinacantán, where the conflict is between the PRD and the Zapatistas, in Larráinzar the Zapatistas and PRD have united against the PRI. The differences in strategy further illustrate that the Zapatistas in both communities are breakaway groups from the main, hierarchical Lacandon Zapatistas who have maintained for 15 years, that involvement in parties and elections sullies their objective of revolutionary change.

In Larráinzar, despite the split over schools and churches, the groups do find ways to work together. Both governments organize basketball tournaments, and some players cross-register to participate on the other group's team, showing that "not everyone considered it indispensable, in every aspect of social life, to treat the separation as a fight to the death in which no one could maintain their neutrality" (Aguilar Hernández et al. 2010, 382). Even more important, a decision made by the assembly of landowners (*comuneros*) in 1996 showed the limits of separate governance structures. Land resources are not fungible and cannot be divided the way local government authority had been. Consequently, the two sides agreed at the start that neither would try to make incursions in that area. The PRI supporters won the all-important communal lands commissioner job by a close vote in 1996, but the PRI candidate set a tone of compromise (Aguilar Hernández et al. 2010, 382–385) by including members of the losing ticket in his administration. As argued throughout this book, constructivist individuals, indigenous and otherwise, have found ways to soften the rigid communitarian rhetoric of the Zapatistas.

The state government of Chiapas, for all its initial anti-Zapatista rhetoric, has also tried to soften the movement's rigidity, by staying in close communication with the Zapatista leadership. Although the national PRD's failure to intercede against the Zinacantán PRD during its confrontation with the Zapatistas was a point of contention, the PAN-PRD coalition that governed Chiapas between 2000 and 2006 ensured that back channels remained open through the secretary of government's office (Luna Luján interview 2005) and the special representative for peace and agreement (González Esponda interview 2007). Indeed, even as analysts widely criticized the federal commissioner for Chiapas's failure to start a dialogue with the Zapatista leadership during the Fox administration, the commissioner himself, Luis H. Álvarez, noted that he maintained some informal contacts and that state authorities claimed to have a high-level, ongoing dialogue with the rebels during the first opposition governorship of Pablo Salazar (2000–2006) (Álvarez interview 2005). Chiapas' present governor, Juan Sabines Guerrero (2006–2012) of the PRD, has tried to maintain unofficial relations with the Zapatistas, but is widely regarded as less successful than his predecessor.

And the Zapatista presence has continued to dwindle. "Zapatista groups, by virtue of their desertions or other necessities, are every day soliciting more state government programs," according to González Esponda (2007 interview). "There exists less of an attitude of rejection, which has to do directly with the government of Pablo Salazar, because the government was no longer of the PRI." The EZLN hired public hygiene promoters, usually sympathetic medical students from Mexico City, to help conduct outreach in Zapatista communities to reduce hygiene-related maladies like diarrhea by learning to purify water (Estrada Saavedra 2007, 411–412). Zapatista schools were also often run by teachers trained outside the area, who were not paid and thus difficult to keep. Other services such as home and sports fields construction; provision of water and electricity; and delivery of specialized goods like bakery and nonperishable foods were also provided when possible (Estrada Saavedra 2007, 415–416).

But as the years since the rebellion stretched into decades, international donors lost their patience with the Zapatistas, and moved their assistance elsewhere. Against this backdrop of increasing discontent and decreasing membership, the Zapatistas created the Good Government Councils. According to Subcommander Marcos, these Councils were established to ensure better distribution of resources to communities beyond easy access by paved roads and to shake up the disfunctional relationship that had been established whereby the public "conduct[s] marches and file[s] petitions and the government [gives] them help" (Castellanos 2008, 37). These local Zapatista government outposts were intended to serve as decision-making bodies for their respective geographic zones regarding the provision of social services. Marcos argued that the Zapatistas had to provide these services because:

> Our generation does not expect anything from the government. We know we have to solve our problems ourselves directly. And what we have to do is get help from people outside [Mexico] who want to give, but not allow interference, even from those people, in deciding what should be done and how. (Castellanos 2008, 37)

But Estrada Saavedra's (2007) former Zapatista interviewees asserted that the Good Government Councils served more of a strategic military purpose than a social service role. Indeed, Estrada Saavedra (2007, 536–541) writes that these councils were a continuation of the Zapatistas' effort to discipline and consolidate their insurgency, as per the guerrilla tactics used in neighboring Central America in the 1980s, rather than a real bid for indigenous autonomy.

Whatever their intentions, the Good Government Councils did provide social services and established a governing structure parallel to that of the official government. Zapatista authorities acknowledged the establishment of a permanent contradiction of their jurisdiction with that of the state (as in the aforementioned Larráinzar case), as they agreed to offer services to all citizens in Zapatista-held areas to quiet the increasing numbers of citizens who sought to undermine the Zapatistas by receiving government services, which in turn diminished Zapatista morale. Despite their nonexistent tax base and lack of any sustainable economic development plan, the Zapatistas stated that their services would be available to all citizens, regardless of whether they were Zapatistas. The Good Government Councils established schools and clinics and managed to resolve some local disputes. As in Larráinzar, citizens chose pragmatically between Zapatista-provided and non-Zapatista-provided social service options, seeking to weigh their individual benefits against the communitarian commitments.

School Choice: Zapatista Followers Turn Statists

Openly seeking state services was embarrassing in Zapatista-held areas for several years, but throughout Chiapas, Zapatista supporters are now turning back to the state once again for the provision of core services, exacerbating the breach between the movement's ideological purists and its pragmatists. The ideologues insist on staying true to the cause by accepting no government support, while the pragmatists argue that the movement must diminish the hardships experienced by members if it wants to survive. In this battle, education has become a central point of disagreement. According to Burguete (2004a, 174–175): "The EZLN rejects any type of relationship between rebel education programs and the government ... but many Zapatista families have accepted negotiations [to send their children] with government schools, causing a friction point within the ranks of the rebellion, which sometimes results in ruptures [between the Zapatistas and some followers]." This conflict between parents who want to ensure that their children receive state-accredited schooling and Zapatista leaders who want to maintain ideological purity and coherence has become more and more relevant as the EZLN's movement has gone from being a low-intensity guerrilla war to a permanent opposition party. (Accreditation is vital as only high school students with accredited diplomas can enroll in postsecondary education).

The Zapatistas' original educational objectives were quite noble. Before the uprising, the majority of Chiapas' indigenous people were illiterate and most rural Lacandon communities had no schools. "In the communities where they did [have schools], most teachers were absent or the children mistreated (Rodriguez 2006, 65)." After expelling many teachers throughout the occupied communities in 1995 "under suspicion that they had become government spies (Rodriguez 2006, 66)," the Zapatistas began constructing new schools. They had completed 80 by 2004. The schools were built in partnership with the *Enlace Civil* and *Semillitas del Sol* NGO, which ran an adult literacy campaign, and a group of teachers in Mexico City who ran six-month training programs for education promoters (unlicensed teachers). Urban intellectuals created most of the didactic materials used to train educators in Zapatista-run schools, and "most of them were readers on social movements or on the history of Mexico and of the EZLN (Rodriguez 2006, 77)" and fell short on teaching practical skills like math and science. The Good Government boards provided infrastructure and resources with international assistance from European donor NGOs like International Forum and Operation Dagsvoerk in Denmark (Rodriguez 2006, 78).[5]

[5] Claims that the Zapatistas receive their funding from European donors seem to be made by some opponents to discredit the regional and national origins of the group, but would also help explain the group's survival. A recent media account ("Ex zapatista revela estructura

The Zapatistas have been able to at least partly address the public school system's chronic failure to teach indigenous languages as well as Spanish, and Zapatista education promoters claimed in 2005 that contemporary youth "have a political, technical, and cultural training that those of us who initiated the Zapatista movement did not possess" (Baronnet 2008, 112). However, many of the young Zapatista educational volunteers (many of whom have only completed sixth grade) have complained that the communal structure of the education system has not been universally popular with parents, leading to huge variations in outcomes. Zapatista schools rely on parents and community members to contribute a day of work or an equivalent in corn or other commodity to the school each week, but these commitments are only sporadically met (Rodriguez 2006).

Gutiérrez Narváez (2005) notes in his study of Zapatista schools in Simojovel that the political divisions often ran along religious lines. There, Protestants split from the PRD and the EZLN to join the Workers' Party (PT) and stayed in government-run schools. The Catholics, linked to the liberation theology of the Dioceses of San Cristóbal de las Casas, joined the EZLN-based school that taught a "communal cosmovision" and emphasized local language and knowledge. The alternative curriculum of the Zapatista schools caught on in the Lacandon but not in the highlands, where a majority of the Zapatistas continued sending their children to official schools or changed back to official schools in 2000 when the government started offering scholarships and hot breakfasts. In 2004, eighty-three autonomous schools were opened by the California-based NGO *Escuelas para Chiapas*, but many of those closed almost immediately when teachers were not paid regularly and left (Villafuerte Solis and Montero Solano 2006, 172).

In general, early enthusiasm for the Zapatista cause has dissipated because the economic condition of rural indigenous populations has not markedly improved over the last fifteen years. The North American Free Trade Agreement (NAFTA), which passed on the same day in 1994 that the Zapatistas launched their campaign, has done more to boost economic indicators than the homegrown rebellion. NAFTA has provided incentives for converting land from corn crops to cattle ranching and increased

actual del EZLN," *Reforma*) included allegations from a dissident former Zapatista that, in 2010, Italians and Basques delivered 150,000 Euros to the Autonomous Governing Councils and then delivered 750,000 and later 350,000 Euros to the Good Government Board in La Garucha (municipality of Ocosingo) where the nearly 600 active members of the Zapatista militia keep their weapons, which include AK-47 and M-16 machine guns.

income in Chiapas through remittances and tourism. Villafuerte Solís (2009, 16) argues that the Zapatistas have not stimulated economic development: "The process [of developing autonomy, especially in the realm of education and health care] has not been exempt from difficulties, in the terrain of human and financial resources as well as in the existence of a tense environment due to the presence of armed forces, government institutions and even the very social organizations which cohabitate the Zapatistas' zones of influence and fight for resources, especially land." Now, instead of rising up to challenge the state, impoverished Chiapanecans are simply leaving.[6] Migration has also the economic coping strategy of rural Oaxaca.

New Partners: Capitalism Meets Customary Cargos

The municipality of Santa Ana del Valle in Oaxaca does not allow citizens living abroad, more than half of the community's population, to vote absentee in *usos y costumbres* elections. The community has one of the highest out-migration rates in all of Mexico. More than one thousand of the town's three thousand residents live abroad (including two-thirds of the male population between nineteen- and sixty-years-old).[7] Of course, even though these migrants are excluded from voting, they are still expected to contribute to Santa Ana's communal well-being.

Activist Primo Aquino wants to change this by allowing *usos y costumbres* elections to be conducted over the Internet. "The culture of Santa Ana is not dying, and does not need to be rescued," said Aquino in an interview (2009) at his home. A large wooden loom of the type ubiquitous throughout Santa Ana partly filled the room. "[Our culture] ... has evolved, and in this era of the Internet and globalization and migration, culture needs to change. Evidence of this happening is that they now celebrate *mayordomias* [parties in honor of the community's religious saint] on the 25th of July in Los Angeles." Aquino added that expatriate communities have implemented Santa Ana barbecues, contests for expatriate

---

[6] Census data show that as of 2007 the majority of young people from more than 20 percent of Chiapas' 2,495 *ejidos* had migrated to urban areas, the United States, or elsewhere in Chiapas. In Oaxaca, the majority of young people from more than 43 percent of the state's 1,474 *ejidos* had migrated (Villafuerte Solís 2009, 17).

[7] According to the National Population Council (Conapo), Santa Ana del Valle has the highest "index of migration intensity" of any municipality nationwide. Population data is from 2000 census, although the ratio of 360 males between 19 and 60 present in town to 608 absent was established in 2003 (Molina Ramirez 2006).

143

weavers and dancers, and celebrations of All Saints Day (*Dia de los Muertos*), which are just as legitimate and authentic as the concurrent celebrations in Santa Ana. "People say that if you want your culture you have to come back home," according to Aquino. "But absence and nostalgia also make you want them," and economic opportunities in the United States force people to adapt their hometown cultural practices to their new locations (interview 2009).

But while migrants have brought their cultural abroad, Santa Ana has done less to keep them politically connected back home. Unable to participate remotely in community assemblies to select leaders, they nevertheless must fulfill *cargo* obligations or risk expulsion from the community. No expulsions have yet occurred because migrants have begun paying errand runners at home to handle the jobs they have been summoned to do.[8] However, Aquino noted (interview) that water service was recently cut to one migrant-led household where a migrant was named to a prominent position on the city council for which substitutions are not allowed and failed to come home and serve.

Throughout Mexico, migrants are figuring out new ways to serve their communities without returning home. In 2007, remittances to Mexico (nearly all from the U.S.) exceeded $26 billion; This figure fell in 2008 and 2009 as a result of the global recession, to a low of about $21 billion in 2009 (Latin American Herald Tribune 2010), before starting to rise again in 2010 (Buchanan 2010). Recent studies have found that stepped-up border security has also made repatriation more costly (Cornelius and Lewis 2006). In Oaxaca, *usos y costumbres* requirements that citizens must return to volunteer for a 12-month term of service as frequently as every three years have further complicated migrants' relations with their hometowns. Sorroza's (2009) analysis of our 2008 Survey of Oaxaca, Mexico Customary Law Municipalities found that 39.4 percent of the state's UC municipalities receive money from migrants to support *tequio* (unrenumerated labor); 40.1 percent require migrant participation in fiestas; 31.9 percent require migrant participation in religious *cargos*; and 22 percent require migrant participation in civil *cargos*.

Monetization of Mexico's rural economy and other aspects of globalization seem to make the perpetuation of this hyper-traditional version of *usos y costumbres* untenable in the long term. As huge majorities of the adult male population in Oaxaca's rural municipalities migrate to the U.S.,

[8] In 2003, 105 out of 235 positions were "contracted out," according to Molina Ramirez (2006).

Table 6.1. *Monetization of* Usos y Costumbres *Institutions*

UC Institution	Number	Percent
Monetization Index	90	27.61
Tequio	63	18.31
Religious Cargos	57	16.86
Civic Cargos	36	10.56
Authority Cargos	17	5.09

Source: 2008 Survey of Oaxaca, Mexico Customary Law Municipalities. Directed by Moisés Jaime Bailón Corres, Michael S. Danielson, Todd A. Eisenstadt, and Carlos Sorroza and sponsored by Higher Education in Development (HED), the United States Agency for International Development (USAID), and the Benito Juárez Autonomous University of Oaxaca (UABJO).

fealty to a strict interpretation of customary law is eroding (Pichardo Peña 2001; Ibarra Templos 2003; Kearney and Besserer [449–466] in Fox and Rivera-Salgado 2004; VanWey, Tucker and Díaz McConnell 2005). As per Table 6.1, 28 percent of Oaxaca's 418 *usos y costumbres* municipalities have integrated some level of monetization.

But as further explored in the following section, advocates argue that these global forces create a compelling reason to strive all the more diligently to preserve historic cultural traditions, even if in adapted forms.

Individual versus Communal Rights in Santa Ana del Valle and Beyond

In Santa Ana, migrant attempts to either have a role in community assemblies or to be ruled ineligible for *cargo* and *tequio* drafts have been unsuccessful. In 2004, migrants in California submitted a list of four candidates representing their interests by fax to the assembly, but the candidates were not approved. While the number of service committees needing volunteers has been limited somewhat, migrants voted into service by their compatriots still have no means of avoiding it. Lesser *cargos* can be filled by paid substitutes, but service to the local government cannot be rendered by anyone except the titular citizen (usually male) or his wife.

The idea of allowing virtual participation of U.S. migrants in assemblies is not unprecedented. The town of San Pablo Macuiltianguis in Oaxaca's Zapotec-speaking northern mountains held a virtual town assembly wherein the mayoral ballots were set, elections in San Pablo and Los

Angeles were held simultaneously, and the absentee vote totals were faxed to municipal authorities and added to the official sum (Hernández-Díaz, and Juan Martínez 2007, 152). Santa Ana's migrants have been as yet unable to arrange a similar process, but they have made inroads toward validating other migrant contributions from abroad, such as paying young people in the town to fill their low-level *cargos*.

City council positions are different, however, because remuneration is not an option. No one gets paid for elected municipal service. The nation-wide municipal reforms of 1983 started a flow of federal taxes into munic-ipal treasuries, but that has not led to a professionalization of local posts in most *usos y costumbres* municipalities. "Those who have served in the past argue, 'If I wasn't paid, why will you be?' Yes, we lose days and hours, but that's how *usos y costumbres* is" explained former Santa Ana regent Francisco López Garcia (interview 2009). Similarly, Aquilino Arellanes, the former mayor of Santa Catarina Minas, argued that citizens are only willing to serve as volunteers if their fellow townspeople do too (interview 2009). In other words, there is a very real fear that if you pay one person, you have to pay everybody.

For Aquino, the migrant rights controversy in Santa Ana directly pits individualism against communalism. "We have to arrive at an equilibrium between individual and communal rights in which no one is discriminated against. It's very delicate. We have not yet reached this point." To him, there is no solution except patience and flexibility, and a willingness to accept the inevitable continued evolution of UC traditions (Aquino interview 2009). Hernández-Díaz and Juan Martínez (2007) view the evolution of the migrants' role in Santa Ana as "a process of seeking consensus through a reasoned process in which all sectors participate" and a "demonstration of the capacity of the system to adapt and innovate" (144).

Hobsbawm's Dark Side: New Synchronicity or Old Authoritarianism?

To Hobsbawm, the "invention of tradition" was the result of three innova-tions in Europe (and particularly France) during the Age of Nationalism. The first was the "development of a secular equivalent of the church – primary education, imbued with revolutionary and republican principles and content (1994, 77);" the second was the invention of public ceremonies (such as Bastille Day, dated to 1880); and the third was the "mass production of public monuments" (78). Hobsbawm contrasted the successful invention of tradition in France with Germany's more limited success during its uni-fication. Bismarck consolidated power but opted for vague national sym-bols that avoided idealization of a nonexistent democratic political culture. Buildings and statues were erected, but they did not emphasize philosophical ideals (Hobsbawm 1994).

What would Hobsbawm say about the symbolic politics of the indige-nous rights movements in Chiapas and Oaxaca? He might note that neither the Zapatistas nor leaders of Oaxaca's more authoritarian *usos y costumbres* communities have shown any hesitation about casting even their most plainly political maneuvers as grandly symbolic events motivated solely by dedication to the cause. These groups are both fighting decades, even cen-turies, of arbitrary authoritarian rule, to be sure. But their actions have not always had a basis in authentic ancestral traditions, as they have almost always claimed.[9] Recognition of UC itself was probably the most cynical effort to cloak contemporary politics under the veil of ancestral mandate. Movement leaders use the symbolism and myth surrounding ancestral practices because it strikes a chord with their intended indigenous audi-ences. But, having conjured up and stoked sentimentality about tradition, it is wrenching for communities when the instrumentalism behind leaders' use of these symbols becomes apparent.

Consider cases where supposed defenders of traditional practices manip-ulate and deform these practices to retain power for themselves and pre-clude participation by members of their community. This is what happened in Santa Catarina Minas in 2001 and in San Miguel Tlacotepec in 2007. Gender discrimination was the issue in Santa Catarina Minas, where women were precluded from participating in the 2001 election shortly before the vote, even though they had been participating in elections for decades. The outgoing mayor tried to disallow participation by women in this election because a candidate he opposed was strenuously campaigning for the votes of a large female bloc. "The argument was that … [women's] participation had been induced, which does not cast doubt on their quality as citizens but rather on their ethic as citizens" (Hernández-Díaz and Ángeles Carreño 2007, 311). Women were ultimately allowed to vote, but the results were

---

[9] The following of ancestral desire as a justification for current policies is widespread in many countries. Even the U.S., without legitimate claims to oral tradition like the Zapotec or Tzotzil people, debates the "intent of the founders" regularly with regard to Supreme Court rulings. The assumption seems to be that founder-ancestors lived during a time when concern was for the public good alone and were unfettered by the base motivations that guide contemporary politics.

extremely controversial. A fight broke out as the final votes were tallied on the community chalkboard on October 7, 2001. Opponents of the winner, Sebastian Mendoza Arellanes, argued that he did not have the right to assume office because the election had violated *usos y costumbres* by allowing the women to participate and because he allegedly had not fulfilled *cargos* assigned by the assembly (Services for an Alternative Education, 2002, 79).

On these trumped up charges, Mendoza Arellanes was disqualified and the third-place finisher, Heliodoro Rios Arellanes, took office. "The disappointment of the population was widespread," according to Services for an Alternative Education (2002, 79), "including among *PRIistas* of the town who affirmed that they were not in favor because the friends, family, and colleagues of Heliodoro had always occupied the municipal presidency." Complaints were brought before the state Electoral Institute and the state Human Rights Commission. The state Electoral Institute ultimately ratified Mendoza Arellanes as mayor. Even though the case of Santa Catarina Minas was resolved in favor of the women and others who were disenfranchised, Ángeles Carreño argues that the incident left citizens much less confident in their local authorities and the community divided.

Usos y costumbres has lent itself to discrimination.... Slowly the organization of our society has undone our community. Many of our people migrate to the U.S. and the problem is that they come back in bad shape, with drugs, problems of identity, etc. The women remain in charge of everything, but we don't have the rights of citizenship. We are halfway citizens. (interview 2009)

This social strain posed by migration was felt throughout Oaxaca, pitting the participation of individual migrants against long-standing communitarian traditions. However, in some cases, the strains had little to do with migrants and their rights and more to do with the role of returnee migrants as an interest group.

In San Miguel Tlacotepec in 2007, arbitrary changes in the *usos y costumbres* process were made for purely instrumental reasons and permitted to stand, and the community remains bitterly divided. Orlando Molina Maldonado was a candidate for mayor in this Mixtec-speaking town of San Miguel Tlacotepec. (Twenty-one percent of adults there speak Mixtec.) But according to Molina Maldonado, and corroborated by other accounts (Cornelius et al. 2008, 218), candidate eligibility rules were changed at the last minute under the guise of *usos y costumbres* in order to render him ineligible. The rules, approved by a municipal assembly on November 18, 2007 and posted several weeks later, stated that citizens could not vote for former municipal presidents, current municipal or communal resources officials, or anyone not living in Tlacotepec proper, and that only those who had served in the community and fulfilled all their *cargos* were eligible. It also specifically noted that one could "vote for women who meet the previously listed requirements" (Cornelius et al. 2008, 218). Molina Maldonado was excluded according to these new rules because he worked in Santiago Juxtlahuaca, even though he claimed to return to nearby Tlacotepec every evening, and because he had allegedly not served his community *cargos*.

Molina Maldonado claims to have completed the *cargo* of *mayordomo* [financier/organizer of the annual party for the patron saint] in 1994, but municipal records credited his father, who had originally been named *mayordomo* but died before completing the service. Maldonado assumed the responsibility after his father's death, but was never given official credit. "Tlacotepec should just be governed by parties," said Norma Molina Maldonado, the candidate's sister. "These are not uses and customs," she said, referring to the irregular imposition of candidate requirements at an unadvertised meeting. "These are abuses and customs" (interview 2009).

In Tlacotepec, residents in the town's five *agencias* cannot vote, although they must still sign the electoral acts, and women have the right to vote and serve in *cargos*, "except that no one lets them" (Norma Molina Maldonado interview 2009). Orlando Molina Maldonado claims that although UC elections are supposedly nonpartisan he was precluded from winning the election by members of the FIOB (the Binational Oaxacan Indigenous Front), a group of migrant returnees affiliated with the PRD.[10] "UC is totally disguised," he said. "Juan Gutiérrez' supporters are from the PRD and mine are from the PRI. Everyone knows this. Why do we have to whisper behind closed doors at night? Why can't we be more open and just conduct the elections by parties?" (Orlando Molina Maldonado interview 2009).

"What is the rule about applying UC?" Orlando Molina Maldonado asked the outgoing municipal officials who conducted the contest. "It's however you apply it," they told him. Despite his claim of having received the most votes, Orlando Molina Maldonado was relegated to regent of health, the lowest position in municipal government, as a means of punishing him and his supporters. The municipality remains rigidly divided along partisan lines, and *usos y costumbres* seems to have created opportunities

---

[10] Siblings Norma and Orlando Molina Maldonado were interviewed in their home on the central plaza of Juxtlahuaca, Oaxaca, where a large PRI banner draped from the third floor in anticipation of Mexico's July 2009 congressional elections.

for arbitrary rule but little harmony. Although no Oaxaca municipality has thus far sought to change its electoral regime from *usos y costumbres* back to political parties, at least some of Tlacotepec's PRI supporters strongly advocate such a change.

Even that would likely not diminish the degree of conflict in Villa Hidalgo Yalálag, where the battle lines are drawn between ethnic groups and have endured for decades. In Yalálag, a *usos y costumbres* town in mountainous northeastern Oaxaca where 92 percent of the population speaks Zapotec or Mixe (and 19 percent do not speak Spanish at all), tradition enthusiasts led by Zapotec intellectual Joel Aquino Maldonado have sought to revive the indigenous culture by forming a band to play traditional music, starting a radio station to broadcast Zapotec content, and designing a Zapotec computer keyboard. Critics of the effort (including some of the Zapotecs, most of the Mixes, and many non-indigenous residents in the area), claim that these new measures are actually reinterpreting the past rather than reviving it. Furthermore, they say, Aquino Maldonado's labors are selectively benefiting members of the Uken ke Uken Cultural Center and that he is utilizing valuable resources (such as international grants) to "rediscover" Zapotec culture at the expense of more pressing community needs (Aquino and Emilio Bautista interview 2004; Martínez interview 2000).

The conflict in Yalálag has deep roots. It began in the late 1970s with the creation of the Grupo Comunitario (GC), headed by Joel Aquino Maldonado. According to Aquino Maldonado, the GC supports "unconditional respect for the traditional Zapotec laws over communitarian government, *tequio* and municipal government, which are the basic institutions that give the population the character of an indigenous community" (cited in Juan Martínez, 2000, 205). This division, founded on differences of clans and families, festered, and grew ideologically polarized over time, through several historic governance conflicts.

However, the case for restoring and retaining Zapotec traditions gained credibility. In 1989, a controversial decision was made to convene a council of elders and it was given a role, along with municipal officials, in deciding who would take over as the town's municipal and traditional authorities. (Some critics like Emilio Bautista argued that the council idea was not original to *usos y costumbres* and was, in fact, taken from Greco-Roman culture. Bautista, a doctor and lifelong resident of Yalálag, said, the *cacique* at the time "did a little reading of universal history and came up with the idea of the council of elders" [Bautista interview 2004].)

Aquino Maldonado's advocacy of indigenous rights won a larger audience after the Zapatista rebellion of 1994, and he became an important Oaxaca-based spokesman for the national indigenous rights movement and an advisor to the Zapatistas. His importance grew when Oaxaca officials started to fear a possible insurrection. Repeated attempts to sabotage Yalálag's precarious telephone antennas during the mid-1990s seemed to confirm that unrest was brewing (Juan Martínez 2007, 212). Those opposed to Aquino Maldonado's movement, including members of the Coordinadora 11 de Octubre, a Mixe group founded in 1998, said that the movement was taking liberties with history, radicalizing the town, and offering selective benefits to movement leaders.

Great disagreements emerged between the factions over the *cargo* system. Primordialist practitioners like Aquino Maldonado sought to preserve the old ways, whereas more liberal adherents wanted to ensure the survival of *usos y costumbres* via adaptation. A big point of contention was whether citizens should be paid for their work. To Aquino Maldonado, this represented a betrayal of tradition. To others, like José María Vargas Mestes (the only woman on the Yalálag city council from 2002 to 2005), refusing to pay guaranteed the services of less qualified officials only, and that public officials would underperform. She said that by refusing to pay police, for example, Yalálag was exposing itself to danger and argued that some used the municipal conflict as an excuse to not pay property taxes (interview 2004). Moderates like Bautista argued that since the state's human rights commission had ruled that noncooperative citizens could not be forced to offer voluntary labor, leaders could no longer enforce these rules. But Bautista was also concerned that a loosening of UC practices would destabilize the community. "*Usos y costumbres* doesn't have rules," Bautista complained (interview). "If we had statutes or even unwritten rules the system would work. But here, we haven't achieved that."

The unification of the Coordinadora and the election of an anti-CG candidate in 1998, even though he was rejected by the council of elders and was unable to take office, hardened the positions of both sides. The state legislature dissolved the local government and tried to solve the problem by naming an agent of the governor municipal administrator. But Yalálag's annual municipal elections offered plenty of additional opportunities for escalation and, eventually, violence. After years of GC dominance, a Coordinadora ally won the election in 2000. This election was declared invalid by the state Electoral Institute, but Coodinadora supporters occupied the city hall. In the course of their forcible removal, one person was killed, several more were injured, and twenty-three were arrested (Juan Martínez 2007, 221).

Should communities be allowed to update and invent *usos y costumbres*, or should their observance be limited to forms that have been used in the past? And if change is allowed, what should be the parameters? The debate in Yalálag has played out across Oaxaca in one way or another. The defense of past traditions and efforts to maintain them in present circumstances is eloquently advocated by adherents like Aquino Maldonado and Flores Cruz (interviews 2004). But as they promote the cultural practices that speak to them and their followers, shouldn't these leaders acknowledge the danger of harnessing the symbolic power of the past in the service of momentary political gain? In candid moments, some indigenous advocates will make such an acknowledgment, and admit that some change is inevitable, but argue that they need to steer the direction of change so that it remains loyal to the tenets of the past. Given that Oaxacan indigenous practices vary from town to town (and even within towns), it is hardly surprising that the isolated and highly centralized Zapatistas could not promote one set of beliefs and attitudes to speak to all of Chiapas. There, a similar question must be asked: Did the co-optation and adaption of *Zapatismo* by second-wave activists diminish the original movement or give it a new life?

Decline of Zapatismo *as End; Rise of* Zapatismo *as Means*

The end of first-wave *Zapatismo*, which since 1996 had relied on indigenous rights claims to promote an essentially class-based demand for greater socio-economic and political equality, was subtly acknowledged through Marcos communiqués in 2005 and more powerfully declared with the launch of the Zapatista's "Other Campaign" on January 1, 2006. According to Estrada Saavedra's (2007, 599–600) detailed analysis, the Other Campaign was conducted:

without the active and visible participation of indigenous people and without support in an ethnic discourse. Distancing themselves from indigenous topics and struggles, the EZLN has started to appeal to the solidarity of other political groups from the 'anticapitalist left' with the hope of making *zapatismo*, through a network of alliances, a national movement, a movement not limited by Chiapas' geography nor the indigenous membership.

The movement's original emphasis on indigenous autonomy attracted international attention and supporters who liked the "romanticization of the indigenous Zapatistas and their 'otherness,' which recalls Eurocentric prejudices about the 'noble savage'; purity of motives and superior forms of social cooperation, politics, and relating to nature, among other things (Estrada Saavedra 2007, 439)." But the movement faced severe internal conflicts, partly as a result of that international assistance, which was disproportionately distributed in easy-to-access areas (Estrada Saavedra 2007, 468) and was sometimes unusable because of local technology or customs.[11]

The Zapatistas' military might and influence also diminished over the last decade. The military structure had grown from five militants in 1983 to an armed fighting force of 1,500 in the mid-1990s, but shrunk hugely after 2000. The group's claim to practice *mandar obedeciendo* (command by obeying) is belied by former Zapatistas' claims that "authoritarianism and despotism" were the real modus operandi and that Subcommander Marcos and other high officials cultivated personalistic rather than institutionalized leadership styles (Estrada Saavedra 2007, 455).

Perhaps most confounding was the movement's inability to attract new supporters from its traditional base. The organization had been built on alliances with land reformers and religious activists, but as described in Chapter 4, the land tenure reforms in the late 1990s sometimes pitted agrarian rights supporters against Zapatista stalwarts, and the religious alliances diminished with the reassignment of Archbishop Samuel Ruiz in 1999. Moreover, the election of PAN-led opposition governments at the federal and state levels in 2000 usurped the more moderate elements of the movement agenda. Repression and neglect were replaced after 2000 by watchful neutrality, which didn't solve any core problems but was a recruitment killer for extremist groups like the Zapatistas because it also did not further polarize conditions or reaffirm the state's role as the oppressor. Governor Pablo Salazar (2000–2006) sought to co-opt Zapatista sympathizers by offering services in movement strongholds with tacit approval from autonomous region leaders.

And the Zapatistas had always expected a lot of self-sacrifice from supporters, a position which became less and less tenable as the movement

---

[11] Stories still abound about the Zapatista communities' roadside sales of non-perishable foods they had received from international donors that were not part of their diet (like tuna fish). Estrada Saavedra further relates that the electrical generator of La Realidad Trinidad was usually broken because, while international donors helped fix it, they did not succeed in training the Zapatistas to maintain it (Estrada Saavedra 2007, 442).

failed to achieve its communal goals. As mentioned in Chapter 4, practices that favored the strategic interests of the movement at the expense of followers' well-being were commonplace. For example, good land would be left fallow to preserve the promise of a future reward, rather than granted and allowed to "distract" revolutionaries with farming. Residents in support base areas had to pay wartime tithes to the Zapatistas, which they gave less willingly over time, particularly when food and other resources were not distributed efficiently to the soldiers. One of Estrada Saavedra's interviewees (2007, 463) reported that Zapatista troops had to plant their own food.

Furthermore, Zapatista leadership consisted predominantly of young people who rose up through the clandestine ranks and bypassed more traditional means of establishing social influence and prestige. They clashed with conventional local authorities, were not terribly seasoned or resourceful, and "were unable to improvise in coordinating actions, and thus fell into authoritarianism" (Estrada Saavedra 2007, 477). According to some, the democratic promise of *mandar obediciendo* became more a catch phrase than a policy. When inexperienced field officers failed to resolve local matters adequately, they would simply fall back on the time-tested formula of requiring unquestioning loyalty. Extreme opposition to the Zapatistas also increased over time, reports Estrada Saavedra, with people cutting off their relations with Zapatista-sympathizing friends and family, even those they'd known "from the second grade (Estrada Saavedra 2007, 502)." Opponents in Zapatista-controlled areas found cover in social groups formerly allied with the movement that had broken ranks.

Internal disagreements spread as the state government's efforts to supplant the Zapatistas with public services that people needed started to work. Chiapas' first non-PRI governor since the 1930s quietly and respectfully made services available, and the needy responded. As stated by one disillusioned former Zapatista leader, "People want their *Progresa* [social program], their *Procampo* [agrarian subsidy] but they [the Zapatista leadership] will not let them receive these … Now there aren't that many left in the EZLN, but the highest leaders have cars, steer, and homes, and the people are screwed" (Estrada Saavedra 2007, 501). This ex-Zapatista was still loyal to the ideals of the movement, however, if not to its leadership. Many interviewees seemed to believe that the Zapatista vision had been derailed somehow, not that the vision was wrong.

In Their Own Words: Individual Agency and Being Indian by Choice

One lesson may be that efforts to devolve governance to indigenous areas like Chiapas and Oaxaca are virtuously conceived but of little practical use in fostering large-scale economic development and political enfranchisement in areas where indigenous (and non-indigenous) residents need basic assistance in the form of food, education, and health care. After all, as important as ethnic pride and self-determination are, you can't eat them for dinner. Writing about the Mixtecs, although this applies to many of Oaxaca's indigenous peoples, Nagengast and Kearney (1990, 65) noted: "[They] know themselves as those who originate in *lugares tristes* [sad places], villages in the Mixteca where food is often scarce, a decent living is difficult to obtain, and children die of preventable diseases ... Mixtecs do not glamorize their poverty by claiming that it is traditional."

Some of Mexico's Indians, especially those in remote areas that have not experienced rule by any other than old-style PRI *caciques*, have faced their fate with resignation and accepted government efforts to maintain a corporatist paternalistic hold. In some areas, the Zapatista were able to break the inertia and empower local people to rise up and demand greater equity and justice. A movement participant from Cruz del Rosario said in 2004, "[D]espite the fact that it is not easy and the government attacks us, we have found a way to live in our struggle. We have lived 10 years without taking anything from the government and we have learned that we can survive with our effort and collective work. Although our children go around with shitty clothes, we have not sold our dignity nor the values we have" (Estrada Saavedra 2007, 428).

But protest is not the same as progress. The Zapatista did find a means to draw attention to Mexico's deficient social policies. But by framing the Mexican government's failings in purely ethnic terms, the Zapatistas ultimately wrought confusion and misdirection. In Chiapas' troubled city of Acteal, the site of the 1997 massacre mentioned in Chapter 2, one young girl said, "We govern ourselves. What is the government good for if we have no light, water, roads, hospitals or schools? ... I do not see a reason to have any relationship with the government" (Burguete in Rus, Hernández Castillo and Mattiace 2003, 212)." But is it really ethnicity or even the need for self-determination that explains this young girl's antigovernment position? Or is the fact that she's never known a government that provided adequately for her needs? If she is like the vast majority of respondents to my survey discussed in Chapter 3, the answer is resoundingly the latter. Rigorous, thoughtful analysis can help de-ethnicize residents' perceptions of Chiapas' social problems and bring the debate back to basics: isolation, economic deprivation, hopelessness, and corruption. Although this may not sound like a particularly uplifting platform for a social movement, it is at least concrete and more empirically grounded than the current stalemate over optimal degrees of indigenous autonomy.

7

Reconciling Individual Rights, Communal Rights, and Autonomy Institutions

LESSONS FROM CHIAPAS AND OAXACA

As much as the Chiapas-based Zapatista insurgency has to teach about political rhetoric, the motivations behind collective action, and instrumental communalism, the indigenous rights phenomena in Oaxaca may be more informative about how individuals negotiate the tensions between individual and group rights day in and day out. In the end, the Zapatistas drew important attention to the indigenous rights agenda, but seem to have became utterly preoccupied by internal strategic concerns. The Oaxacan movement, by contrast, never achieved the unity of purposes or collective strength of the Zapatistas (see Chapter 2), but advocates there have grappled directly, even daily, with how to enact indigenous group rights in the modern world community by community.[1]

It may be possible from a theoretical perspective to put individual rights on one side of the ledger and collective rights on the other. But one of the most basic lessons of Oaxaca's experience with *usos y costumbres* is that these neat categories break down in practice, creating enormously messy grey areas. The case of Santa Ana del Valle, where migrants are disenfranchised from elections but must serve the community, even if from abroad, is a great example of how difficult it can be for communities to navigate this complex and fraught terrain. While the situation was clearly an affront to the individual rights of migrants in Santa Ana del Valle, there were

---

[1] For example, Orlando Molina Maldonado (interview 2009) argued that in San Miguel Tlacotepec, where he was embroiled in a controversy over proper UC procedures, the debate only mattered in the municipal seat (*cabecera*). In the outlying communities (*agencias*), elections were not even held. "They are just forced to sign the results," he said. In Santa Catarina Minas, different neighborhoods have different UC traditions, and there is constant disagreement over which rules to follow. The argument once became so heated that a brawl occurred on the village basketball court, according to Ángeles Carreño (interview 2009).

credible communitarian rights claims being made as well. In this chapter, I will discuss how these individual versus communitarian rights demands are reconciled in southern Mexico and compare that to how conflicts are adjudicated in the Andean nations of Bolivia and Peru. Interestingly, on the Bolivian side of Lake Titicaca, the Aymara people have developed a strong indigenous rights movement, whereas the Aymara on the Peruvian side of Lake Titicaca have created no such movement.

Also, I will directly address an issue that until now I have only addressed indirectly: group autonomy. "Autonomy" as a concept contains a slew of meanings, connotations, and frames. In this case, I am referring to the degree to which groups can operate independently from the state and its dominant culture as well as the degree to which individuals are free to make conscious decisions about the institutions, parties, and practices they support. I will use the examples given throughout the book to begin to analyze the proper unit (individual, interest group, community, region) for granting of autonomy and constructing support institutions. I conclude that only a frank consideration of the trade-offs between individual and communitarian rights can yield the kind of self-aware multiculturalism that simultaneously respects the rights of groups and their individual members. Normatively, one form this could take is the adoption of "conditional multiculturalism" (Danielson and Eisenstadt 2009, 153, 156), whereby institutions of autonomy are constructed that allow groups to revere and sustain whatever cultural norms they choose, but with the stipulation that they respect citizens' constitutional rights and include an "opt out" clause so that individuals can choose not to participate without penalty or the loss of group rights. While Mexican law has scarcely taken up these normative issues, the Colombian Constitutional Court has found perhaps the best standards to date for mediating between individual and communitarian rights.

Workaday Conflicts: Communal Norms and Individual Rights in Oaxaca

The Oaxacan experience with UC recognition has provided a wealth of information about how tensions between individual and communal rights are negotiated on the ground within indigenous groups and also between UC municipalities and the state, the nation, and the international community. Over the last fifteen years of UC practice, several issues have arisen time and again as major, seemingly intractable, sticking points between individualists and communitarians: women's rights, migrants' rights, and globalization.

The case of Eufrosina Cruz, who was elected and then stripped of office simply for being a woman, drew enormous attention from the national and international media[2] and her case had resonance with liberal Western elites. It raised the profile of gender discrimination under UC as a serious issue (see Chapter 5), such that even national Mexican officials, including the Federal Electoral Tribunal president, María del Carmen Alanis Figueroa, said that gender discrimination in indigenous communities was a problem that needed to be addressed, albeit at state and local levels (Tapia 2010). The cases of gender discrimination in Santa Catarina Minas and Asunción Tlacolulita were somewhat more ambiguous, given that women themselves were potentially making individual rights demands to serve temporal political ends. In general, however, Zafra's systematic study of electoral results shows a lack of female political representation of epic proportions. Female municipal officials, former officials, and candidates from UC communities who were interviewed (Ángeles Carreño 2009, Molina Maldonado 2009, and Cruz 2008) all independently decried "abUC" [abuses and customs] of women's political rights under the UC system.

Immigration also poses persistent challenges to UC administration. In many communities at the moment, migrants are caught in a triple bind. There is an economic imperative to go to the U.S. to seek work, but they are completely disenfranchised while they are gone. If they stay in the U.S. long enough to be able to send substantial remittances, they can lose their rights and land in Oaxaca. If they return to Oaxaca, they are not always well received because of the fear that migrants will bring new habits, including drug use and gang activity, back with them (López Valencia interview 2009).

Furthermore, as the debates over the *escalafon* (the practice of selecting leaders via the ladder of *cargos*) show, economic development imperatives are presenting a whole other set of challenges to the practice of UC. Traditionally, leaders have been selected based on their loyalty to the community and record of past service, regardless of their individual skills or merit. As stated by Martínez Luna (interview 2005), who espouses a philosophy of *comunalicracia*: "In democracy, votes are defined by rhetoric. In *comunalicracia*, your work is what defines you." The essential question

---

[2] Cruz has become a role model for womens' rights, receiving extensive coverage in international media like the *Los Angeles Times* (Tobar and Uribe 2008) and *El País* (Relea 2008) and visits from dignitaries like Margarita Zavala (Mexico's First Lady) and Michelle Obama (United States' First Lady).

for voters in *comunalicracia* is whether candidates have served the *cargos* they have been called to serve and whether they have earned respect in the community. While this approach is true to Oaxaca's communalist tradition, some people have begun to argue that merit deserves more weight. Shouldn't those people with particular skills or talents be able to use them to benefit the collective? Wouldn't it make sense to allow a college-trained accountant to run for municipal secretary without having to first serve as an errand runner, police officer, cemetery caretaker, or church-bell ringer? San Miguel Tlacotepec's mayor, Esperón Angón (interview 2009), lamented the fact that all of the talented and ambitious young people had migrated, and that no one left spoke Mixtec or observed traditional rules. His colleague, San Miguel Tlacotepec's treasury regent, Gumesindo Bollaños Berra (interview 2009), said that *cargos* discriminate against the poor: "For those who have the economic conditions, serving [*cargos*] offers a break. But for those who don't have the economic conditions, it is not beneficial, because your family suffers."

One of the distinctive features of Oaxaca's UC system is that it represents a very real attempt to sow group autonomy from below. In most other places in Mexico and Latin America, group autonomy has been imposed from above. This was certainly the case in Zapatista Chiapas, and that movement failed to result in greater indigenous autonomy.[3] Elsewhere in Latin America, movements to allow subnational geographical and minority group autonomy are growing. But here too, efforts to allow more local control have often been top-down, driven by governments or international development banks and other agencies. Ironically, these programs sometimes simply serve to concentrate power in the hands of those who decide how to allocate resources to decentralized bodies.

National Parties and the Quest for Autonomy

In order to win UC recognition, a bargain was struck: the PRI-state would largely leave local administrations to govern their territories and, in exchange, UC winners would agree to be registered as PRI members. In other words, the PRI got rural legitimacy and the UC communities got

---

[3] This is not to diminish the accomplishments of the Zapatistas in drawing attention to the plight of Chiapas' destitute indigenous peasants, achieve land reform when no other means seemed possible, and inspire "imaginary Zapatistas" throughout Chiapas, Mexico, and Latin America. However, as a model for sustainable development, few can argue that the movement has been a success.

a modicum of independence. Formal recognition of UC ensured the PRI's stranglehold in rural Oaxaca to the point that opposition parties were unable to make inroads for decades. Moreover, local autonomy was constricted by the fact that authoritarian governors could send their minions to take over as administrators whenever electoral conflicts became too intense.

This willingness on the part of the government to use rights and services as leverage in order to command political support from citizens has a long history in Mexico. One recent example was President Carlos Salinas's (1988–1994) bid to decentralize welfare spending as a means of resuscitating the PRI in rural Mexico. Instead of sending out checks from the federal government, he channeled welfare spending through regional and local solidarity committees composed of PRI allies, technocrats, and cronies. The public then came to see these local PRI groups as the face of social welfare. "Hunger is tough," said one Oaxacan PAN leader (PAN has traditionally opposed UC). "If you give someone food for one day, they feel beholden to raise up their hand for you in an assembly" (López interview 2005). Indeed, the power of the state to decide who eats and who doesn't is well known in rural Oaxaca, where legions of administrators have directed resources in a way to maximize support for their political party. In this context, arguments for greater indigenous autonomy from the state carry understandable salience.

In Chiapas, the situation was even more disempowering for local populations. The state government was so authoritarian that the heavily exploited indigenous populations had no voice at all against the *latifundista* agrarian elites. Chiapas' repressive system did start to recede in 2000, however, when the state's first-ever opposition governor, Pablo Salazar, was elected by a left-right coalition of PAN and PRD voters. The Zapatista insurgency was able to scare the state into negotiating additional land reforms. However, the lack of local venues for dialogues between Zapatista sympathizers and detractors, especially before the 2003 declaration of the Good Government Councils, has rendered local governments easy prey for *caciques* and predatory interest groups. Paramilitaries representing landholders and, on occasion, some of the more belligerent squatter groups claiming to represent *Zapatismo* have undermined local authority.

In Mexico and other nations with long histories of patronage and repression, the advantages of devolving authority to locals must be weighed against the vulnerability of local systems to corporatist power grabs and clientelism. Patron-client relationships are easily established and manipulated under a guise of communitarianism under which political bosses paternalistically declare to be the "authentic" voice of the movement and know what is best for their supporters. These supporters and the silent bystanders who may not even be sympathetic to the movement must simply abide by the leader's decisions without getting to express their own views or deliberate. Apparent shows of communal decision-making, even if they are theater merely to reaffirm decisions already taken in back rooms, win credibility for local movement leaders, who are then able to claim to speak for the collective and, if so inclined, translate that aggregation of interests into support for local bosses, patronage networks, and national parties.

In some cases, group solidarity has actually been manipulated by outsiders, usually interlocutors seeking to build support for a particular politician who could not otherwise access a linguistically indigenous community (Rus 1994; Hernández-Díaz and Juan Martínez 2007; Recondo 2007). Bilingual teachers are the quintessential example, but not the only one. San Juan Chamula is dominated by alcohol distributers seeking to monopolize sales (Rus 2002), and Burguete confirmed (2007 interview) that monopolistic commodities providers still battle for market control by taking sides in local political battles. In much of Mexico's destitute south, individuals sell votes for roof laminate, sewing machines, and canned goods (Eisenstadt 2004, 255), and receive little from the government between election seasons.[4]

Would experiments in self-governance by southern Mexico's indigenous citizens have fared better if they had included more expansive autonomy rights? Critics, like the former director of the Oaxaca electoral institute, Flores Cruz, say greater autonomy would have prompted the state to abandon autonomous areas. He argues that the more extreme groups who have sought indigenous autonomy in Mexico (i.e., the Zapatistas) do not actually wish to govern and "will not define, nor execute, nor evaluate" policies (interview 2005). Ultimately, this would leave the region's interests totally unrepresented at the national level, where the overwhelming amount of Mexico's public resources is doled out. Flores Cruz argues that better representation of indigenous positions within existing government and partisan structures is what's needed. In their ideological migration from revolutionary Marxists to ethnic warriors to social democrats, the Zapatistas seem to have implicitly acknowledged this.

The broader point is that autonomy must be coupled with strong local governance in order to deliver communities the independence they seek

---

[4] Burguete (interview 2008) called this "the politics of the roof laminate shingle," which is reminiscent of Africanist Jean-Francois Bayart's (1993) reference to "the politics of the belly."

from the state. Autonomy coupled with weak local governance will be manipulated and disenfranchise the very groups it is intended to empower. To Burguete (2009), autonomy has four preconditions: 1) some sort of territorial definition, 2) internal self-government, 3) set jurisdiction over territory and internal governance, and 4) "specific, constitutionally-established competences and powers" (2009, 13). What the Zapatistas showed was that recognition without a share of state resources or competent governance is of limited use. Autonomy is only beneficial to communities that have the resources and capacity to effectively call their own shots.

And how can local autonomy for communitarian practices be reconciled with participation in a larger nation-state that is constitutionally committed to individual rights? According to Oaxacan anthropologist Martínez Luna, "Here and in all communities there are moments where individual preoccupations dominate, like getting a house and paying your children's school tuition. But there are also moments when the community clamps down on us and we have to serve a *cargo*, go to assemblies, do *tequio* and share our resources. The individual is diminished, but we in no way deny individual aspirations" (interview 2005).

Ethnic Political Movements in Latin America: Bolivia and Peru[5]

Efforts to objectively study instances of subnational autonomy in Mexico have frequently demonstrated a bias on the part of researchers to be sympathetic toward the underdogs, namely, the outside agitators. Bobrow-Strain (2007, 18) confronted this issue by defying his own impulse to study the "dualism of 'good' indigenous peasants and 'bad' *ladino* landowners around which much discussion of Chiapas had revolved." Instead, he constructed a narrative from the landowners' perspective and captured their fears about the post-1994 land redistributions in Chiapas. (These reforms and the creation of hundreds of new *ejidos* coincided with a dramatic decline in the viability of the *ejido*-centric model of farming and ranching that had long dominated Mexican agriculture.[6]) In the context of this book, one way to correct for this bias is to consider a case where an autonomous government has won elections and is now in power. Bolivia's recent experiment with

[5] Shannan Mattiace coauthored portions of this section as part of a 2006 grant proposal. While I am extending the argument, Mattiace and I initially worked on this question together. (thank shannan in the acknowledgements.)
[6] For more on the decline of the *ejido* and the simultaneous rise of the *ayuntamiento* (municipal government) as the unit of governance in rural Mexico, see Torres-Manzuera (2009).

autonomy provides some insight into what happens when an indigenous rights movement is at least partly able to implement its agenda.

In December 2005, Evo Morales was elected Bolivia's first indigenous president. This, coupled with the passage of a new constitution in early 2009, has trained intense international focus on that country as a laboratory of indigenous power and participation. Bolivia's new constitution grants multicultural rights to the Quechua, Aymara, and other indigenous groups to a degree not equalled by many countries. The interesting thing for comparative purposes is that the Aymara do not all live within Bolivia's borders. A large number of Aymara-speakers also live across Lake Titicaca in Peru. But those who live in Bolivia have demonstrated a much stronger indigenous identity. I ask whether the reasons that the Aymara in Bolivia are so much more communitarian than their brethren in Peru are similar to the reasons for the communitarian/individualistic split between Oaxaca's and Chiapas's indigenous groups. Although the discussion is more suggestive than conclusive, this hypothesis does appear to hold promise. That is, it seems that indigenous identity in Bolivia grew out of an organized social movement (as in Chiapas), whereas it was repressed or rechanneled in Peru via state corporatism (as in Oaxaca). If differences in agrarian institutions also prove to be explanatory variables, it would suggest that the Mexican model has some predictive power.

As in Mexico, there is much variability in how and when traditional customary law has been applied in the Andes. Examples can be found where traditional practices defy human rights norms, such as during the 2004 lynchings in El Callao, Peru, and Ayo Ayo, Bolivia, which were conducted in the name of traditional law (Mulligan 2004). Examples also abound of the social capital generated by indigenous networks that was harnessed to defend villages against Shining Path terrorists in Peru (Starn 1999), and of the empowering effect of *ayllu* communitarian institutions on local democracy in Bolivia (Ticona et al. 1995; Fernández Oslo 2004; Lucero 2008; Andolina, Laurie, and Radcliffe 2009).[7] Such traditional practices have tended to occur in parallel with the state in Peru, while they have been integrated into Bolivia's political institutions over the last decade. At the level of the nation-state, a wide range of policies and practices fall under the broad rubric of "decentralization" and include political, economic (or functional), and administrative decentralization.

---

[7] *Ayllus* are extended family and community structures and their importance is rooted in pre-Conquest Andean social and political practices.

Following Willis, Garman, and Haggard's approach (1999, 8), I define political decentralization as the establishment or reestablishment of elected autonomous subnational governments capable of making binding decisions in at least some policy areas. Economic, or functional, decentralization involves the transfer of responsibilities for expenditure and revenue-raising powers to subnational governments (Willis, Garman, and Haggard 1999, 8). Administrative decentralization involves the transfer of management responsibilities to subnational governments but does not include the power to raise or allocate resources (Rodríguez 1997, 10). If we place decentralization policies on a continuum ranging from weak to strong, simple deconcentration would be at the weak end. Deconcentration generally involves a transfer of functions, power, and resources to the state offices of central (federal) agencies (Rodríguez 1997, 11). A strong decentralization policy involves transferring power to popularly elected local governments and providing local governments with greater political authority (e.g., to convene local elections or establish participatory processes), increased financial resources (e.g., through transfers or greater tax authority), and/or more administrative control.

During the 1990s, almost all Latin American countries experienced some political decentralization (Willis, Garman, and Haggard, 1999).[8] Decentralization initiatives were the result of two major events in the region: 1) the debt crisis, and subsequent structural adjustments and neoliberal economic policies; and 2) the transition to democracy. Great pressure was brought to bear on Latin American leaders by international financial institutions responding to the debt crisis who wanted to see greater decentralization to guard against a repeat crash. At the same time, Willis, Garman, and Haggard (1999) suggest political liberalization and democratization also provided powerful motives to decentralize. They argue that democratic opposition movements and parties pushed for the decentralization of political power because they believed that they would have more success winning local offices than competing at higher levels of government. Democratic reforms during the 1980s and 1990s brought previously marginalized actors into the political process and subtly altered the terms of the decentralization debates. Blair (2000, 25) notes that decentralization reforms in the 1990s were different from the 1950s-era initiatives which

---

[8] Eaton and Dickovick (2004) have suggested that a recentralization of political power is occurring in at least some countries that decentralized during the 1980s and early 1990s. Nevertheless, the overall trend in the region continues to favor decentralization.

sought to enhance the efficiency of public administration in the developing world. The new decentralization efforts placed more emphasis on democratic local governance and focused on citizen participation and accountability of local government for its decisions.

The effects of decentralization policies on ethnic identity in Mexico and South America have been intensely debated by scholars, in part because the policies vary significantly throughout the region, as does the strength of indigenous mobilization. In Mexico, decentralization of administrative authority has not been met with commensurate decentralization of discretion over revenue generation or decision-making with regard to governance. In Bolivia, while the new multicultural laws are still being implemented, it would appear that decentralization has contributed to indigenous mobilization.

This is not surprising when one looks more closely at the context. For one thing, communal attitudes have been more prevalent in Bolivia for generations as a result of organizing by tin worker and coca grower unions. At the same time, the state had been less effective in propagating state corporatism in the countryside. In Peru, where labor movements and collective actions have not been able to take hold nationwide, land reform has helped promote peasant rather than indigenous identities in agrarian areas. In addition, Peru has experienced extreme levels of political violence at the hands of brutal Shining Path Maoist insurgents, which effectively demobilized and silenced the indigenous population and obstructed state involvement of any kind in those victimized communities.

Bolivia's Decentralization: Origins and Legal Framework

Legally, Bolivia has a centralized political system with three layers of government: national, departmental, and municipal. In 1994, President Gonzalo Sánchez de Lozada launched one of the most comprehensive decentralization programs in Latin America, shifting the balance of power noticeably toward municipal governments. According to Grindle (2000), in the face of formidable governability challenges, the Sánchez de Lozada administration viewed decentralization as a way of making government more responsive and markets more efficient. First, decentralization diffused the power of regional elites without causing a direct confrontation that could divide the country. Second, decentralization was viewed as a way of reducing corruption by taking power out of the hands of central elites who traded votes for partisan advantage and patronage. Third, transferring responsibilities to municipalities was intended to lead to greater efficiencies. Fourth, decentralization, it was hoped, would bring the government closer to the people, thus enhancing governmental legitimacy.[9]

The central pillar of Sánchez de Lozada's decentralization initiative was the 1994 Law of Popular Participation (LPP).[10] "An idea generated by a small team of advisors, [the LPP] was taken up by a national political entrepreneur [Sánchez de Lozada] as a solution to ineffective state management and troublesome demands for regional autonomy" (Grindle 2000, 98). The LPP established the municipality as the basic unit of local government throughout the country, and 311 new municipalities were created. Prior to 1994, only a few dozen municipal governments existed in the country, mainly in urban areas (Van Cott 2003). The law established that 20 percent of government revenue would be transferred to municipal governments, based on population size. The LPP also authorized the direct election of mayors and municipal councils. Before 1994, mayors had been appointed. In an effort to promote accountability at the local level, the LPP stipulated that each municipality set up a "vigilance committee" charged with overseeing the mayor and reviewing and approving local budgets and an annual operating plan. The vigilance committees would be comprised of members of new local organizations called "base territorial organizations" (OTBs). These OTBs would be organized around three groups: indigenous peoples, peasant communities, and neighborhood organizations (*juntas vecinales*). Even though the results have been mixed, the OTB system gave political power to indigenous organizations and their customary leaders for the first time. After the legislation was passed, new municipalities were created quickly and promised funds were delivered to local governments (Grindle 2000, 126). As a direct result of the LPP, hundreds of elected positions opened up at the local level. Some political activists believe that the creation of these new positions was the single greatest impetus behind the dramatic indigenous rights movement that brought Evo Morales to prominence in the late 1990s and garnered him the support needed for his presidential election in 2005 and reelection in 2009. Before 1994, subnational elections in Bolivia

---

[9] Hiskey and Seligson (2003) argue that decentralization can bolster citizen support for the national political system. They caution this strategy can backfire if the performance of local institutions falters.

[10] The second legislative piece of Sánchez de Lozada's initiative was passed in 1995, the Law of Administrative Decentralization. This law decentralized federal management of social services and devolved administrative responsibilities for transportation, tourism, environment, rural electrification, and investment fund management to the department (or regional government) level.

featured contests over some 262 positions. After the LPP went into effect, 2,900 positions were contested (Grindle 2000, 121).[11] But while Bolivia's LPP may have catalyzed the country's national indigenous movement, the decentralization of social services may also have helped build local patronage networks and spur corruption (on the latter, see Blanes 2000). LPP was in many ways a victory for communitarian local organizations, but even policy architects have acknowledged that individual incentives are also needed to harness the new institutions efficiently.[12]

Like Mexico, which decentralized on paper but not financial flows, Peru has also realized almost none of Bolivia's benefits of decentralization. During his 1985–1990 term in office, President Alan García initiated a decentralization bid, making governors elected rather than appointed, to bolster his political support in Peru's regions. This was almost immediately undone by his successor, Alberto Fujimori (1990–2000), whose radical recentralization in 1992 outlawed gubernatorial elections and postponed mayoral elections. Fujimori promulgated Decree Law 776, which reduced local taxation authority and made the transfer of resources to local governments discretionary (O'Neill 2003, 1072). Post-Fujimori, Peruvian authorities have again made some tentative moves toward decentralization such as reinstituting gubernatorial elections and bolstering local budgetary rules. Many hope that García, reelected in 2006, albeit with a smaller mandate than he had at the start of his earlier term, will attempt a more comprehensive set of reforms in his present administration (2006–2011).

Like Chiapas, Bolivia has constructed a pan-ethnic movement which originally started as a class rebellion by Evo Morales' coca growers' union. Unlike the Zapatistas, however, the Movement Toward Socialism (MAS) adopted an electoral strategy early, broadened their appeal as a political party, and proceeded to govern in Bolivia. That Andean nation's economic elites, concentrated geographically in the city of Santa Cruz and surrounding *Media Luna* (Half Moon) region, have been politically marginalized, but retained their economic power. In Chiapas, the traditional landowners have been victimized by the turmoil in the Zapatista zones of conflict, as have the

---

[11] Van Cott has suggested that the LPP reforms have been a boon to indigenous parties in terms of winning elections. Writing about the 2002 elections in which two indigenous parties combined and won an unprecedented 27 percent of the national vote, she argued that municipal decentralization (and the conversion of sixty-eight seats in the Chamber of Deputies to uninominal districts in 1997) significantly boosted the fortunes of indigenous movements and parties (Van Cott 2003).

[12] Ivan Arias, one of the designers of the 1994 law, has acknowledged that it required anticorruption and accountability incentives to keep local politicians in line (interview 2005).

landless peasants (see Bobrow-Strain 2007 for a poignant account of how "the rich also cry, " to quote a Mexican phrase). While the analogy needs further study, Bolivia seems to have followed the more communitarian rights-oriented Chiapas model of indigenous mobilization. Bolivia broadened its institutional spaces of local participation via the LPP in 1994 and via further decentralization in the 2006–2009 constituent assembly and new constitution; Chiapas, as a mere subnational federal unit, was unable to execute such institutional reforms, although it did attend partly to the Zapatistas' most concrete demand by executing the state's greatest land redistribution ever (even if much of the reform was sabotaged by special interests).

Both of these spaces of contention – Bolivia and Chiapas – used primarily communitarian solidarity appeals of a type that were not effective historically in Peru or in southern Mexico's Oaxaca region. Rather than permeating the countryside with corporatist interest-promoting carrots and sticks, the state largely failed to even penetrate insurgent-infested Peru until the 1990s, and in Oaxaca, the post-colonial pattern of benign neglect made indigenous leaders *caciques* (as per the elaborate Knight definition in footnote 12 of Chapter 2), but who were left to govern themselves when not delivering tribute to the Spanish, the post-colonial Mexican government, or more recently, the burgeoning PRI-state. Peru has registered few wide-scale efforts to decentralize authority and grant autonomy to indigenous or other groups, whereas Oaxaca has symbolic state laws on the books, but no real commitment to implementation or enforcement, and no buy-in by the federal judiciary, or any other branch of the national government.

What Disaggregating to the Level of the Individual Can Teach Us

The survey of Mexico's indigenous populations and brief preliminary extension of the Chiapas/Oaxaca comparison to Bolivia and Peru showed that ethnicity is less correlated with respondents' political attitudes than other concomitant circumstances such as historical development, economic conditions, state policies and land tenure institutions, and isolation. The lesson here is that efforts to decentralize governance and legalize indigenous forms of local leader selection in Bolivia may carry symbolic weight but be of little use to indigenous participants who are struggling to meet their basic human needs. This is a moment of flux in Bolivia's political institutions, and it will be interesting to see how politicians across the political spectrum grapple with the outcomes of the constituent assembly. Lawmakers elsewhere might also consider adopting consociational institutions (such as a proportionally representative legislature, plural language laws, etc.) to promote multicultural rights and greater power sharing with long-ignored ethnic minority groups.

Bolivia's highly mobilized indigenous communities are quite different from the silent indigenous majority in Peru's demobilized society. Peru may offer a sobering but vital case study in the prolonged effects of widespread social violence on social capital and community development. A decade after the twenty years of ruthless Shining Path insurgency and vicious military reprisals in many of the Aymara-speaking and Quechua-speaking regions, the time is now right for analyzing the medium-term effects of this convulsive episode on Peru's social history. Data collected by Peru's Truth Commission provides tremendous insights into exactly where violence was centered and how it affected those communities.

President Morales's Movement Toward Socialism (MAS) clearly struck a chord with its Indian-ized take on the perennial calls from the countryside to address the country's failed social policies. However, in recasting Bolivian government failings in indigenous terms, President Morales and his party may have complicated the debate, much like the Zapatistas in Chiapas. In Mexico, survey data shows that indigenous people name isolation, economic deprivation, lack of opportunities, and a repressive and unresponsive state as their principal concerns. Indigenous rights come much farther down on the list. If a similar survey were conducted in Bolivia, these findings might help focus resources and channel development assistance from the United States to programs that address poverty alleviation first. The new indigenous electoral districts in Bolivia, and partial adoption of UC there may be beneficial in further decentralizing governance. But survey research there – and an inventory of how indigenous rights are practiced "on the ground" – would, from a practical policy perspective, help determine the broader viability of traditional indigenous cultural practices.

Surveying the indigenous populations in Bolivia and Peru, as was done in Chiapas and Oaxaca, would also shed light on the vitality of customary law institutions (such as *ayllus* in Bolivia and *rondas campesinas* in Peru) by asking respondents how pervasive these practices are in their communities, how effective they are relative to government institutions, and how they substitute for or compliment government agencies. According to many ethnographic accounts, recognition of communitarian rights makes local leaders more accountable, gives indigenous communities more direct representation, unifies communities by reinforcing pride in their traditions, and makes resource distribution more equitable by eliminating intermediaries between indigenous communities and the state. However, caution is also warranted. Customary law traditions have been demonstrated to discriminate against minorities within majority-indigenous communities, ignore human rights and due process, lead to conflicts over sovereignty, and empower authoritarian leaders who claim to speak for entire groups.

Surveying the Silence of Mexico's Indigenous Peoples: Constructing Autonomy Institutions

As I have argued throughout the book, one possible pitfall of studying collective action and communitarianism is assuming that movement leaders speak for movement followers. Instead of taking such a facile approach, I have attempted to disaggregate group data to the level of the individual in order to understand better the perspective of the people who movement leaders claim to represent. In the remaining sections, I consider how individual attitudes and preferences are driving the development of proposals in southern Mexico (but also in Bolivia – and Ecuador – but not Peru) for new autonomous indigenous institutions that would support indigenous rights.

"Constitutional multiculturalism," as recognized in Latin America (Van Cott 2000), refers to a set of reforms that recognize the rights of groups and is based in part on the work of liberal rights activist Kymlicka (1995). Kymlicka attempts to solve the problems of discrimination against minorities by creating a multiculturalism "paradigm" that "does not accept allowing ethnic groups themselves to make the decisions, to exercise control over their own members, or to decide about their cultural, economic, religious, social and political life, since doing so could put the individual rights of the group's members at risk" (Burguete 2009, 12). These efforts to recognize group rights as long as they do not violate the human rights of individual members contrasts sharply with other Latin American calls for autonomy like those of Diaz-Polanco (2008). For him, autonomy is not autonomy without the aforementioned four attributes: territory, self-government, jurisdiction over this self-government, and specific legal powers that reinforce the first three elements (cited by Burguete 2009, 13). Burguete argues that the recent Latin American indigenous rights movements, including the Zapatistas (but not the Oaxacans), "mobilized ... deploying arguments that used the language of autonomy. They were answered with policies that were constructed using the language of multiculturalism" (Burguete 2009, 14).

Some institutions have emerged in southern Mexico that afford a minimal degree of autonomy to indigenous peoples, and which the government formally tolerates. In practice, since the San Andrés Accords, federal authorities have done little more than allow weak municipalities in the most rural parts of Oaxaca to engage in Darwinian postelectoral conflicts to decide who governs, often replacing whoever survives with governor-dispatched municipal administrators. Federal electoral courts have heard cases from Oaxaca and even overturned some elections there, but in the precedent-setting case of Asunción Tlacolutita, for example, federal court rulings were ignored by local officials and federal authorities refused to take any further action to enforce them.[13] The Mexican Supreme Court's official investigation of state government repression of APPO and teacher protestors in Oaxaca in 2006 was also weak. And despite regulatory changes in Chiapas and Oaxaca calling for the creation of indigenous courts to arbitrate disputes over traditional legal norms within indigenous communities, these courts have no docket and insufficient numbers of translators have been hired to mediate for indigenous citizens. In other words, southern Mexico's indigenous citizens have received lip service, but little in the way of real change.

Indigenous Autonomy in Contemporary Chiapas and Oaxaca

The San Andrés Accords have not been adhered to, the decentralized Zapatista administrative units have not managed to contribute visibly to governance in their areas of influence, and the Zapatistas' Other Campaign (an alternative electoral campaign without candidates or new platforms) has not further concretized the ideological imperatives the Zapatistas presented in the mid- and late 1990s. The uprising's genuine achievements – offering an alternative frame for second-wave reformers and raising concerns about the concentration of poverty and repression in indigenous areas – seem mostly to be in the past. The material benefits of increased state spending in the region, land redistribution in the conflict area, extensive international assistance, and infrastructure expansion financed by the

---

[13] The Electoral Court of the Judicial Power of the Federation (TEPJF) did enforce some rulings, starting with its landmark Yucatán verdict in 2000. The electoral judges ruled that the state had selected an illegal electoral commission and ultimately sent officials to enforce the creation of a new electoral commission after the governor refused to comply with the court's ruling (see Eisenstadt 2004, 244–252).

military and the state have also abated. Chiapas is no longer governed by a PRI-dominated oligopoly, but the movement's goal of formal indigenous autonomy remains far out of reach. Not only have the Zapatistas' more extravagant aims gone unrealized, my survey findings (presented in Chapter 3) show that ethnic claims are actually less central to the political beliefs of indigenous people in Chiapas and Oaxaca than their political history, economic condition, and forms of local land tenure. While the movement had undeniable emotional power, as an empirical matter, it could not solve the problems it so sharply diagnosed.

The fact that Zapatista collective rights claims have dominated the conversation during a decade when neoliberal globalization, deregulation, and open markets were just beginning to bear down on rural Latin Americans had real costs. Despite these large-scale economic transformations, the Zapatistas kept their focus dogmatically trained on indigenous autonomy rather than on the broader issue of rural sustainable development that encompasses indigenous autonomy. Liberalization of corn commodities markets in 2005 hit Mexican rural dwellers especially hard. As stated by Otero (2007, 76) in a salient critique of Yashar, this narrow "ethnic politics" focus "misses important class-structural aspects behind the fight for autonomy, such as control over land and territory," and furthermore equates corporatism only to ethnic-based organization (i.e., that which is "not indigenous") rather than as a system of interest articulation that can occur around class or economic interests.

President Calderón did not further Mexico's prospects for rural development when he abolished the Secretariat for Agrarian Reform in the summer of 2009, markedly weakening the future of both *ejidos* and communal lands as state-supported non-private forms of land tenure. While the effort to survey and title all lands during the Fox and Calderón administrations did not succeed in rural southern Mexico to the same extent as it did in the more privatized North,[14] most observers assume that Mexico's interest in using land reform as a redistributive mechanism to help bolster livelihood in the countryside has ended. Rural dwellers, without state supports for agricultural products, have increasingly had to sell their land and move to Mexico's cities or to the U.S.

[14] While recent data is harder to find because the program has officially ended, Chiapas and Oaxaca were Mexico's least cooperative states with the surveying and titling of *ejido* and communal lands, as of 2003. By that time, the program, called PROCEDE, had registered between 70 and 100 percent of publicly held lands in every other state, but just over 50 percent of these lands in Chiapas and Oaxaca (Rivera Nolasco 2004, 134).

For those who have stayed behind in Oaxaca, UC continues to repress individuals and minorities in indigenous communities, including Protestants and other non-Catholic groups, residents of outlying towns not connected to municipal seats, and women. Oaxaca human rights activists like Méndez (interview 2005) still believe that individual and communal rights can be reconciled: "We understand that the community has to reproduce itself, but on the other hand, we want authorities to consider the position of individuals and it is time for rights to be recognized from inside communities as well as just from the outside." Assuming that the Oaxacans can articulate a coherent vision for reform of UC, despite the indigenous movement's history of disunity there, it could offer the most useful model of partially autonomous institutions for places like Bolivia and other burgeoning Latin American rights movements.

Conclusion: Balancing Custom, Individual Rights, and Autonomy

While giving some consideration to autonomy "on the ground," little attention has been paid to how autonomy laws should be constructed at the level of a national constitution. That is, what citizenship rights must a nation-state cede to regional groups to grant them autonomy, and what price must the exercise of citizenship pay for this national-level redirection of rights, especially individual rights? The question has been suggested in considering the wills of non-Zapatistas stuck in Zapatista-held areas where state services, like health care and education, have been withdrawn, and in the case of women like Eufrosina Cruz who must sacrifice their political participation as individual citizens to achieve a time-honored collective vision of customary law and order. Texts on the impact of the 2001 constitutional reforms on indigenous rights in Mexico (Rabasa Gamboa 2002; Bailón Corres 2003) carefully trace the genealogies of the latest reforms, but make almost no mention of any actual cases or jurisprudence at all. For real cases and the precedents they set, we must consider the Colombian Constitutional Court, which has compiled perhaps the most extensive corpus of rulings and doctrinal consistency in the hemisphere.

Straddling the line between individual and communitarian rights, the Colombian Constitutional Court "has developed a jurisprudence that seeks to maximize the autonomy of indigenous communities and to respect their ways of doing justice without embracing an unconditional cultural relativism" (Assies n.d., 11). While the court's decisions have often been controversial, such as 1997 Case T-523, allowing to stand an indigenous consultative verdict that a political enemy of the victim was to be punished for instigating the murder at the hands of *guerrillas* (by denouncing the deceased to *guerrillas* as a paramilitary fighter shortly before he was slain). The sentence was that the denouncer of the victim should be whiplashed sixty times, expelled from the Northern Cauca, Colombia community where he resided and committed the offense, and lose all political rights there (Assies n.d., 7).

The court's decision was roundly condemned by human rights groups but consistent – after a finding that the whippings and expulsion did not constitute torture – with the court's doctrine that judges should be guided by cultural relativism and as full a view as possible, based on extensive anthropological research, of the social context and meaning and purpose of sanctions. The Colombian Constitutional Court has elsewhere (perhaps most famously in 1998 decision U-510) further specified that conflicts are inevitable between the sphere of liberties and collective rights, and that indigenous communities are to be treated as unique and diverse pluriethnic communities, but that said diversity is limited by the rights delineated in the national constitution (Sánchez Botero 2010, 300 – 307). More broadly, Sánchez Botero summarized the court's position as accepting three universally sacrosanct individual rights: 1) the right to life; 2) the right to preserve the integrity of one's body; and 3) the right to due process (however codified in a given cultural context).[15]

The Colombian Constitutional Court standard seems to allow violations of the women's vote in Oaxaca and the denial of water to the "imaginary Zapatistas" of Zinacantán. Furthermore, it seems to deny many external protections of minority groups and individuals, as per those mentioned in Kymlicka's (1995) effort to develop a theory of multicultural rights but which parts from the assumption of strong individual rights. But the Colombian Constitutional Court has taken a provocative and bold stand, and moved the debate from abstractions to concrete cases. While the Zapatistas of Chiapas did an excellent job of diagnosing the problems of southern Mexico's rural indigenous peasants, Oaxaca seems to be the setting for the next stage of addressing these grievances in Mexico. If the national and state courts start taking responsibility for rulings rather than

---

[15] Sánchez Botero added a fourth minimal condition, "freedom of expression and from slavery" in a talk at the 7th International Congress of the Latin American Network of Legal Anthropology (RELAJU) in Lima, Peru (August 2, 2010).

just throwing up their hands and letting the *caciques* rush in, Oaxaca's many savvy indigenous rights movements with their deliberative leaders and broad arrays of options, may be able to help advance the development of legal and political institutions to protect group and individual rights. If they can incorporate and systematize cases from the nearby heavily indigenous states of Guerrero, Michoacán, Puebla, Quintana Roo, Tabasco, Tlaxcala, Veracruz and Yucatán, as well as Chiapas, they may be able to build a national consensus emanating from the south, for a change.

In Mexican – and universal – culture and literature, individualism is often associated with base instincts, selfishness, and neo-liberalism, whereas indigenous communalism is associated with purity, heritage, stewardship of the land, and authenticity. Mexico's recent history with collective rights calls into question the accuracy of these associations. Starting with the federal government's post–World War II assimilationist policies to support a uniform "cosmic race" and running all the way to 2000 and the collapse of the PRI-state and its associated corporatist structures like the National Indigenous Institute (INI), communalism's good name has taken some blows. Even sincere efforts to build multicultural institutions in Chiapas, Oaxaca and at the national level have led to some distasteful outcomes. The 2001 indigenous rights constitutional reforms have not been implemented (Bailón Corres 2009), the 1996 San Andrés Accords have languished, and the Zapatistas' communitarian rallying cries do not resonate like they used to.

And efforts by Mexico's opposition government to dismantle the PRI's corporatist machines have been slowed down in a few holdout states, like Oaxaca, where authoritarian governance persisted to 2010 – in part – as an unintended consequence of UC recognition and the ease with which authoritarian governors and local bosses could manipulate UC outcomes. The absence of any legal baseline standards for resolving UC disputes in Oaxaca – or anywhere in Mexico, really – opened the system to abuse by local *caciques* and the governor. The failure of APPO and the teachers' union to unify and broaden their calls for change in 2006 demonstrates how successful Oaxaca's political elites have been in dismantling rural threats and narrowly channeling urban ones. It was largely the hint of threat and urgency contributed by the Zapatistas in Chiapas that halted the further regression of rights recognition and gave a much-need boost to the multicultural movement in Oaxaca.

If Oaxaca's indigenous rights movement is going to move forward and rescue their weak autonomous structures from PRI domination, it will need to be reconceptualized as a long-term political struggle and local differences will need to be transcended to form regional power centers. Mexico's federal government and courts will also have to make some choices and then enforce them, as the Colombians have. Only then will Oaxaca's indigenous people start to develop the kinds of subnational power-sharing institutions that consociationalists from Lijphart (1999) to Norris (2008) have found best represent plural societies like those in southern Mexico. The Oaxaca experiment may have a more enduring legacy than the violent insurgency in Chiapas, although without the Zapatistas, there would be no UC recognition. Furthermore, the Zapatistas' partial reconstitution as a social democratic interest group holds promise for representing the broader population along the lines of MAS in Bolivia, but only if they change tactics and allow themselves, finally, to try changing the political system from within.

The Zapatistas may have been among the first indigenous peoples to be heralded for ushering in a more authentic and natural form of democracy in the age of globalization. Chiapas scholars acknowledging primordialist elements, like Gossen (1994) and Hernández Castillo (2006), and the new generation of constructivists like Estrada Saavedra (2007), Inclán (2008), and Trejo (2004) alike have noted the difficult internal contradictions faced by movement leaders. Perhaps Engle (2010), in her masterful study of the rise of the late 20th century worldwide indigenous rights movement in international law said it best. Engle observes that their small numbers and relative powerlessness requires that indigenous peoples everywhere justify the urgency of their claims for cultural protection through "strategic essentialism." (Engle 2010, 156) In other words, they must make indigenous cultures and cosmovisions sufficiently attractive to outsiders that they can recruit international bystanders into their cause. The irony is that indigenous leaders must wrap their movements in authentic traditional garb and beliefs to gain international recognition for the substance of their very real struggles, but that "however valuable this recognition [from the international stage] might be ... the costumes and dances are what are remembered." (Engle 2010, 153)

Returning to Stoll's Chapter 1 admonition, but perhaps now with greater solidarity for indigenous leaders and their movements, as captured by the slogan "We are all Marcos!," it may be time to acknowledge that indigenous movements feel they must pander to the broader crowds if they are to receive any of the outside resources they desperately need. It may also be time for the broader public to move beyond the nostalgic longing for authentic times and places we think that indigeneity restores to us all in this otherwise impersonal era of globalization and decentering. Many justifiably hunger for leadership from Latin America's indigenous movements to construct more humane and location-specific models of democratic representation and citizenship which are elsewhere lacking. As part of this longing, we romanticize the achievements of vanguard indigenous movements, while underplaying the fact that even if they are somehow imbued with special powers their heritage and authenticity must grant them, they are still poor and marginalized and victims of a large and growing development gap in Latin America's shrinking countrysides.

Surveying the silence in southern Mexico has demonstrated that the Zapatistas (and other indigenous rights movements) often project much larger than life. To say the least, they are not without bystanders and a growing number of opponents. These subdued citizens on the sidelines must be helped to also find their voice and express themselves more forcefully, even in the indigenous rights movements hitherto monopolized by the strategic and essentialist Zapatista "true believers." If they can, then they, and the citizens who empathize with them, will finally avail themselves of a more nuanced reality which can be – gradually – understood, and then perhaps changed for the better.

But this book has sought also to show why movement leaders and followers make the individual choices they do. These leaders seek to remove their movements from victimhood and paternalism and ascribe to them the individual agency that often goes unnoticed due to an unconscious collusion between analysts of indigenous movements, movement leaders, followers and bystanders, who all reify indigenous mobilizations as moral crusades as well as social movements. Rather than depicting change via static and reductionist classism and economic structures, or indigeneity and cultural structures, these leaders strive to serve social transformations as change agents in their own right.

In the process, sometimes they exaggerate primordial or essentialist claims, and the importance of intangible aspects of their indigeneity (for tangible elements, like language, costumes, and traditions, if allowed to represent the essence of what these groups stand for, can be taken from indigenous groups and stored in museums). Ultimately, a power-sharing model based on moderate, constructivist assumptions that serves as a hemisphere-wide example of communal rights recognition within a liberal society, can only be created by understanding geographical, historical, psychological, socioeconomic – as well as the ethnic – group incentives, and complementary individual motivations. These individual motivations are the ones that guide indigenous peoples, indigenous people, and the rest of us, in choosing from among the identity choices available to us at a given concrete moment.

Movements of particular times and places have increasingly universal value in this era of globalized homogenization. We must all do a better job of contextualizing them, understanding them, and putting them into a framework that recognizes the virtue of the specific, but also the virtue of the universal, which sometimes gets lost in the rhetoric.

Bibliography

Secondary Sources

Agudo Sanchíz, Alejandro. 2009. "Actores, lenguajes y objetos de confrontación y conflicto en la Zona Chol de Chiapas," in Marco Estrada Saavedra, ed. *Chiapas Después de la Tormenta: Estudios Sobre Economía.*

——— 2010. "Rumores' Zapatistas: el pragmatism de las identidades histórico-políticas en El Limonar (Tila)," in Marco Estrada Saavedra and Juan Pedro Viquera, eds. *Los indígenas de Chiapas y la rebelión Zapatista: Microhistorias políticas.* Mexico City: El Colegio de México, 240–289.

Aguilar Hernández, Eufemio, Díaz Teratol, Martín and Juan Pedro Viqueira. 2010. "Los otros acueredos de San Andrés Larráinzar, Chiapas (1959–2005)," in Marco Estrada Saavedra and Juan Pedro Viqueira, eds. *Los indígenas de Chiapas y la rebelión Zapatista: Microhistorias políticas.* Mexico City: El Colegio de México, 240–289.

Anaya-Muñoz, Alejandro. 2002. "Governability and Legitimacy in Mexico: The Legalisation of Indigenous Electoral Institutions in Oaxaca." Department of Government, University of Essex, Ph.D. thesis.

Alvaro García Linares. 2003. "El zapatismo: indios insurgentes, alianzas, y poder," in Observatorio Social de América Latina, eds. *La Guerra del Gas en Bolivia: A diez años del levantamiento zapatista.* Buenos Aires: Consejo Latinoamericano de Ciencias Sociales, 293–300.

Anderson, Benedict. 1994. "Imagined Communities," in John Hutchinson and Anthony D. Smith, eds. *Nationalism.* New York: Oxford University Press, 89–96.

Andolina, Robert, Nina Laurie, and Sarah A. Radcliffe. 2009. *Indigenous Development in the Andes: Culture, Power, and Transnationalism.* Durham, NC: Duke University Press.

Aquino Centeno, Salvador and María Cristina Velásquez Cepeda. 1997. *Usos y costumbres para la renovación de los ayuntamientos de Oaxaca.* Oaxaca City: Centro de Investigaciones y Estudios Superiores de Antropología Social/Instituto Estatal Electoral de Oaxaca.

Aquino Moreschi, Alejandra. 2002. "Acción Colectiva, Autonomía y Conflicto: La Reinvención de la Identidad entre los Zapotecas de la Sierra Juárez," M.A.

thesis in political sociology, Instituto de Investigaciones, Dr. José María Luís Mora. Typescript.

Arellanes Meixueiro, Anselmo. 1999. *Oaxaca: reparto de la tierra, alcances, limitaciones y respuestas*. 2nd ed. Oaxaca City, Mexico: Universidad Autónoma Benito Juárez de Oaxaca.

Arias, Arturo, ed. 2001. *The Rigoberta Menchu Controversy*. Minneapolis, MN: University of Minnesota Press.

Ascencio Franco, Gabriel. 2008. *Regularización de la Propiedad en la Selva Lacandona: Cuenta de Nunca Acabar*. Tuxtla Gutiérrez, Chiapas: Universidad de Ciencias y Artes de Chiapas.

Assies, Willem. n.d. "Indian Justice in the Andes: Re-Rooting or Re-Routing." Typescript.

Aziz Nassif, Alberto and Juan Molinar Horcasitas. 1990. "Los Resultados Electorales" in Pablo González Casanova, ed. *Segundo Informe la Democrácia: México el 6 de Julio de 1988*. Mexico City: Siglo Veintiuno Editores, 138–171.

Bailón Corres, Moisés Jaime. 2009. "Legislación federal y estatal en materia de derechos indígenas; saldos al 2009," in Victor Leonel Juan Martínez and Maria Clara Galvis, eds. *Derecho y Sociedad Indígena en Oaxaca*. Washington, DC: Due Process of Law Foundation.

2008. *Derechos de los Pueblos Indígenas en las Entidades Federativas*. Mexico City: Comisión Nacional de los Derechos Humanos.

2007. "La Medusa y el Caracol: Derechos Electorales y Derechos Indígenas en el Siglo XIX – los Orígenes del sistema político oaxaqueño," in Jorge Hernandez-Diaz, ed. *Ciudadanías diferenciadas en un estado multicultural: los usos y costumbres en Oaxaca*. Mexico City: Siglo XXI, 87–110.

2006. "Las reformas constitucionales indígenas de 2001 en México: Avances Nacionales y Regionales a Cinco años de su apropiación," paper presented at the 2006 meeting of the Latin American Studies Association, March 15–18 (San Juan).

2003. *Derechos Humanos y Derechos Indígenas en el Orden Jurídico Federfal Mexicano*. Mexico City: Comisión Nacional de los Derechos Humanos.

2002. *Pueblos Indios, Élites y Territorio – Sistemas de Dominio Regional en el Sur de México – Una historia política de Oaxaca*. 2nd ed. Mexico City: El Colegio de México.

Baronnet, Bruno. 2008. "Rebel Youth and Zapatista Autonomous Education," *Latin American Perspectives* 35 (July), 112–124.

Barry, Brian. 2001. *Culture and Equality: An Egalitarian Critique of Multiculturalism*. Cambridge, MA: Harvard University Press, 293–328.

Barth, Frederik. 1969. *Ethnic Groups and Boundaries*. Boston, MA: Little, Brown and Co.

Bayart, Jean-Francois. 1993. *The State in Africa: The Politics of the Belly*. London: Longman Publishers.

Bazant, Jan. 1975. Cinco Haciendas Mexicanas. Tres siglos de vida rural en San Luís Potosí (1600–1910). México: Colegio de México, 176.

Benhabib, Seyla. 2002. *The Claims of Culture: Equality and Diversity in the Global Era*. Princeton, NJ: Princeton University Press.

Bibliography

Benítez Manaus, Raúl, Andrew Selee, and Cynthia J. Arnson. 2005. "Frozen Negotiations: The Peace Process in Chiapas," *Mexican Studies/Estudios Mexicanos* 22 (1), Winter 2006, 131–152.

Benjamin, Thomas. 1996. *A Rich Land – A Poor People: Politics and Society in Modern Chiapas*. Revised edition. Albuquerque, NM: University of New Mexico Press.

Benton, Allyson Lucinda. 2006. "The Effects of Electoral Rules on Indigenous Voting Behavior in Mexico," paper presented at the 2006 meeting of the Midwest Political Science Association, April 19–23 (Chicago).

Blair, Harry. 2000. "Participation and Accountability at the Periphery: Democratic Local Governance in Six Countries." *World Development* 28.1, 21–39.

Blanes, José Jiménes, ed. 2000. *Mallkus y Alcaldes: La Ley de Participación Popular en Comunidades Rurales del Antiplano Paceño*. La Paz, Bolivia: PIEB; CEBEM.

Bob, Clifford. 2005. *The Marketing of Rebellion: Insurgents, Media, and International Activism*. New York: Cambridge University Press.

Bobrow-Strain, Aaron. 2007. *Intimate Enemies: Landowners, Power, and Violence in Chiapas*. Durham, NC: Duke University Press.

Boone, Catherine. 2007. "Property and Constitutional Order: Land Tenure Reform and the Future of the African State," in *African Affairs* 106/425, 557–586.

Bourdieu, Pierre 1986. "The Forms of Capital," in John Richardson, ed. *Handbook of Theory and Research for the Sociology of Education*. New York: Greenwood Press, 241–258.

Brass, Paul R. 1997. *Theft of an Idol – Text and Context in the Representation of Collective Violence*. Princeton, NJ: Princeton University Press.

——— ed. 1985. *Ethnic Groups and the State*. London: Croom Helm.

Brysk, Alison. 2000. *From Tribal Village to Global Village: Indian Rights and International Relations in Latin America*. Stanford, CA: Stanford University Press.

Burguete Cal y Mayor, Araceli. 2009. "Constitutional Multiculturalism in Chiapas: Hollow Reforms to Nullify Autonomy Rights," paper presented at the conference "Reconciling Liberal Pluralism and Group Rights: Oaxaca, Mexico's Multiculturalism Experiment in Comparative Perspective," February 20, American University, Washington, D.C.

——— 2006. "Los concejos municipales: un recurso oficial y oficioso para la transición política en Chiapas," in *Anuario 2005* of the Centro de Estudios Superiores de México y Centroamérica, Tuxtla Gutiérrez Chiapas, Universidad de Ciencias y Artes de Chiapas: 135–186.

——— 2004a. "Desplazando al Estado: la política social zapatista," in Pérez Ruiz, Maya Lorena, ed. *Tejiendo historias: Tierra, género, y poder en Chiapas*. Mexico City: Instituto Nacional de Antropología e Historia: 143–187.

——— 2004b. "Ayuntamientos indígenas de facto en el Chiapas postzapatista (1994–2004): una tipología," paper presented at the XXI meeting of the Latin American Studies Association, October 9, 2004 (Las Vegas).

——— 2003. "The De Facto Autonomous Process: New Jurisdictions and Parallel Governments in Rebellion," in Jan Rus, Rosalva Aída Hernández Castillo, and Shannan L. Mattiace, eds. *Mayan Lives, Mayan Utopias*. Lanham, MD: Rowman & Littlefield Publishers, 191–218.

2000. *Agua que nace y muere – Sistemas normativos indígenas y disputas por el agua en Chamula y Zinacantán*. San Cristóbal de las Casas: Programa de Investigaciones Multidisciplinarias sobre Mesoamérica y el Sureste, Universidad Nacional Autónomo de México.

Burguete Cal y Mayor, Araceli and José Antonio Montero Solano. n.d. "Morir en la impunidad: Violencia política en regiones indígenas de Chiapas – Cronología 1974–1988." Typescript.

Burguete Cal y Mayor, Araceli and Miguel Gómez Gómez. 2008. "Multiculturalismo y gobierno permitido en San Juan Cancuc, Chiapas," in Xochitl Leyva, Araceli Burguete and Shannon Speed, eds. *Gobernar (en) la diversidad: experiencias indígenas desde América Latina: Hacia la investigación de co-labor*. Mexico City: Centro de Investigaciones y Estudios Superiores en Antropología (CIESAS).

Cancian, Frank. 1992. *The Decline of Community Life in Zinacantán: Economy, Public Life, and Social Stratification, 1960–1987*. Stanford, CA: Stanford University Press.

Castellanos, Laura. 2008. *Corte de Caja: Entrevista al Subcomandante Marcos*. Mexico City: Grupo Editorial Endira.

Castro Rodríguez, Angelica, Marcos Arturo Leyva Madrid, and Miguel Angel Vásquez de la Rosa, eds. 2009. *Oaxaca: Un Régimen Agrietado – Informe Publico sobre Democracia y Derechos Humanos en Oaxaca, 2007–2009*. Oaxaca City: Servicios para una Educación Alternativa (EDUCA), A.C.

Chance, John K. 1986. "Colonial Ethnohistory of Oaxaca," in Ronald Spores, ed. *Supplement to the Handbook of Middle American Indians – Volume 4*. Austin, TX: University of Texas Press, 165–189.

Chandra, Kanchan. 2004. *Why Ethnic Parties Succeed: Patronage and Ethnic Head Counts in India*. New York: Cambridge University Press.

Cohen, Jeffrey. 2009. "Migration and Southern Mexico: Patterns, Politics and Meaning in Oaxaca and Beyond," paper presented at the conference "Fifteen Years after the Zapatistas: Social and Political Change in Mexico and Chiapas since 1994," David Rockefeller Center for Latin American Studies, Harvard University, April 10, 2009.

Collier, George A. and Elizabeth L. Quaratiello. 1999. *Basta! Land and the Zapatista Rebellion in Chiapas*. 2nd ed. Oakland, CA: Food First Books, Institute for Food and Development Policy.

Connor, Walker. 1994. *Ethno-nationalism: The Quest for Understanding*. Princeton, NJ: Princeton University Press.

Cornelius, Wayne A., David Fitzgerald, Jorge Hernández-Díaz, and Scott Borger, eds. 2008. *Migration from the Mexican Mixteca: A Transnational Community in Oaxaca and California*. Boulder, CO: Lynne Rienner Publishers.

Cornelius, Wayne A. and Jessa M. Lewis, eds. 2006. *Impacts of Border Enforcement on Mexican Migration: The View from Sending Communities*. La Jolla: Center for Comparative Immigration Studies, University of California-San Diego.

Corstange, Daniel. 2005. "Ethnic Politics and Surveys: How Do We Measure What We Want to Measure," paper presented at the December 9–10, 2005 meeting of the Laboratory in Comparative Ethnic Processes (LiCEP) at the University of California, San Diego.

Bibliography

Cress, Daniel M. and David A. Snow. 2000. "The Outcomes of Homeless Mobilization: The Influence of Organization, Disruption, Political Mediation, and Framing," *American Journal of Sociology* 105, 1063–1104.

Danielson, Mike S. 2009. "Effects of International Migration on Customary Practices: Preliminary Findings from the 2008 *Usos y Costumbres* Catalog," paper presented at the conference "Reconciling Liberal Pluralism and Group Rights: Oaxaca, Mexico's Multiculturalism Experiment in Comparative Perspective," February 20, American University, Washington, D.C.

Danielson, Michael S. and Todd A. Eisenstadt. 2009. "Walking Together, but in Which Direction? Gender Discrimination and Multicultural Practices in Oaxaca, Mexico," *Politics & Gender* 5, 153–184.

De Vos, Jan. 2002a. "El Lacandón: Una introducción histórica," in Juan Pedro Viqueira and Mario Humberto Ruz, eds. *Chiapas – Los Rumbos de Otra Historia*. Mexico City: Universidad Nacional Autónoma de México, 330–361.

2002b. *Una tierra para sembrar sueños: Historia reciente de la Selva Lacandona, 1950–2000*. Mexico City: Centro de Investigaciones y Estudios Superiores en Antropología Social.

Deere, Carmen Diana. 2006. "Married Women's Property Rights in Mexico: A Comparative, Latin American Perspective and Research Agenda," paper prepared for 2006 meeting of Latin American Studies Association (San Juan).

Dennis, Philip A. 1987. *Intervillage Conflict in Oaxaca*. New Brunswick, NJ: Rutgers University Press.

Díaz Montes, Fausto. 1992. *Los municipios: la lucha por el poder local en Oaxaca*. Oaxaca: Instituto de Investigaciones Sociales-UABJO/Gobierno del Estado de Oaxaca.

Díaz-Polanco, Héctor. 2008. "La insoportable levedad de la autonomía: la experiencia Mexicana," in Natividad Gutiérrez Chong, ed. *Estados y autonomías en democracias contemporáneas: Bolivia, Ecuador, España y México*. Mexico City: Instituto de Investigaciones Sociales, Universidad Nacional Autónoma de México and Plaza y Valdés Editores, 245–271.

2003. *Autonomía Regional – la Autodeterminación de los Pueblos Indios*. Mexico City: Siglo Veintiuno Editores.

Eaton, Kent and J. Tyler Dickovick. 2004. "The Politics of Re-centralization in Argentina and Brazil," *Latin American Research Review* 39.1, 90–122.

Eisenstadt, Todd A. 2009. "Agrarian Tenure Institution Conflict Frames, and Communitarian Identities: The Case of Indigenous Southern Mexico," *Comparative Political Studies* 42.1, 82–113.

2007a. "The Origins and Rationality of the 'Legal versus Legitimate' Dichotomy Invoked in Mexico's 2006 Post-Electoral Conflict," *PS: Political Science and Politics* 40 (January), 39–43.

2007b. "*Usos y Costumbres* and Post-Electoral Conflicts in Oaxaca, Mexico, 1995–2004: An Empirical and Normative Assessment," *Latin American Research Review* 42.1, 52–77.

2004. *Courting Democracy in Mexico: Party Strategies and Electoral Institutions*. New York: Cambridge University Press.

Eisenstadt, Todd A. and Viridiana Ríos. 2010. "Multiculturalism and Political Conflict in Indigenous Latin America: The Oaxaca 'Experiment' in Comparative Perspective," paper presented at the 2010 meeting of the Latin American Studies Association, Toronto, October 6.

Engle, Karen. 2010. *The Elusive Promise of Indigenous Development: Rights, Culture, Strategy.* Durham, NC: Duke University Press.

Escárzaga, Fabiola and Raquel Gutiérrez, eds. 2005. *Movimiento indígena en América Latina: resistencia y proyecto alternativo.* Puebla: Benemérito Universidad de Puebla.

Estrada Saavedra, Marco. 2007. *La Comunidad Armada Rebelde y el EZLN – Un studio histórico y sociológico sobre las bases La de apoyo zapatistas en las cañadas tojolabales de la Selva lacandona (1930–2005).* Mexico City: El Colegio de México.

Fearon, James D. and David D. Laitin. 2003. "Ethnicity, Insurgency, and Civil War," *American Political Science Review* 97.1, 75–90.

1996. "Explaining Interethnic Cooperation," *American Political Science Review* 90.4, 715–735.

Fernández, Marcelo Oslo. 2004. *La Ley del Ayllu – Práctica de jach'a justicia y jusk'a justicia (Justicia Mayor y Justicia Menor) en comunidades aymaras.* 2nd ed. La Paz: Programa de Investigación Estratégica en Bolivia.

Fox, Jonathan. 2002. "La relación recíproca entre la participación ciudadana y la rendición de cuentes: la experiencia de los Fondos Municipales en el México rural," *Política y Gobierno* IX.1, 95–133.

García Torres, Ana Esther, Esmeralda López Armenta and Alma Nava Martínez. 1999. "Municipio Autónomo de Polhó" en *Revista Chiapas* No. 8, Año 1999. México: ERA-Instituto de Investigaciones Económicas. http://www.ezln.org/revistachiapas/No8/ch8garcia-nava.html (accessed on June 16, 2006).

Geertz, Clifford. 1973. *The Interpretation of Cultures.* New York: Basic Books.

Gellner, Ernest. 1994. "Nationalism and Modernization," in John Hutchinson and Antony D. Smith, eds. *Nationalism.* New York: Oxford University Press. 55–62.

Gibson, James. 2005. "Boundary Control: Subnational Authoritarianism in Democratic Countries," *World Politics* 58.1, 101–132.

Giraudy, Agustina. 2009. "Subnational Undemocratic Regime Continuity after Democratization: Argentina and Mexico in Comparative Perspective." Dissertation in Political Science, University of North Carolina, Chapel Hill.

Gómez Cruz, Patricia Jovita and Christina María Kovic. 1994. *Con un pueblo vivo, en tierra negada – Un ensayo sobre los derechos humanos y el conflicto agrario en Chiapas, 1989–1993.* San Cristóbal de las Casas: Centro de Derechos Humanos Fray Bartolomé de las Casas.

González Compeán, Miguel and Leonardo Lomeli. 2000. *El Partido de la Revolución: Institución y Conflicto (1928–1999).* Mexico City: Fondo de Cultura Económica.

González Oropeza, Manuel and Francisco Martínez Sánchez. 2002. *El derecho y la justicia en las elecciones de Oaxaca – Tomo II.* Oaxaca: Tribunal Estatal Electoral.

Goodman, Gary L. and Jonathan T. Hiskey. 2008. "Exit Without Leaving: Political Disengagement in High Migration Municipalities in Mexico," *Comparative Politics* 40.2, 169–188.

Bibliography

Gossen, Gary H. 1994. "From Olmecs to Zapatistas: A Once and Future History of Souls," *American Anthropologist* 96.3, 553–570.

Greenberg, James B. 1989. *Blood Ties – Life and Violence in Rural Mexico*. Tucson, AZ: University of Arizona Press.

Grindle, Merilee S. 2000. *Audacious Reforms: Institutional Invention and Democracy in Latin America*. Baltimore: Johns Hopkins University Press.

Guerra Pulido, Maira Melisa. 2000. "Usos y costumbres o partidos políticos: una decisión de los municipios oaxaqueños." Undergraduate thesis in political science, Centro de Investigación y Docencia Económicas (CIDE), Mexico City. Typescript.

Guillén, Diana. 1998. *Chiapas 1973–1993: Mediaciones, política e institucionalidad*. Mexico City: Instituto Mora.

Gutiérrez Narváez, Raúl de Jesús. 2005. "Escuela y Zapatismo Entre los Tsotsiles; Entre la Asimilación y la Resistencia," MA thesis in anthropology, Centro de Investigaciones y Estudios Superiores en Antropología Social (CIESAS).

Gutiérrez, Natividad. 1999. *Nationalist Myths and Ethnic Identities – Indigenous Intellectuals and the Mexican State*. Lincoln, NE: University of Nebraska Press.

Hansen, Roger D. 1971. *The Politics of Mexican Development*. 2nd ed. Baltimore: Johns Hopkins University Press.

Hardin, Russell. 1995. *One for All: The Logic of Group Conflict*. Princeton, NJ: Princeton University Press.

Hardy, Clarisa. 1984. *El Estado y los campesinos: La Confederación Nacional Campesina (CNC)*. Mexico City: Centro de Estudios Económicos y Sociales del Tercer Mundo (CEESTEM) and Editorial Nueva Imagen.

Harvey, Neil. 1998. *The Chiapas Rebellion: The Struggle for Land and Democracy*. Durham, NC: Duke University Press.

Hechter, Michael. 1986. "A Rational Choice Approach to Race and Ethnic Relations," in David Mason and John Rex, eds. *Theories of Race and Ethnic Relations*. New York: Cambridge University Press.

Hernández Castillo, Rosalía Aida. 2002. "National Law and Indigenous Customary Law: The Struggle for Justice of Indigenous Women of Chiapas," in Maxine Molyneux and Shahra Razavi, eds. *Gender, Justice, Development and Rights*. Oxford: Oxford University Press, 384–413.

2006a. "Hacia una Concepción Multicultural de los Derechos de las Mujeres: Reflexiones desde México," paper presented at 2006 meeting of Latin American Studies Association (San Juan).

2006b. "The Indigenous Movement in Mexico: Between Electoral Politics and Local Resistance," *Latin American Perspectives* 147.33, 115–131.

Hernández-Díaz, Jorge and Victor Leonel Juan Martínez. 2007. *Dilemas de la Institución Municipal – Una Incursión en la Experiencia Oaxaqueña*. Mexico City: Miguel Ángel Porrúa Publishers.

Hernández Navarro, Luis. 1995. *Chiapas: La Guerra y La Paz*. Mexico City: ADN Editores.

Higgins, Nicholas P. 2004. *Understanding the Chiapas Rebellion: Modernist Visions and the Invisible Indian*. Austin, TX: University of Texas Press.

Hiskey, Jonathan and Mitchell Seligson. 2003. "Pitfalls of Power to the People: Decentralization, Local Government Performance, and System Support in Bolivia," *Studies in Comparative International Development* 37.4, 64–88.

Hobsbawm, Eric. 1994. "The Nation as Invented Tradition," in John Hutchinson and Anthony D. Smith, eds. *Nationalism*. New York: Oxford University Press, 76–82.

Huntington, Samuel. 2006. *Political Order in Changing Societies*. New Haven, CT: Yale University Press.

Ibarra Templos, Yuribi Mayek. 2003. "Espacios alternativos de poder: participación de las mujeres en una comunidad transnacional." Undergraduate thesis in social anthropology, Universidad Autónoma Metropolitana – Unidad Iztapalapa, Mexico City. Typescript.

Inclán María. 2009. "Sliding Doors of Opportunity: Zapatistas and Their Cycle of Protest," *Mobilization: An International Journal* 14.1, 85–106.

_____. 2008. "From the *Ya Basta* to the *Caracoles*: Zapatista Protest Mobilization under Transitional Conditions," *American Journal of Sociology* 113.5, 1316–1350.

Inglehart, Ronald and Wayne E. Baker. 2000. "Modernization, Cultural Change, and the Persistence of Traditional Values," *American Sociological Review* 65.1, 19–51.

Inglehart, Ronald and Pippa Norris. 2004. *Rising Tide – Gender Equality and Cultural Change Around the World*. New York: Cambridge University Press.

Jackson, Jean E. and Kay B. Warren. 2005. "Indigenous Movements in Latin America, 1992–2004: Controversies, Ironies, New Directions," *Annual Review of Anthropology* 34, 349–573.

Juan Martínez, Victor Leonel. 2007. "Yalálag: Las contradicciones de una lucha por la autonomía," in Jorge Hernández-Díaz, ed. *Ciudadanías diferenciadas en un estado multicultural: los usos y costumbres en Oaxaca*. Mexico City: Siglo XXI Editorial, 199–228.

Jung, Courtney. 2008. *The Moral Force of Indigenous Politics: Critical Liberalism and the Zapatistas*. New York: Cambridge University Press.

Kearney, Michael and Francisco Besserer. 2004. "Oaxacan Municipal Governance in Transnational Context," in Jonathan Fox and Gaspar Rivera-Salgado, eds. *Indigenous Mexican Migrants in the United States*. La Jolla, CA: Center for US-Mexican Studies, University of California, San Diego, 449–466.

Keck, Margaret and Kathryn Sikkink. 1998. *Activists Beyond Borders: Advocacy Networks in International Politics*. Ithaca, NY: Cornell University Press.

Knight, Alan. 2005. "*Caciquismo* in Twentieth-Century Mexico," in Knight, Alan and Wil Pansters, eds. *Caciquismo in Twentieth-Century Mexico*. London: Institute for the Study of the Americas, University of London, 1–50.

Kymlicka, Will. 1995. *Multicultural Citizenship*. New York: Oxford University Press.

Laitin, David. 1985. "Hegemony and Religious Conflict: British Imperial Control and Political Cleavages in Yorubaland," in Peter B. Evans, Deitrich Rueschemeyer, and Theda Skocpol., eds. *Bringing the State Back In*. New York: Cambridge University Press, 285–316.

León Pasquel, Lourdes, ed. 2001. *Costumbres, leyes y movimiento indio en Oaxaca y Chiapas*. Mexico City: Centro de Investigaciones y Estudios Superiores en Antropología Social (CIESAS) and Miguel Ángel Porrúa.

Bibliography

Lewis, Stephen E. 2008. "Unmasking Chiapas: Recent Scholarship on Subcomandante Marcos, Dissident Women, and Impotent Thugs," *Latin American Perspectives* 163.35, 179–185.

Leyva Solano, Xochitl and Araceli Burguete Cal y Mayor, eds. 2007. *La remunicipalización de Chiapas: Lo político y la política en tiempos de contrainsurgencia.* Mexico City: Centro de Investigaciones y Estudios Superiores en Antropología Social (CIESAS) and Miguel Ángel Porrúa.

Lichbach, Mark. 1994. "Rethinking Rationality and Rebellion: Theories of Collective Action and Problems of Collective Dissent," *Rationality and Society* 6, 10–20.

Lijphart, Arend. 1999. *Patterns of Democracy: Government Forms & Performance in Thirty Six Countries.* New Haven, CT: Yale University Press.

Lin, Ann Chih. 1998. "Bridging Positivist and Interpretivist Approaches to Qualitative Methods," *Policy Studies Journal* 26.1, 162–180.

López Bárcenas, Francisco. 2002. *Legislación y derechos indígenas en México.* Juxtlahuaca, Oaxaca: Centro De Orientación y Asesoría a Pueblos Indígenas.

López y Rivas, Gilberto. 1995. *Nación y Pueblos Indios en el Neoliberalismo.* Mexico City: Plaza y Valdes Editores.

Lucero, José Antonio. 2008. *Struggles of Voice: The Politics of Indigenous Representation in the Andes.* Pittsburgh, PA: University of Pittsburgh Press.

Madrid, Raúl. 2005. "Indigenous Voters and Party System Fragmentation in Latin America," *Electoral Studies* 24.4, 689–707.

2008. "The Rise of Ethnopopulism in Latin America," *World Politics* 60.3, 475–508.

Mahoney, James and Gary Goertz. 2006. "A Tale of Two Cultures: Contrasting Quantitative and Qualitative Research," *Political Analysis* 14.3, 227–249.

Mallon, Florencia. 1995. *Peasant and Nation: The Making of Post-colonial Mexico and Peru.* Berkeley, CA: University of California Press.

Marshall, T. H., ed. 1973. *Class, Citizenship, and Social Development – Essays by T.H. Marshall.* Westport, CT: Greenwood Press.

Martínez Vásquez, Víctor Raúl. 2007. *Autoritarismo, Movimiento Popular y Crisis Política: Oaxaca 2006.* Oaxaca City: Universidad Autónoma Benito Juárez de Oaxaca.

Mattiace, Shannan L. 2009. "Multicultural Reforms for Mexico's 'Tranquil' Indians: Indian Rights Legislation in Yucatán," paper presented at the conference "Reconciling Liberal Pluralism and Group Rights: Oaxaca, Mexico's Multiculturalism Experiment in Comparative Perspective," February 20, American University, Washington, D.C.

2003. *To See with Two Eyes: Peasant Activism and Indian Autonomy in Chiapas, Mexico.* Albuquerque, NM: University of New Mexico Press.

McAdam, Doug. 1996. "Conceptual Origins, Current Problems, and Future Directions," in Doug McAdam, John D. McCarthy, and Mayer N. Zald, eds. *Comparative Perspectives on Social Movements – Political Opportunities, Mobilizing Structures, and Cultural Framings.* New York: Cambridge University Press, 1–26.

McAdam, Doug, Sidney Tarrow and Charles Tilly. 2001. *Dynamics of Contention.* New York: Cambridge University Press.

McCammon, Holly J. 2001. "Stirring Up Suffrage Sentiment: The Emergence of the State Woman Suffrage Organizations, 1866–1914," *Social Forces* 80.2, 449–480.

Mestries Benquet, Francis. 2001. "Antecedentes y motivos del movimiento indígena zapatista," *Estudios Agrarios* 16, 118–136.

Meyer, David S. 2004. "Protest and Political Opportunities," *Annual Review of Sociology* 30, 125–145.

Mill, John Stuart. 1970 (1888). "Two Methods of Comparison," in Amitai Etzioni and Fredric Dubow, eds. *Comparative Perspectives: Theory and Methods*. Boston, MA: Little, Brown, 205–213.

Minnesota Advocates for Human Rights and the Heartland Alliance for Human Needs & Human Rights. 1996. *The Rule of Lawlessness in Mexico: Human Rights Violations in the State of Oaxaca*. Minneapolis, MN: Minnesota Advocates for Human Rights and the Heartland Alliance for Human Needs & Human Rights.

Molina, Oscar and Martin Rhodes. 2002. "Corporatism: The Past, Present, and Future of a Concept," *Annual Review of Political Science* 5 (June 2002), 305–331.

Molinar Horcasitas, Juan. 1991. "Counting the Number of Parties: An Alternative Index," *The American Political Science Review* 85.4, 1381–1383.

Molinar Horcasitas, Juan and Jeffrey Weldon. 1994. "Electoral Determinants and Consequences of National Solidarity," in Wayne Cornelius, Ann Craig, and Jonathan Fox, eds. *Transforming State-Society Relations in Mexico: The National Solidarity Strategy*. La Jolla, CA: Center for US-Mexican Studies.

Monroy, Mario B., ed. 1994. *Pensar Chiapas, Repensar México*. Mexico City: Convergencia de Organismos Civiles por la Democracia.

Morales Canales, Lourdes. 2008. "Conflicto electoral y cambio social: el caso de San Miguel Quetzaltepec, Mixes," in Jorge Hernández-Díaz, ed. *Ciudadanías diferenciadas en un estado multicultural: los usos y costumbres en Oaxaca*. Mexico City: Siglo XXI Editorial, 151–174.

Moreno Derbez, Carlos. 2009. "Territorio y conflictos agrarios," in Victor Leonel Juan Martínez and Maria Clara Galvis, eds. *Derecho y Sociedad Indígena en Oaxaca*. Washington, DC: Due Process of Law Foundation. 49–63.

Nagengast, Carol and Michael Kearney. 1990. "Mixtec Ethnicity: Social Identity, Political Consciousness, and Political Activism," *Latin American Research Review* 25.2, 61–91.

Niezen, Ronald. 2003. *The Origins of Indigenism – Human Rights and the Politics of Identity*. Berkeley, CA: University of California Press.

Norris, Pippa. 2008. *Driving Democracy: Do Power-Sharing Institutions Work?* New York: Cambridge University Press.

North, Douglass C. and Barry R. Weingast. 1989. "Constitutions and Commitment: The Evolution of Institutions Governing Public Choice in Seventeenth-Century England," *The Journal of Economic History* 49, 803–832.

Olson, Mancur. 1971. *The Logic of Collective Action – Public Goods and the Theory of Groups*. Cambridge, MA: Harvard University Press.

O'Neill, Kathleen. 2003. "Decentralization as an Electoral Strategy," *Comparative Political Studies* 36.9 (November), 1068–1091.

Bibliography

Onoma, Ato. 2006. "Securing Property Rights in Land: Politics on the Land Frontier in Postcolonial Africa." Doctoral dissertation. Northwestern University, Evanston, IL.

Osorno, Diego Enrique. 2007a. *Oaxaca sitiada: La primera insurrección del siglo XXI.* Mexico City: Grijalbo Editores.

Otero, Gerardo. 2007. "Review Article: Class or Identity Politics? A False Dichotomy," *International Journal of Comparative Sociology* 48.1, 73–80.

Pallares, Amalia. 2002. *From Peasant Struggles to Indian Resistance: The Ecuadorian Andes in the Late Twentieth Century.* Norman, OK: University of Oklahoma Press.

Pérez Ruiz, Maya Lorena. 2004. *Tejiendo historias: Tierra, género y poder en Chiapas.* Mexico City: Instituto Nacional de Antropología e Historia.

Pichardo Peña, David. 2001. "Migración y cambio sociocultural en la zapoteca sur, Oaxaca." Undergraduate thesis in social anthropology, Universidad Autónoma Metropolitana – Unidad Iztapalapa, Mexico City. Typescript.

Pineda Pineda, Luz Olivia. 2002. "Maestros Bilingües, Burocracia y Poder Político en los Altos de Chiapas," in Juan Pedro Viqueira and Mario Humberto Ruz, eds. *Chiapas: Los Rumbos de Otra Historia.* Mexico City: Universidad Nacional Autónoma de México, 279–300.

Plutarch, Pedro. 2004. "The Zapatistas and the Art of Ventriloquism," *Journal of Human Rights* 3.3, 291–312.

Popkin, Samuel. 1979. *The Rational Peasant – The Political Economy of Rural Society in Vietnam.* Berkeley, CA: University of California Press.

Posner, Daniel N. 2003. "The Colonial Origins of Ethnic Cleavages: The Case of Linguistic Divisions in Zambia," *Comparative Politics* 35.2, 127–146.

Rabasa Gamboa, Emilio. 2002. *Derecho Constitucional Indígena.* Mexico City: Universidad Nacional Autónoma de México.

Ragin, Charles. 1987. *The Comparative Method: Moving Beyond Qualitative and Quantitative Strategies.* Berkeley, CA: University of California Press.

Recondo, David. 2007. *La política del gatopardo: Multiculturalismo y democracia en Oaxaca.* Mexico City: Centro de Investigaciones y Estudios Superiores en Antropología Social (CIESAS).

2006. "Las costumbres de la democracias: multiculturalismo y democratización en Oaxaca," paper presented at the 2006 Meeting of the Latin American Studies Association, March 15–18 (San Juan).

2001. "Usos y costumbres, procesos electorales y autonomía indígena en Oaxaca," in Lourdes de León Pasquel, ed. *Costumbres, leyes y movimiento indio en Oaxaca y Chiapas.* Mexico City: Centro de Investigaciones y Estudios Superiores en Antropología Social and Miguel Ángel Porrúa, 91–113.

Regino Montes, Adelfo. n.d. "Foro Indígena Nacional – La Autonomía: Una Forma Concreta de Ejercicio del Derecho a la Libre Determinación y sus Alcances," typescript. San Cristóbal de las Casas: Servicios del Pueblo Mixe.

n.d. "Taller 2: Libre Determinación de los Pueblos Indígenas," typescript.

Reyes Ramos, María Eugenia. 1992. *El Reparto de Tierras y la Política Agraria en Chiapas, 1914–1988.* Mexico City: Universidad nacional Autónoma de México.

Reyna, José Luis and Richard S. Weinert, ed. 1977. *Authoritarianism in Mexico.* Philadelphia: Institute for the Study of Human Issues.

Ríos, Viridiana. 2006. "Conflictividad postelectoral en los Usos y Costumbres de Oaxaca." Undergraduate thesis in political science, Instituto Tecnológico Autónomo de México (ITAM).

Rivera Nolasco, Marco A. 2004. "Reporte de Investigación: Controversias Agrarias y su Relación con el Avance del PROCEDE 1992–2003," *Estudios Agrarios* 26, 121–148.

Robles Berlanga, Héctor and Luciano Concheiro Bórquez. 2004. *Entre las fábulas y la realidad, los ejidos y comunidades con población indígena.* Mexico City: Universidad Autónoma Metropolitana and Comisión Nacional para el Desarollo de los Pueblos Indígenas.

Rodríguez, Victor. 2006. "Awakening to the Dream: Education, Leadership, and Political-Cultural Formation in Four Neo-Zapatista Communities of Chiapas." MA Thesis in Latin American Studies. Simon Frasier University.

Rodríguez, Victoria. 1997. *Decentralization in Mexico: From Reforma Municipal to Solidaridad to Nuevo Federalismo.* Boulder, CO: Westview Press.

Ronfeldt, David, John Arquilla, Graham Fuller, and Melissa Fuller. 1998. *The Zapatista "Social Netwar" in Mexico.* Santa Monica, CA: RAND Corporation.

Rus, Jan. 2002. "Rereading Tzotzil Ethnography: Recent Scholarship from Chiapas, Mexico," in John M. Watanabe and Edward F. Fischer, eds. *Pluralizing Ethnography: Comparison and Representation in Maya Cultures, Histories, and Identities.* Santa Fe, NM: School of American Research.

———. 1994. "The 'Comunidad Revolucionaria Institutional': The Subversion of Native Government in Highland Chiapas, 1936–1968," in Gilbert M. Joseph and Daniel Nugent, eds. *Everyday Forms of State Formation: Revolution and the Negotiation of Rule in Modern Mexico.* Durham, NC: Duke University Press, 265–300.

Rus, Jan, Rosalía Aída Hernández Castillo, and Shannan L. Mattiace, eds. 2003. *Mayan Lives, Mayan Utopias: The Indigenous Peoples of Chiapas and the Zapatista Rebellion.* Lanham, MD: Roman & Littlefield.

Sánchez Botero, Ester. 2010a. *Justicia y Pueblos Indígenas de Colombia.* 3rd ed. Bogotá: Universidad Nacional de Colombia.

———. 2010b. "Como entender el derecho en contextos de diversidad cultural?" presentation at 7th International Congress of the Latin American Network of Legal Anthropology (RELAJU), Lima, Peru, August 2.

Serrano Carreto, Enrique, Arnulfo Embriz Osorio and Patricia Fernández Ham, eds. *Indicadores socioeconómicas de los pueblos indígenas de México, 2002.* Mexico City: Instituto Nacional Indigenista.

Silva Herzog, Jesús. 1960. *Breve Historia de la Revolución Mexicana – tomo I.* Mexico City: Fondo de Cultura Económica, 20.

Snow, David and Robert Benford. 1988. "Ideology, Frame Resonance, and Participant Mobilization," in Bert Klandermans, et al., eds. *International Social Movement Research* 1, 197–217.

Bibliography

Snyder, Richard. 2001. *Politics after Neoliberalism: Reregulation in Mexico.* New York: Cambridge University Press.

Sonnleiter, Willibald. 2001. *Los indígenas y la democratización electoral – Una década de cambio político entre los tzotziles y tzeltales de Los Altos de Chiapas (1988–2000).* Mexico City: El Colegio de México/Instituto Federal Electoral.

Sonnleiter, Willibald. forthcoming. *Elecciones Chiapanecas del Régimen Post-Revolucionario al Desorden Democrático.* Mexico City: El Colegio de México.

Sorroza Polo, Carlos. 2009. "Political Subsystems in Oaxaca's Usos y Costumbres Municipalities: An Analysis of the Civil-Religious Service Background of Mayors," paper presented at the conference "Reconciling Liberal Pluralism and Group Rights: Oaxaca, Mexico's Multiculturalism Experiment in Comparative Perspective," February 20, American University, Washington, DC.

Stahler-Sholk, Richard. 2007. "Resisting Neoliberal Homogenization: The Zapatista Autonomy Movement," *Latin American Perspectives* 34.2 (March), 48–63.

Starn, Orin. 1999. *Nightwatch: The Politics of Protest in the Andes.* Durham, NC: Duke University Press.

Stephen, Lynn. 2002. *Zapata Lives! Histories and Cultural Politics in Southern Mexico.* Berkeley, CA: University of California Press.

Strom, Kaare. 1990. "A Behavioral Theory of Competitive Political Parties," *American Journal of Political Science* 34, 565–598.

Tarrow, Sidney G. 1998. *Power in Movement: Social Movements and Contentious Politics.* 2nd ed. New York: Cambridge University Press.

Taylor, Charles, Amy Gutmann, Kwame Anthony Appiah, Jurgen Habermas, Stephen C. Rockefeller, Michael Walzer, and Susan Wolf. 1994. *Multiculturalism: Examining the Politics of Recognition.* Princeton, NJ: Princeton University Press.

Thibault, Simon. 1998. "The Zapatista Uprising." Norman Paterson School of International Affairs, Carleton University, Ottawa. Typescript.

Ticona, Estéban, Gonzalo Rojas and Xavier Albó. 1995. *Votos y Wiphalas – Campesinos y Pueblos Originarios en Democracia.* La Paz: Centro de Investigación y Promoción del Campesinado (CIPCA).

Torres-Manzuera, Gabriela. 2009. "The Decline of the *Ejido* and *Ayuntamiento* Emergence Reconfiguring Local Powers: New Actors, Old Practices." Paper presented at the conference, "Fifteen Years after the Zapatistas: Social and Political Change in Mexico and Chiapas since 1994," David Rockefeller Center for Latin American Studies, Harvard University, April 10, 2009.

Trejo, Guillermo. 2004. "Indigenous Insurgency: Protest, Rebellion, and the Politicization of Ethnicity in 20th Century Mexico," Ph.D. dissertation in political science, University of Chicago.

Van Cott, Donna Lee. 2000. *The Friendly Liquidation of the Past – the Politics of Diversity in Latin America.* Pittsburgh, PA: University of Pittsburgh Press.

2003. "Institutional Change and Ethnic Parties in South America," *Latin American Politics and Society* 45.2, 1–39.

2005. *From Movements to Parties in Latin America – The Evolution of Ethnic Politics.* New York: Cambridge University Press.

Van der Haar, Gemma. 2001. *Gaining Ground: Land Reform and the Constitution of Community in the Tojolabal Highlands of Chiapas, Mexico.* Amsterdam: Utrecht University Press.

VanWey, Leah K., Catherine M. Tucker and Eileen Díaz McConnell. 2005. "Community Organization, Migration, and Remittances in Oaxaca," *Latin American Research Review* 40.1, 83–107.

Velásquez Cepeda, María Cristina. 2000. *El nombramiento – Las elecciones por usos y costumbres en Oaxaca.* Oaxaca: Instituto Estatal Electoral de Oaxaca.

2004. "Migrant Communities, Gender, and Political Power in Oaxaca," in Jonathan Fox and Gaspar Rivera-Salgado, eds. 2004. *Indigenous Mexican Migrants in the United States.* La Jolla, CA: Center for US-Mexican Studies, University of California, San Diego.

2003. "Mujeres Indígenas Gobernando en Municipios de Oaxaca?" *México Indígena* 2.5, 24–31.

Villafuerte Solís, Daniel, Salvador Meza Díaz, Gabriel Ascencio Franco, María del Carmen García Aguilar, Carolina Rivera Farfán, Miguel Lisbona Guillén and Jesús Morales Bermúdez. 1999. *La Tierra en Chiapas – Viejos problemas nuevos.* 2nd ed. Mexico City: Plaza y Valdés Editores.

Villafuerte Solís, Daniel and José Montero Solano. 2006. *Chiapas: La Visión de los Actores.* Mexico City: Ediciones Casa Juan Pablos.

Viqueira, Juan Pedro and Mario Humberto Ruz, eds. 2002. *Chiapas: Los Rumbos de Otra Historia.* Mexico City: Universidad Nacional Autónoma de México, 279–300.

Wasserstrom, Robert. 1983. *Class and Society in Central Chiapas.* Berkeley, CA: University of California Press.

Whittier, Nancy. 2002. "Meaning and Structure in Social Movements," in David S. Meyer et al., eds. *Social Movements: Identity, Culture, and the State.* Oxford University Press, 289–308.

Willis, Eliza, Christopher da C.B. Garman and Stephan Haggard. 1999. "The Politics of Decentralization in Latin America," *Latin American Research Review* 34.1, 7–56.

Wolf, Eric R. 2001 (1957). "Closed corporate peasant communities in Mesoamerica and Central Java," in *Pathways of Power: Building an Anthropology of the Modern World.* Berkeley: University of California Press. http://ark.cdlib.org/ark:/13030/kt2z09q1jj/

Womack, John. 1999. *Rebellion in Chiapas: An Historical Reader.* New York: New Press.

Yashar, Deborah J. 2005. *Contesting Citizenship: The Rise of Indigenous Movements.* New York: Cambridge University Press.

Zafra, Gloria. 2009. "Por la ley o la costumbre: obstáculos en la participación política de las mujeres en el sureste mexicano," in Victor Leonel Juan Martínez and Maria Clara Galvis, eds. *Derecho y Sociedad Indígena en Oaxaca.* Washington, DC: Due Process of Law Foundation, 63–73.

Zald, Mayer N. 1996. "Culture Ideology and Strategic Framing," in Doug McAdam, et al., eds. *Comparative Perspectives on Social Movements.* Cambridge: Cambridge University Press, 261–274.

Bibliography

Zoomers, Annelies and Gemma van der Haar, eds. 2000. *Current Land Policy in Latin America: Regulating Land Tenure under Neo-liberalism.* Amsterdam: Royal Tropical Institute.

Primary Sources

Amnesty International. 2009. "Mexico: New Investigation into Acteal Massacre is Essential," accessed online February 10, 2010 at http://www.amnesty.org/en/for-media/press-releases/mexico-new-investigation-acteal-massacre-essential-20090813.

Attorney General for Agrarian Concerns, Office of Studies and Publications. 2004. Provision of data on collective agrarian conflicts registered by that office between April 1992 and November 2004 in three of Mexico's states in correspondence with author.

Chiapas State Government, Secretary for Rural Areas, Subsecretary for Agrarian Affairs. 2006. 2006–2012 Development Plan memo. Typescript.

Commission for Historical Clarification. 1999. *Guatemala: Memory of Silence.* Report of the Commission for Historical Clarification. Accessed online February 1, 2006 at http://shr.aaas.org/guatemala/ceh/report/english/concl. html.

Electoral Tribunal of the Judicial Power of the Federation. 2001. *Colección Sentencias Relevantes No. 4: Elección de Concejales al Ayuntamiento del Municipio de Asunción Tlacolulita, Estado de Oaxaca, por Usos y Costumbres (Caso Oaxaca).* Mexico City: Tribunal Electoral del Poder Judicial de la Federación.

Federal Electoral Institute (IFE). 2004. *Atlas electoral federal de México, 1991–2003.* México: Instituto Federal Electoral.

Federal Institute for Information Access (IFAI). 2005. List of states with IFAI laws. Online at http://www.ifai.org.mx/test/eym/estatales.htm

International Service for Peace (SIPAZ). 2003 (June), "Forced Evictions in Montes Azules: Conserving Biodiversity – With or Against Indigenous Villages?" Accessed online April 6, 2010 at http://www.sipaz.org/fini_eng.htm

National Indigenous Forum (Foro Nacional Indígena): 1996. "Comunidad y Autonomia: Derechos Indígenas," typescript.

National Institute for Federalism and Municipal Development (CEDEMUN). 2003. *Sistema Nacional de Información Municipal, versión 7.* Mexico City: Instituto Nacional para el Federalismo y el Desarrollo Municipal. CD-ROM and also accessible at www.inafed.gob.mx

National Institute of Statistics, Geography, and Information Processing (INEGI). 2001a. *XII Censo General de Población y Vivienda 2000 – Principales Resultados.* Mexico City: Instituto Nacional de Estadística, Geografía e Informática. CD-ROM.

National Institute of Statistics, Geography, and Information Processing (INEGI). 2001b. *XII Censo General de Población y Vivienda 2000 – Principales Resultados por Localidad.* Mexico City: Instituto Nacional de Estadística, Geografía e Informática. CD-ROM.

National Institute of Statistics, Geography, and Information Processing (INEGI). 2001c. *Resultados del VIII censo ejidal (special provision of data)*. Mexico City: Instituto Nacional de Estadística, Geografía e Informática. Accessed online January 10, 2006 at http://www.inegi.gob.mx/est/contenidos/espanol/proyectos/coesme/programas/rel_biblio.asp.

National Institute of Statistics, Geography, and Information Processing. 2002a. *XII Censo General de Población y Vivienda 2000 – Sistema para la Consulta de Información Censal/Chiapas*. Mexico City: Instituto Nacional de Estadística, Geografía e Informática. CD-ROM.

National Institute of Statistics, Geography, and Information Processing. 2002b. *XII Censo General de Población y Vivienda 2000 – Sistema para la Consulta de Información Censal/Oaxaca*. Mexico City: Instituto Nacional de Estadística, Geografía e Informática. CD-ROM.

National Institute of Statistics, Geography, and Information Processing. 2002c. *XII Censo General de Población y Vivienda 2000 – Sistema para la Consulta de Información Censal/Zacatecas*. Mexico City: Instituto Nacional de Estadística, Geografía e Informática. CD-ROM.

National Plural Indigenous Rights Assembly for Autonomy. 1995. "Iniciativa de Decreto para la Creación de las Regiones Autónomas," typescript. San Cristóbal de las Casas: Asamblea Nacional Indígena Plural por la Autonomía.

National Statistical Institute. 2003. *Bolivia: Características Sociodemográficas de la Población Indígena*. La Paz: Instituto Nacional de Estadística.

National Statistics and Informatics Institute. 2001. *2000 National Household Survey (ENAHO)*. Lima: Instituto Nacional de Estadística e Informática.

Oaxaca State Electoral Institute. 2009. *Compendio de Legislación Electoral*. Oaxaca: Instituto Estatal Electoral de Oaxaca.

Oaxaca State Legislature. 1993. Registry of Legislative Decrees 13, 1992–1995. Typescript.

Secretariat of Agrarian Reform, 2008. "Asuntos Concluidos 2003–2007," Internal document. Chiapas Special Representative of Secretaria de Reforma Agraria.

Secretariat of Agrarian Reform, 2005a, internal presentation regarding the Lacandon common lands zone, Chiapas Special Representative of Secretaria de Reforma Agraria.

Secretariat of Agrarian Reform, 2005b. "Diagnóstico Agrario – Región Desempeño-Valle Santo Domingo," Internal document. Chiapas Special Representative of Secretaria de Reforma Agraria.

Services for an Alternative Education. 2005. *Informe: Observación Electoral en Municipios Indígenas que Rigen por Sistemas Normativos Internos*. Proceso Electoral 2004. Oaxaca City: Servicios para una Educación Alternativa, A.C., 77–81.

Services for an Alternative Education. 2002. *Informe de Observación Electoral en Municipios de Usos y Costumbres, Oaxaca 2001*. Oaxaca City: Servicios para una Educación Alternativa, A.C. and Comisión Diocesana de Pastoral Social, 77–81.

Truth and Reconciliation Commission. 2003. *Data Base of the Truth and Reconciliation Commission*. CD-ROM and data files. Lima: Comisión de la Verdad y Reconciliación.

Bibliography

Media

"A Political Awakening: Indigenous people in South America," *The Economist*, February 21, 2004.

Becerril, Elio. 2003. "Desplazados de Montes Azules Buscan Tierras ante el Incumplimiento de PROFEPA," *La Jornada* (May 27), accessed online on March 5, 2010 at http://www.nodo50.org/pchiapas/chiapas/montes/montes27.htm

Bellinghausen, Herman. 2002. "Se alistan fuerzas de seguridad para desalojar 35 comunidades de la reserva Montes Azules," *La Jornada* (March 16), accessed online October 20, 2005 at http://www.jornada.unam.mx/2002/03/16/015n1pol.php?printver=1.

Buchanan, Ronald. 2010. "Remittances from US to Mexico Drop 14%," *Financial Times* (January 5), accessed online on October 19, 2010 at www.remittancesgateway.or/index/php/press-clippings/flows-information/441-remittances-from-us-to-mexico-drop-14.

Camacho, Dolores and Arturo Lomelí. 2004. "El ascenso de la violencia en Zinacantán," *La Jornada Suplemento Hojarasca* 84 (April).

Del Collado, Fernando. 2003. "Murat, Retrato de un Cacique: Entrevista con José Murat," *Enfoque* insert to *Reforma* (October 19), 13–18.

"Ex zapatista revela estructura actual del EZLN," *Reforma* (March 27, 2010), accessed online September 15, 2010 at www.terra.com.mx/oticias/articulo/898733/Ex+zapatista+revela+estructura+actual+del+EZLN.

Guillén, Guillermina, "Planean más desalojos en Montes Azules: Existen otros grupos que permanecen ilegalmente en la zona, denuncian lacandones," in *El Universal*, January 1, 2003, accessed online March 5, 2010 at http://www2.eluniversal.com.mx/pls/impreso/noticia.html?id_nota=48006&tabla=estados

Guillén, Guillermina and Alejandro Almazán. 2002. "Esperan Que Choles Dejen Tierras Desprotegidas," *El Universal* (December 19), 22.

Guillén, Guillermina, Jorge Octavio Ochoa, and Fredy Martín. 2003. "Requiere millones reubicar a desplazados de Montes Azules," *El Universal* (May 29), accessed online October 18, 2005 at http://www2.eluniversal.com.mx/pls/impreso/noticia.html?id_nota=49474&tabla=estados_h.

Izquierdo, Martha. 2006. "Anulan su triunfo por ser mujer. Elección celebrada por el sistema de usos y costumbres," *Reforma* (December 5), accessed online October 1, 2009 at http://www.e-local.gob.mx/wb/INAFED2006/INAF_Diciembree05#oaxaca2.

Juan Martínez, Víctor Leonel. 2000. "Yalálag: Historia de una violenta lucha indígena," *En Marcha – Realidad Municipal de Oaxaca* 3.16, 5–9.

Latin American Herald Tribune. 2010. "Remittances to Mexico Up 11.9% in May," *Latin American Herald Tribune* (July 4), accessed online October 19, 2010 at http://www.remittancesgateway.org/index/php/press-clippings/flows-information/744-remittances-to-mexico-up-119-in-may.

Martín Pérez, Fredy. 2003. "Regresan indígenas a 'Montes Azules,'" *El Universal* (November 16), accessed online October 21, 2005 at http://www2.eluniversal.com.mx/pls/impreso/noticia.html?id_nota=51433&tabla=estados_h.

Bibliography

2004. "Se oponen Zapatistas a salir de 'Montes Azules,'" *El Universal* (February 4), accessed online October 21, 2005 at http://www2.eluniversal.com.mx/pls/impreso/noticia.html?id_nota=52294&tabla=estados_h.

Molina Ramirez, Tania. 2006. "El viento del norte sopla en las comunidades oaxaqueñas: La migración transforma los usos y costumbres," *Masiosare* 421 (January 15).

Mulligan, Mark. 2004. "Bolivian demonstration ends in lynching," *The Financial Times* (June 16).

Osorno, Diego Enrique. 2007b. "Todo Está Mal en Oaxaca," *Letras Libres*. January 2007, accessed online September 9, 2010 at http://www.letraslibres.com/index.php?art=11755.

Regino Montes, Adelfo. 1996. "Los derechos indígenas, en serio," *La Jornada* (October 22), accessed online June 11, 2000 at http://www.jornada.unam.mx/1996/oct96/961022/adelfo.html.

Relea, Francesc, 2008. "La rebelión se llama Eufrosina Cruz," *El País* (February 10), accessed online April 27, 2010 at http://www.elpais.com/articulo/internacional/rebelion/llama/Eufrosina/Cruz/elpepiint/20080210elpepiint_1/Tes.

Salazar González, Claudia. 2003. "Versión estenográfica de la entrevista de prensa que concedió el Procurador Agrario, Dr. Isaías Rivera Rodríguez, a la reportera Claudia Salazar González, del periódico *Reforma*, la cual tuvo lugar este día en el despacho del titular de la Procuraduría Agraria," *Reforma* (June 3), accessed online October 20, 2010 at http://www.pa.gob.mx/boletines/entrevistas/016.htm.

Sarabia, Ernesto and Verónica Galán. 2005. "Vive País de remesas y Gobierno del crudo," *Reforma* (May 11), A-1.

Sosa, Yadira, 2010. "Eufrosina con Michelle Obama," *El Imparcial* (April 13), A-1, accessed online April 27, 2010 at http://www.imparcialenlinea.com/?mod=leer&id=118026&sec=primera&titulo=Eufrosina_con_Michelle_Obama.

Tapia, Alma Alejandra. 2010. "Prevalece marginación de mujeres en materia electoral: Alanís Figueroa," *La Jornada-Zacatecas* (March 10), 1, accessed September 16, 2010 at http://www.trife.gob.mx/comunicacionsocial/resumen/resumen/pdf/2010/140310.pdf.

Tobar, Hector and Maria Antonietta Uribe, 2008. "Refusing to take men for an answer," *Los Angeles Times* (April 5), A-1, accessed April 27, 2010 at http://articles.latimes.com/2008/apr/05/world/fg-suffrage5.

Velásquez, Luis Ignacio. 2010 . "Sobre estructura del IEEA montó Cipriano operativo electoral," *Noticias: Voz e Imagen* (July 8), accessed September 14, 2010 at www.noticiasnet.mx/portal/principal/sobre-estructura-del-ieea-monto-cipriano-operativo-electoral.

Interviews

Aguilár, Hugo, lawyer for Servicios al Pueblo Míxe legal advocacy group, Oaxaca City, Oaxaca, May 12, 2005.

Alcántara Guzmán, Armando, Oaxaca delegate of the Commission of Indigenous Rights (CDI), Oaxaca City, Oaxaca, July 17, 2004.

Bibliography

Álvarez, Luís H, federal government Commissioner for the Dialogue and Negotiation in Chiapas, Mexico City, May 23, 2005.

Ángeles Carreño, Graciela, former secretary of Santa Catarina Minas and poll worker during 2001 post-electoral conflict, Santa Catarina Minas, Oaxaca, June 22, 2009.

Aquino Maldonado, Joel, leader of Zapoteco indigenous rights movement, Villa Hidalgo Yalálag, Oaxaca, July 24, 2004.

Aquino, Primo, Commissioner of Common Lands (*bienes comunales*) Santa Ana del Valle, Santa Ana del Valle, Oaxaca on June 26, 2009.

Arellanes, Aquino, former mayor of Santa Catarina Minas, Santa Catarina Minas, Oaxaca, June 23, 2009.

Arias, Ivan, a designer of Bolivia's 1994 law of Popular Participation, La Paz, Bolivia, December 6, 2005.

Arnaud Viñas, Enrique, former finance director for Oaxaca Governor Diodoro Carrasco, Oaxaca City, Oaxaca, June 29, 2009.

Bautista, Emilio, medical doctor and political activist, Villa Hidalgo Yalálag, Oaxaca, July 24, 2004.

Bollaños Berra, Gumesindo, regent of finances at San Miguel Tlacotepec, San Miguel Tlacotepec, Oaxaca, June 24, 2009.

Burguete Cal y Mayor, Araceli, senior researcher at Centro de Investigaciones y Estudios Superiores en Antropología Social (CIESAS), San Cristóbal de las Casas, Chiapas, June 13, 2007, and June 6, 2008.

Burguete Carlos, advisor to the secretary for Indigenous Affairs of the State of Chiapas, San Cristóbal de las Casas, Chiapas, July 29, 2004.

Chambor Yuk, Carmelo, former commissioner for common lands, Lacandon Comunal Zone, Lacanja hamlet in Ocosingo, Chiapas, September 26, 2005.

Cortés López, Elías, Oaxaca PRI sub-secretary of elections, Oaxaca City, Oaxaca, November 26, 1998.

Cruz, Eufrosina, former mayoral candidate in Santa María Quegolani, August 6, 2008, Oaxaca City, Oaxaca.

Cruz Iriarte, Rodrigo, staff representative of the Oaxaca State Human Rights Commission, Oaxaca City, Oaxaca, August 6, 2008.

Cruz López, Oscar, PRD state legislator, Oaxaca City, Oaxaca, July 20, 2004.

Díaz Gordillo, Martha Cecilia, Chiapas Special Representative for Agrarian Reform, Lacanja hamlet in Ocosingo, Chiapas, September 26, 2005.

Díaz Solís, Pedro, Lacandon communal zone, Lacanja hamlet in Ocosingo, Chiapas, September 26, 2005.

Embruz, Arnolfo, director of research for the National Indigenous Rights Commission (CDI), Mexico City, July 15, 2004.

Esperón Angón, Cesar Eric, municipal president of San Miguel Tlacotepec, San Miguel Tlacotepec, Oaxaca, June 24, 2009.

Fernández, Tania, leader of "Cinco Señores" barricade during 2007 Oaxaca APPO movement and UABJO graduate student in sociology, Oaxaca City, Oaxaca, June 29, 2009.

Flores Cruz, Cipriano, advisor to the PRI and ex-director of the Oaxaca State Electoral Institute, Oaxaca City, Oaxaca, July 22, 2004 and May 17, 2005.

Frias López, Ricardo, biologist of the CONANP (National Commission for Protected Natural Areas), Tuxtla Guttierrez, Chiapas, June 12, 2006.

Gijón Cernas, Mauricio, Oaxaca delegate of National Agrarian Registry, Oaxaca City, Oaxaca, July 23, 2004.

Gómez Hernández, Caralampios, director of Emiliano Zapata Proletariat Organization (OPEZ), Tuxtla Gutierrez, Chiapas, July 28, 2004.

González Esponda, Juan, commissioner, Chiapas Governor's Commission for Reconciliation of the Communities in Conflict (Comisionado para la Reconciliación de Comunidades en Conflicto), Poder Ejecutivo del Estado de Chiapas, San Cristóbal de las Casas, November 7, 2002 and June 18, 2007.

González, Gerardo, rural doctor and external affairs liason, El Colegio de la Frontera Sur, Tuxtla Gutierrez, Chiapas, June 6, 2007.

González Hernández, Juan, former traditional judge, San Juan Chamula, Chiapas, July 30, 2004.

Guzmán Alcántara, Armando, Oaxaca delegate of the National Indigenous Rights Commission (CDI), Oaxaca City, Oaxaca, July 17, 2004.

Hernández Fernández, Sylvia, teacher in Section 22 and leader of Popular Revolutionary Front (Frente Popular Revolucionario – an APPO component group), Oaxaca City, Oaxaca, June 28, 2009.

Hernández, Samael, advisor to the Oaxaca state government's State Institute of Public Education (IEPO), Oaxaca City, Oaxaca, June 30, 2009.

Hidalgo Vasqúez, Manuel, communal property holder in The House of the People, Venustiniano Carranza, Chiapas, July 29, 2004.

Jiménez Gaeta, Gustavo, managing partner of fishery/restaurant "Rio Colornises," Ixtlán de Juárez, Oaxaca, May 14, 2005.

Jiménez Moreno, Antonio, land reform negotiator on behalf of citizens of Valle Santo Domingo, Ocosingo, Chiapas, June 16, 2007.

Jiménez Pacheco, Juan José, director of *usos y costumbres* section of Oaxaca Electoral Institute, Oaxaca City, Oaxaca, November 24, 1998.

Jiménez Pérez, José, Municipal Secretary of Zinacantán, Zinacantán, Chiapas, July 30, 2004.

Ledesma, Fermin, department for agrarian affairs official, Office of the Chiapas Special Representative for Agrarian Reform, Tuxtla Gutierrez, Chiapas, September 27, 2005 and June 13, 2007.

Leyva, Marcos, member of APPO executive council and co-director of EDUCA (Servicios para una Educación Alternativa, A.C.), Oaxaca City, Oaxaca, July 30, 2008.

López Garcia, Francisco, Santa Ana del Valle Regent of Goods and Services, Santa Ana del Valle, Oaxaca, June 26, 2009.

López, Leovijildo, Secretary for Doctrine and Policy, Oaxaca state chapter of the National Action Party (PAN), Oaxaca City, Oaxaca, May 12, 2005.

López López, Eric, advisor to the Secretary of Government, Oaxaca State Government, Oaxaca City, Oaxaca, November 24, 1998.

López Valencia, Alan, resident of San Juan Guelavia, San Juan Guelavia, Oaxaca, June 24, 2009.

Bibliography

Luna Luján, C. Jorge Arturo, subsecretary of Secretariat of Government of the State of Chiapas and former subsecretary, Secretariat of Agrarian Development, Tuxtla Gutierrez, Chiapas, July 29, 2005, July 27, 2004 and November 7, 2002.

Marquez Mendoza, Arturo, Chiapas Special Representative of the Attorney General for Agrarian Affairs, Lacanja hamlet in Ocosingo municipality, Chiapas, September 26, 2005.

Martínez Coria, Ramón, director of FORO para el Desarollo Sustentable and former advisor to Chiapas Secretary of Social Development, San Cristóbal de las Casas, Chiapas, June 25 and 26, 2008.

Martínez Luna, Jaime, anthropologist, Gelatao, Oaxaca, May 14, 2005.

Martínez Pérez, José, president of communal property, The House of the People, Venustiniano Carranza, Chiapas, July 29, 2004.

Méndez, Sara, human rights activist at Centro Derechos Humanos Tierra del Sol in Tlaxiaco, Oaxaca City, Oaxaca, May 15, 2005.

Molina Maldonado, Norma, businesswoman and Juxtlahuapa regent for health and sister of Tlacotepec mayoral candidate, Juxtlahuapa, Oaxaca, June 24, 2009.

Molina Maldonado, Orlando, regent for health of San Miguel Tlacotepec and 2007 mayoral candidate, Juxtlahuapa, Oaxaca, June 24, 2009.

Moreno Alcántara, Carlos, PAN representative to the Oaxaca Electoral Institute, Oaxaca City, Oaxaca, November 24, 1998.

Pérez Gómez, Marcos, former commissioner of communal property in Chalchihuitán, San Cristóbal de las Casas, Chiapas, August 1, 2004.

Pérez Hernandez, Mariano de Jesús, Zinacantán resident and member of the Committee of the San Lorenzo Fair, Zinacantán, Chiapas, July 30, 2004.

Pérez Ruiz, Armando, teacher and former commissioner of communal property in Chenalho, Chenalho, Chiapas, August 2, 2004.

Reyes Aguilar, Pablo, Director of Public Works, Municipality of Zinacantán, Zinacantán, Chiapas, June 14, 2007.

Ruíz, Margarito, Chiapas delegate of the National Indigenous Rights Commission (CDI), Tuxtla Gutierrez, Chiapas, July 28, 2004.

Sánchez López, Samuel, land reform negotiator on behalf of citizens in Valle Santo Domingo, Ocosingo, Chiapas, June 16, 2007.

Sánchez Pérez, Pablo, vice mayor (síndico), Aldama, Aldama, Chiapas, August 2, 2004.

Solís Rios, Samuel, department head for agrarian affairs, Office of the Chiapas Special Representative for Agrarian Reform, Tuxtla Gutierrez, Chiapas, September 27, 2005.

Vargas Mestes, José María, regent for finances in Villa Hidalgo Yalálag, Villa Hidalgo Yalálag, Oaxaca, July 24, 2004.

Zenon Flores, Anastasia, tortilla factory owner and women's rights advocate, Asunción Tlacolulita, Oaxaca, July 21, 2004.

Zenteno, Jeronimo, Subsecretary for Rights of Indigenous Peoples, Attorney General for Indigenous Affairs, Oaxaca City, Oaxaca, May 15, 2005.

Index

agencia municipal, 115, 124
agency – by individuals, 16, 17, 45, 50, 56, 71, 94, 96, 100, 104, 155, 178
agrarian reform, 29, 33, 39, 90, 101, 173. *See also* land reform
Agrarian Reform Ministry, 33
Agrarian Registry (RAN), 90
Agrarian Rehabilitation Program (PRA), 34
Alanis Figueroa, María del Carmen, 159
Albores Guillén, Roberto, 136
Álvarez, Luis H., 139
Anaya-Muñoz, Alejandro, 106, 124
Anderson, Benedict, 131
Ángeles Carreño, Graciela, 125, 148, 157, 159
Aquino Maldonado, Joel, 127, 149–152
Aquino, Primo, 143
Arellanes, Aquilino, 146
Article 4, 6, 27, 33, 35, 41, 87, 88, 97
Asamblea Nacional Indígena Plural por la Autonomía (ANIPA), 52
Asamblea Popular de los Pueblos de Oaxaca (APPO), 21, 22, 23, 24, 32, 43, 172, 176
Ascencio Franco, Gabriel, 181
Asociación Rural de Interés Colectivo (ARIC), 87
Attorney General for Agrarian Concerns, 90
Attorney General for Environmental Protection (PROFEPA), 95
authoritarian state, 18, 49, 102, 110, 117, 130, 147
autonomy, 50, 171
    definition, 158

Bailón Corres, Moisés Jaime, xii–xiii, 108
Baja California, 115
Barth, Fredrik, 48
Base Territorial Organizations (OTBs), 167
Bautista, Emilio, 150–151
Benford, Robert, 46
Benhabib, Seyla, 127
Benito Juárez Autonomous University, 22
Benton, Allyson Lucinda, xii, 21, 116
Binational Oaxacan Indigenous Front (FIOB), 149
Blair, Harry, 165
Bolivia, 14, 49, 70, 104, 158, 163–171, 174, 177
Bollaños Berra, Gumesindo, 160
Bourdieu, Pierre, 61
Brass, Paul, 48–49
Burguete, Araceli, 7, 41, 136, 141, 162–163, 171
bystanders, 2, 15, 18, 43, 50, 56, 71, 103, 162, 177–178

cabecera, 53, 113, 114, 157. *See also* municipal seat
Calderón, Felípe, 19, 23, 33, 42, 120, 173
Campillo, Ignacio, 95, 96
Cárdenas, Cuauhtémoc, 112
Cárdenas, Lázaro, 6, 30, 32, 36, 84, 112
cargos, 62, 109, 115, 133, 144–149, 159
Carrasco, Diódoro, 27
Castellanos Domínguez, Absalón, 25, 34
Catholic Church, 25, 30, 34, 38, 85, 107
Central Independiente de Obreros Agrícolas y Campesinos (CIOAC), 40, 91
certificates of non-affectability, 34

Chambor Yuk, Carmelo, 93
Chance, John K., 29
Chankín, Alfonso, 96
Chiapas, 2–5, 12–14, 16–21, 25–26, 42,
    45–71, 104–81, 108, 116, 122, 127,
    129–131, 139, 140, 142, 147, 152,
    154–157, 160–161, 163–164, 168–170,
    172, 176
Acteal, 26, 27, 47, 155
Aldama, 131, 137, 138
Apaz, 135
Buena Vista Pachán, 41
Bonampak, 77
Chankin, 77
Chenalho, 131
El Limonar, 100
Huixtla, 137
Lacandon, 12, 20, 30–34, 40, 42, 56, 77,
    129, 132, 135, 138, 141, 142
Lacantún, 77
Montes Azules Biosphere, 29, 77, 78, 94,
    96, 100
Nachig, 135
Nicholas Ruiz, 131
Oventik, 129, 130
Palenque, 96, 100
Pasté, 133–135
Sabanilla, 131
Salto de Agua, 131
San Andrés Larrainzar, 130
San Andrés Larráinzar, 53, 131, 138
San Cristóbal de las Casas, 132, 133,
    142
San Juan Chamula, 162
Tabasco, 41
Tila, 89, 131
Tumbala, 93, 131
Viejo Velasco Suárez, 100
Yachilán, 77
Zinacantán, 4, 53, 129–139, 175
citizen trust of the Zapatista movement, 3
citizenship, 9–11, 49, 148, 174, 177
class, 4, 5, 7–8, 11, 12, 16, 18, 20, 24–26,
    47, 49, 71, 88, 94, 129, 133, 135, 152,
    168, 173
class conflict, 7, 16, 26
clientelism, 39, 161
collective action, 11, 56, 71, 132, 157, 171
collective rights, 9, 10, 19, 26, 47, 51, 157,
    173, 175

Colombian constitutional court, 158,
    174, 175
communal lands (*tierras comunales*), 8, 12,
    21, 29, 37, 68–69, 77–84, 86, 89,
    97–139, 173
communitarian identity, definition, 2
communitarian rights, 2, 3, 4, 9, 11, 27, 46,
    54, 103, 126, 128, 133, 157, 158, 168,
    170, 175
Compania Forestal de La Lacandona, 83
comunalicracia, 51, 108, 159
conflict – environmental, 63, 74, 129,
    134, 138
conflict – ethnic, 45, 62, 63, 74, 118
conflict – land, 25, 28, 30, 47, 76, 77–102
conflict – municipal, 63, 74, 151
conflict – political parties, 63, 74, 107, 111
conflict – religious, 47, 63, 74
conflict resolution, 42, 52, 61–62
Connor, Walker, 48
constitutional reforms, 27, 47, 48, 51, 103,
    174, 176
constructivist(s), 4, 17, 19, 45, 48, 70, 128,
    139, 177
Coordinadora 11 de Octubre, 151
corporate communities, 4, 13, 37, 60, 68
corporate communities, definition, 5
corporatism, 7, 11, 12, 21–23, 30–35, 37,
    45, 47, 49, 59, 62, 69, 71, 81, 83–87, 91,
    105, 112, 136, 155, 161, 164, 166, 169,
    173, 176
council of elders, 28, 150, 151
Cruz Alcántara, Jorge, 120
Cruz, Eufrosina, 120, 159, 174
customary law, 20, 56, 63, 82, 104, 105,
    116, 124, 127, 137, 144, 164, 170, 174.
    See also usos y costumbres

Danielson, Michael, 121, 122,
    158
de facto land ownership, 37, 68
de jure land ownership, 7, 37, 68
de la Madrid, Miguel, 86
De Vos, Jan, 83
decentralization, 133, 164–169
democratization, 165
Díaz Gordillo, Martha Cecilia, 82
Díaz Ordaz, Gustavo, 32, 82, 84
Díaz Solís, Pedro, 79
discourses, 2, 5, 47, 81, 88, 152

Index

discrimination (especially against women and citizens living outside municipal seat), 28, 48–50, 53, 62, 104, 114, 118, 120, 121, 122, 125–128, 147, 148, 159, 160, 171
drug trafficking, 100

Echeverría, Luis, 32, 77, 79, 80, 82, 84, 94, 104
economic development, 39, 47, 51, 54, 62, 70, 83, 100, 140, 143, 155, 159
economic development gap, 178
Ecuador, 49, 104, 171
education, 11, 13, 24, 52, 54, 61, 85, 91, 100, 115, 128, 141–142, 146, 155, 174
Eisenstadt, Todd, 20, 28, 107, 116, 158, 162
ejido, 6, 8, 20, 29–33, 36–40, 44, 60, 61, 68, 70, 71, 78, 89, 90, 97, 98, 100, 102, 143, 163, 173
electoral court, 54, 114, 118–120, 126
elites, 3, 5, 7, 8, 14, 20, 28, 35, 36, 49, 50, 87, 103, 108, 126, 132, 157, 159, 166, 168, 176
Engle, Karen, 177
Enlace Civil, 141
Escuelas para Chiapas, 142
essentialist, 4, 178
Estrada Saavedra, Marco, 5, 41, 140, 152–154, 177
ethnic identity, 3–5, 8, 12, 16, 19, 27, 45, 48–50, 55, 57–63, 69–70, 71, 79–83, 98, 103, 104, 107, 123, 164, 166

Fearon, James D., 57, 69
Fernández, Tania, 24
Flores Cruz, Cipriano, 118–119, 120, 124, 127, 152, 162
Fox, Vicente, 19, 21–22, 42, 48, 78, 108, 139, 173
free-riders, 1, 15, 71
Frias, Ricardo, 100
Fujimori, Alberto, 168

García Aguilar, María del Carmen, 35
García, Alan, 168
Garman, Christopher da C.B., 165
globalization, 4, 18, 46, 47, 61, 74, 105, 133, 143, 144, 158, 173, 177, 178
Goertz, Gary, 56
González Esponda, Juan, 139

Good Government Councils, 42, 122, 129, 132, 134, 137, 139, 140, 141, 142, 161
Goodman, Gary L., 116
Grupo Comunitario (GC), 150, 151
Guatemala, 15, 78
gubernatorial election, 16
Guerrero, 176
Gutiérrez Narváez, Raúl de Jesús, 142

Haggard, Stephan, 165
hamlet, 57, 62, 70, 113, 115, 118, 126, 129, 130, 134
Harvard Project, 4
health care, 11, 143, 155, 174
Hechter, Michael, 48–50
Hernández Castillo, Aida, 122, 132, 177
Hernández Fernández, Sylvia, 23
Hernández, Samael, 24
Hernández-Díaz, Jorge, 107, 146
Higgins, Nicholas Paul, 4
Hiskey, Jonathan T., 116
Hobsbawm, Eric, 146, 147
human rights, xiii, 5, 15, 19, 20, 27, 78, 105, 118, 120, 123, 148, 151, 164, 171, 174, 175

imaginary Zapatistas, 132, 175
Inclán, María, 16, 56, 177
indigeneity, 4, 177, 178
indigenismo, 24, 84
indigenous autonomy, 1–5, 9–10, 14, 18, 20, 28, 38, 47–49, 51–52, 53–55, 56, 79, 80, 87, 93, 102, 113, 127, 129, 130, 136, 140, 142, 152, 156, 158, 160–164, 167, 169, 171–175
indigenous Mexico, 3, 18, 118, 175
indigenous rights, 2, 3, 5–6, 8–14, 18, 20, 23, 43, 46, 49–53, 54, 56, 81, 82, 87–89, 93, 104, 108, 119, 124, 129, 147, 151, 152, 157, 158, 164, 167, 172, 175
individual rights, 3–4, 9–14, 28, 46–47, 105, 122, 157, 158, 163, 171, 174, 175
informal land reforms, 36, 42
instrumental(ist), 16, 45–46, 49, 50, 70, 129, 147, 148, 157
insurgency, 5–7, 12, 14, 18, 19, 27, 41, 43, 78, 81, 91, 102, 105, 130, 131, 140, 157, 161, 170, 177
interest articulation, 32, 173

interest group, 7, 23, 96, 121, 148,
    158, 161, 177
interest intermediation, 10, 11, 91
internal conflict (Chiapas groups), 54, 129,
    134, 138
internal conflict (Oaxaca groups), 63,
    106, 150
International Labor Organization Treaty
    169 (ILO 169), 26, 87

Jiménez Moreno, Antonio, 101
Juan Martínez, Victor Leonel, 107, 146
Jung, Courtney, 4

Kearney, Michael, 155
Kymlicka, Will, 171, 175

Lacandon agrarian conflict, 13,
    79–102, 129
Laitin, David, D., 57, 69
land distribution, 21, 33, 38, 43, 44

"land and liberty!", 35
land redistribution, 6, 35, 56, 88, 90,
    169, 173
land reform, 6, 32, 36, 42, 87–88, 90,
    91, 102, 166, 173. *See also* agrarian
    reform
land tenure, 3, 8, 12, 13, 20, 26, 36, 43, 45,
    46, 68, 70, 71, 82, 91, 102, 104, 153,
    169, 173
landowners, 21, 34, 35, 47, 86, 90, 94,
    138, 163, 168
Law of Popular Participation (LPP),
    167, 168
leaders framing of social movement, 3, 16,
    26, 81, 155
Leyva Beltrán, Beatriz, 121
Leyva, Marcos, 23
Lin, Ann Chih, 56
Lisbona Guillén, Miguel, 35
local, 4, 22–24
López Portillo, José, 77
Lucero, José Antonio, 2

Mahoney, James, 56
Marx(ist), 4, 26, 162
Mattiace, Shannan, 3, 4, 6, 34, 47,
    87, 155
Mexican Army, 6

Mexican Constitution, 6, 18, 33, 38, 47, 52,
    88, 90, 97, 105, 164, 169, 174, 175
Meza Díaz, Salvador, 35
Michoacán, 176
Mill, John Stuart, 56
Molina Maldonado, Norma, 148
Molina Maldonado, Orlando, 148, 149
Morales Bermúdez, Jesús, 35
Morales, Evo, 164, 167, 168
movement followers, 1, 3, 5, 14, 15, 32, 43,
    50, 56, 132, 141, 152, 154, 171, 178
movement leadership, 1–3, 5, 6, 13–14, 15,
    20, 21, 23–26, 27, 29, 32, 38, 42, 43,
    45, 50, 54, 56, 68, 71, 79, 84, 86, 104,
    107–110, 113, 118, 132, 141, 147,
    151, 153–155, 159, 162, 165, 167,
    169, 171, 176
Movement Toward Socialism, 168, 170
multiculturalism, 11, 46–48, 51, 104, 105,
    118, 126, 128, 158, 171
municipal seat, 13, 53, 106, 109, 114, 118,
    129, 157
Murat, José, 23, 120, 127

Nagengast, Carol, 155
National Action Party. *See* Partido Acción
    Nacional (PAN)
National Indigenous Forum, 9
National Indigenous Institute (INI), 34,
    39, 176
National Peasant Confederation (CNC), 30,
    34, 35, 39, 87, 90, 104
National Union of Education Workers
    (SNTE), 22
nationalism, 8, 16, 131

Oaxaca, 3, 8, 9, 12–14, 16, 18–24, 27–32,
    36–40, 43–44, 48, 51–71, 81–83, 103,
    104–127, 132, 133–135, 143–152, 153,
    155, 157, 162, 164, 173, 175
    Asunción Tlacolulita, 54, 115,
        117–119, 159
    Capulalpam de Mendez, 121
    Cruz del Rosario, 155
    Ixtlán de Juárez, 37
    Oaxaca City, 19, 21, 24, 32
    San Miguel Tlacotepec, 147–149,
        157, 160
    San Pablo Macuiltianguis, 145
    Santa Ana, 143–146

Index

Santa Catarina Minas, 53, 125, 146, 147–148, 157, 159
Santa María Quiegolani, 117, 120
Santiago Juxtlahuaca, 149
Villa Hidalgo Yalálag, 53, 150
Oaxaca 2006 conflict, 18–23. *See also* APPO
tequio, 62, 109, 113, 131, 144, 145, 150, 163
objectivity, 15, 49, 163
Olson, Mancur, 2

paraje, 133–135
Partido Acción Nacional (PAN), 23, 42, 48, 108, 112, 117, 120, 136, 139, 153, 161
Partido de la Revolución Democrática (PRD), 22, 23, 42, 91, 112, 117, 118–121, 129, 130, 132, 134–136, 137–139, 142, 149, 161
Partido Revolucionario Institucional (PRI), 7, 8, 11, 20, 22, 26, 27, 30–34, 35, 39, 43, 47–48, 69, 84, 87, 89–91, 94, 105–107, 110–113, 116–119, 124, 125, 134, 135, 136–139, 149, 150, 154, 155, 160, 161, 169, 173, 176
Partido Unidad Popular (PUP), 124
Party of the Democratic Revolution. *See* Partido de la Revolución Democrática (PRD)
Party of the Institutional Revolution. *See* Partido Revolucionario Institucional (PRI)
peasants, 1–3, 4–5, 11, 12, 13, 20, 21, 25, 30, 34–36, 39, 40, 41, 43, 45, 47, 49, 61, 69, 78, 81, 83, 84–98, 101–103, 104, 112, 130, 136, 163, 166, 167, 168, 175
Pérez, Jacinto, 5
Peru, 14, 158, 163, 164, 166, 168–171
pluralism, 11, 13, 16, 46, 57, 60, 61, 62, 81, 104
political autonomy, 2, 49, 71
political stability, 6
Popkin, Samuel, 11
Popular Revolutionary Army (EPR), 27
post-electoral conflict, xii, 13, 63, 107, 110, 111, 115, 116, 119, 123–125, 172
poverty, 24, 62, 79, 155, 170, 172
power sharing institutions (consociationalism), 170, 178
primordial(ist), 4, 16, 19, 29, 45, 46, 48, 49, 51, 70, 83, 151, 177, 178

Protestant, 34, 53, 85, 131
protests, 18, 21–23, 28, 82, 115, 120, 130, 136
public lands, 61, 70
Puebla, 23, 96, 176

Quintana Roo, 176
Quiptic Ta Lecubtesel, 86

Ragin, Charles, 56
rationality, 45, 98
raza cosmica, 8
Recondo, David, 38, 39, 106, 124
Regino Montes, Adelfo, 9, 52
relative autonomy, 12, 43
relative deprivation, 62, 133
resource distribution, 5, 103, 124, 171
Reyes Aguilar, Pablo, 134
Rios Arellanes, Heliodoro, 147
Ríos, Viridiana, 107
Rivera Farfán, Carolina, 36
Ruíz, Margarito, 88
Ruíz Ortiz, Ulises, 21–24, 112, 117
Ruiz, Samuel, 86
Rus, Jan, xiii, 4, 21, 30, 49, 84, 162

Sabines Guerrero, Juan, 43, 139
Salazar, Pablo, xiv, 42, 136, 139, 153, 161
Salinas, Carlos, 25, 32, 34, 87, 112, 161
San Andrés Accords, 6, 26, 41, 47, 48, 51, 54, 108, 131, 136, 172, 176
Sánchez de Lozada, Gonzalo, 166, 167
Sánchez López, Samuel, 101
Secretariat for Agrarian Reform (SRA), 86, 90, 94, 96, 98, 99, 100, 102
Secretariat of Urban Development and the Environment (SEDUE), 87, 96
Semillitas del Sol, 141
Shining Path, 164, 166, 170
silent majority, 2
Sinaloa, 115
Snow, David, 46
Snyder, Richard, 32
social capital, 61, 63, 70, 164, 170
social services, 5, 34, 54, 85, 93, 140, 167
Sonnleiter, Willibald, 137
Sorroza, Carlos, 144
Sosa, Flavio, 22, 23, 43
southern Mexico, 2, 8, 14, 16, 18, 19, 45, 82, 85, 104, 129, 132, 157, 162, 169, 171, 172, 173, 175, 177, 178

sovereignty, 171
Soviet Union, 4
squatters, 6, 7, 8, 21, 25, 28, 32, 35, 41, 47,
    68, 78, 87, 89, 90, 91, 94–100, 102, 161
Stahler-Sholk, Richard, 4
state legislature, 6, 48, 54, 87, 108, 110, 115,
    117, 151
state services, 14, 90, 91, 140, 154, 174
Stoll, David, 15, 16, 177
Subcommander Marcos, 25, 43, 88, 89, 122,
    131, 134, 137, 139, 152, 153
subjectivity, 15, 49
Supreme Court (Mexican), 19, 22, 27,
    147, 172
survey, 2–3, 8, 12, 14, 15, 16, 19, 28, 46, 50,
    55–57, 62, 69, 70, 71, 81, 86, 97, 103,
    106, 114, 137, 144, 156, 169, 170, 173

Tabasco, 176
Tarrow, Sidney, 20, 46
Taylor, Charles, 46
teachers, 119, 121, 172
Tlatelolco, 30
Tlaxcala, 176
topil, 109
Toro, Olga, 121
Trejo, Guillermo, 16, 34, 49, 85, 86, 177

Unión Tierra y Libertad, 40
usos y costumbres, 13, 20, 27, 28, 39,
    48, 51–56, 62, 104–128, 132,
    143–148, 149–152, 153, 157–161.
    See also customary law

usos y costumbres conflicts, 106, 111, 120,
    123–125

Van Cott, Donna Lee, 3, 49, 167, 171
Vargas Mestes, José María, 151
Velásquez Cepeda, María Cristina, 122
Veracruz, 176
Villafuerte Solís, Daniel, 36, 142
violence, 15, 20, 29, 47, 78, 101, 133, 136,
    151, 166, 170
Vogt, Evon, 129

Willis, Eliza, 165
Wolf, Eric, 5, 13
women, 13, 51, 53, 106, 109, 113–127,
    147–149, 159, 174, 175
women's rights, 51, 104, 118, 122–123, 158
Workers' Party (PT), 142

Yashar, Deborah J., 3, 10, 173
Yucatán, 39, 55, 176

Zacatecas, 3, 55, 70
Zafra, Gloria, xiii, 121, 159
Zapata, Emiliano, 5, 35, 90, 134
Zapatismo, 41, 55, 81, 89, 131, 132, 133, 136,
    137, 152, 161
Zapatista rebellion of 1994, 151
Zapatista social movement, 1, 4, 24, 41, 71,
    93, 101, 103, 132, 141
Zapatista uprising, 51, 86, 90, 105, 130
Zedillo, Ernesto, 6, 26, 33, 47, 84, 136
Zenón Flores, Anastasia, 118, 119

Title in the Series (continued from page iii)

Ralph Thaxton, Jr., *Catastrophe and Contention in Rural China: Mao's Great Leap: Forward Famine and the Origins of Righteous Resistance in Da Fo Village*

Charles Tilly, *Contention and Democracy in Europe, 1650–2000*

Charles Tilly, *Contentious Performances*

Charles Tilly, *The Politics of Collective Violence*

Marisa von Bülow, *Building Transnational Networks: Civil Society and the Politics of Trade in the Americas*

Stuart A. Wright, *Patriots, Politics, and the Oklahoma City Bombing*

Deborah Yashar, *Contesting Citizenship in Latin America: The Rise of Indigenous Movements and the Postliberal Challenge*